Sources of the African-American Past

Primary Sources in American History

Roy E. Finkenbine
University of Detroit Mercy

 LONGMAN

An Imprint of Addison Wesley Longman, Inc.

New York • Reading, Massachusetts • Menlo Park, California • Harlow, England
Don Mills, Ontario • Sydney • Mexico City • Madrid • Amsterdam

D1469078

Executive Editor: Bruce Borland
Supplements Editor: Jessica Bayne
Page Design: Judith Anderson
Cover Design: Kay Petronio
Manufacturing and Production: Rohnda Barnes

Sources of the African-American Past by Roy Finkenbine.

ISBN: 0-673-99202-0

99 00 01 9 8 7 6

Contents

Acknowledgments

Many individuals played a part in the making of *Sources of the African-American Past*.

The staff of Addison Wesley Longman deserves special thanks. Sheila Abbruzzo first recognized the need for this volume and helped convince the press to go ahead with the project. Jessica Bayne proved to be an ideal editor. She regularly expressed her faith in the value of the project and gently nudged it along to a conclusion.

Former colleagues and students helped to shape this volume. I had the good fortune to work with C. Peter Ripley and the staff of the Black Abolitionist Papers Project at Florida State University for more than a decade. They taught me the art of documentary editing and introduced me to many of the sources that appear here. Students in my African-American history courses at Florida State University, Murray State University, and Hampton University inspired this reader. They graciously allowed me to present several of these documents in a classroom environment and offered valuable feedback.

A few former colleagues provided specific assistance and advice. Donald Yacovone, now of the Massachusetts Historical Society, convinced me to use the version of the Henry Highland Garnet speech that appears in chapter six. Scholars and staff at Hampton University also contributed. Steve Rosenthal increased my understanding of African-American participation in the Communist Party during the 1930s, thus influencing the direction of chapter twelve. Carmen Grayson read a sample chapter and suggested improvements. Elizabeth Charity typed several chapters.

My wife Barbara and our four children bore the making of this volume with good humor, understanding, and patience. I suspect that they occasionally doubted that it would ever be finished. But they kept any doubts to themselves, offering instead a substantial measure of encouragement and emotional support. I can't thank them enough!

Livonia, Michigan

"Bones of the Past": Using Primary Sources in African-American History

In *Migrations of the Heart: An Autobiography* (1983), African-American novelist Marita Golden recounted being introduced to her people's past when she was eighteen years old. Although her father had occasionally passed on family stories, the offerings she found in a black nationalist bookstore called the Drum and Spear in 1968 opened a wealth of new understandings about the African-American experience.

> Its shelves stocked a whole range of books on black and African studies, and they finished the stories my father had begun. I learned of slave revolts, W.E.B. Du Bois, black inventors, Carter G. Woodson, Reconstruction, Jean Toomer, Timbuktu, the precarious existence of freed slaves, Duke Ellington, Nat Turner, Bessie Smith. Page after page put flesh and blood on the bones of the past my father had kindled for me in spurts.

Golden's epiphany was necessary because of the way in which the African-American past had been ignored or distorted by the broader American culture. Prior to the late 1960s, blacks rarely appeared in U.S. history textbooks except as faceless slaves. On occasion, the character and accomplishments of Booker T. Washington and George Washington Carver—perceived by many whites as "good Negroes" who "knew their place"—would be mentioned. But there were few other attempts to explore the African-American experience.

Over the past three decades, the importance of African-American history has become widely recognized. The Civil Rights and Black Power Movements of the 1960s stimulated the historical as well as the political consciousness of blacks and whites alike and led to an intensive effort to recover the African-American past. Courses in African-American history are now taught in most colleges and universities and in many secondary schools. Thousands of books and articles have revised our understanding of slavery, emancipation, segregation, and the mass migration of blacks to urban centers in the twentieth century. Dozens of documentary films, feature films, and television miniseries such as *Roots*, *Glory*, and *Malcolm X* have carried aspects of African-American history to a broad general audience.

One of the most exciting areas of change has been the effort to retrieve the primary sources of the African-American past. Primary sources are the documents or other evidence—written, oral, and visual—created during the period being studied or by participants remembering the event. These are the materials historians use to recreate the past. Because earlier generations of Americans placed little importance on black documents, many historians once argued that the necessary primary sources for writing African-American history were not available. However, as a result of the work of committed historians and documentary editors over the last thirty years, many important black historical documents are now widely available in published form.*

This primary source reader is the beneficiary of these extensive efforts to recover documentary evidence from the African-American past. Like Golden's experience at the Drum and Spear, it is designed to "put flesh and blood on the bones of the past." This will be accomplished in two ways. First, it will introduce you to the "flesh and blood" of the African-American experience. A growing number of Americans—black and white— are familiar with the broad outlines of the black experience in the United States. But many have not heard the voices of the participants themselves. Reading the letters, speeches, editorials, interviews, memoirs, petitions, poems, songs, and stories of historic African Americans—whether famous or ordinary—will enrich your understanding of that experience.

Second, this reader will introduce you to "the bones of the past"—the primary sources of African-American history. For scholars, these documents are the skeletal structure from which history is written—or "fleshed out"—much as a paleontologist works from bone fragments to reconstruct the form of a long-dead hominid. As you examine and evaluate the primary sources in this volume, you will gain a better understanding and appreciation for how scholars "do history."

As you read, you will want to examine every document critically. This will involve asking the following questions of each one you encounter in order to "put flesh and blood on the bones of the past."

1. **Who created the document?** A person's perspective on events is usually determined by their experiences and position in life. African-American history is populated by diverse individuals from varied backgrounds. Try to determine the author's gender, class, region, and social status. Clues to this information usually appear in either the headnote or the document. This will help you determine the

---

* Dozens of broadly conceived collections of primary sources in African-American history appeared in the late 1960s and 1970s but most are now out of print. Among those still available are Joanne Grant, ed., *Black Protest: History, Documents, and Analyses, 1619 to the Present* (New York: Fawcett Press, 1968); Thomas R. Frazier, ed., *Afro-American History: Primary Sources*, 2d ed. (Chicago: Dorsey Press, 1988). Also available are several recent volumes, which reprint a range of documents on particular aspects of the African-American experience. On slavery, see John W. Blassingame, ed., *Slave Testimony: Two Centuries of Letters, Speeches, Interviews, and Autobiographies* (Baton Rouge, La.: Louisiana State University Press, 1977). On black abolitionists, see C. Peter Ripley et al., eds., *Witness for Freedom: African American Voices on Race, Slavery, and Emancipation* (Chapel Hill, N.C.: University of North Carolina Press, 1993). On the emancipation experience, see Ira Berlin et al., eds., *Free at Last: A Documentary History of Slavery, Freedom, and the Civil War* (New York: New Press, 1992); Edwin S. Redkey, ed., *A Grand Army of Black Men: Letters from African-American Soldiers in the Union Army, 1861-1865* (New York: Cambridge University Press, 1992). On African-American women, see Dorothy Sterling, ed., *We Are Your Sisters: Black Women in the Nineteenth Century* (New York: W. W. Norton and Company, 1984). On the twentieth-century migrations, see Malaika Adero, ed., *Up South: Stories, Studies, and Letters of This Century's African-American Migrations* (New York: New Press, 1993). On the Civil Rights Movement, see Howell Raines, ed., *My Soul is Rested: Movement Days in the Deep South Remembered* (New York: G. P. Putnam's Sons, 1977); Peter B. Levy, ed., *Let Freedom Ring: A Documentary History of the Modern Civil Rights Movement* (New York: Praeger, 1992). For the writings and speeches of two important black leaders, see James M. Washington, ed., *A Testament of Hope: The Essential Writings of Martin Luther King, Jr.* (New York: Harper and Row, Publishers, 1986); Robert A. Hill, ed., *Marcus Garvey: Life and Lessons* (Berkeley, Calif.: University of California Press, 1987).

author's point of view. An African-born slave woman on a southern cotton plantation, for example, would undoubtedly have a different perspective than a wealthy and educated free black man born in the pre-Civil War North.

2. **Why was the document created?** Was the author a participant or a mere observer of the events being described? Did he or she have a personal interest in what they were describing that would bias their account? Were they trying to persuade someone? Was the document produced for a particular cause or organization such as the Civil Rights Movement?

3. **What was the document's intended audience?** Was it intended to be private—a diary or a letter between family members or friends? Or was it for public consumption—a speech, a newspaper editorial, a published autobiography? Was it written to other blacks? or to influential whites? Was it a petition to Congress or a state legislature, or an argument before a court? Most documents are produced with a particular audience in mind. The nature of that audience usually shapes the document. The two sources in chapter one offer an example. Olaudah Equiano penned his narrative as propaganda to be used in a campaign to abolish the Atlantic slave trade; Venture Smith simply hoped to sell his story to a popular audience. Read both documents. Do you think this affected the tone of the account of the slave trade that each produced?

4. **What type of document is it?** Is it written in ordinary prose? Or is it an example of a particular literary or musical genre, such as a poem or a spiritual? If so, the author may have rearranged (or even changed) some of the facts for artistic effect. How does this alter the usefulness and reliability of the document?

5. **When was the document created?** Was it produced immediately after (or during) the event it describes, within a short span of time, or after many years? Human memory fades and changes over time, becoming less distinct as an event recedes into the distant past. It even deludes us. Sometimes we remember events differently than they actually occurred. A slave still in bondage before the Civil War would likely describe slavery differently than an aging former slave interviewed by the Works Progress Administration in the 1930s.

An excellent example of the importance of this last question is the 1851 speech by Sojourner Truth that appears in chapter six. For more than a century, historians and biographers accepted an account by white feminist Frances D. Gage, written nearly twelve years after the event, as the definitive version of this speech. In Gage's account, Truth speaks in slave dialect and frequently utters the refrain, "And ar'n't I a woman?" In 1991 I joined my colleagues at the Black Abolitionist Papers Project in reprinting an earlier version of this speech, the one that appears here. It had been stenographically recorded by a fellow abolitionist and published in an antislavery journal less than a month after it was delivered.* Notice that both the dialect and the refrain are absent in this earlier version. What does this suggest about the effect of memory?

Sources of the African-American Past will introduce you to eighty-five primary sources produced by many different black men and women between the era of the Atlantic slave trade and the present. Some were slaves, sharecroppers, and factory workers; others were abolitionists, politicians, soldiers, and civil rights activists; a few were preachers, poets, professors, and newspaper editors. As you read their words, remember to examine each document critically. But also try to imagine how they lived. If you can, like Marita Golden, you will "put flesh and blood on the bones of the past" by the time you complete this volume.

---

* For a discussion of the background of the two versions, and the text of Gage's account, see Nell Irvin Painter, "Representing Truth: Sojourner Truth's Knowing and Becoming Known," *American Historical Review* 81 (September 1994): 461-92.

About the Editor

Roy E. Finkenbine is Assistant Professor of History at the University of Detroit Mercy. From 1981 to 1991, he served on the editorial staff of the Black Abolitionist Papers Project at Florida State University, where he coedited the five-volume *Black Abolitionist Papers, 1830–1865* (1985–92) and *Witness for Freedom: African American Voices on Race, Slavery, and Emancipation* (1993). He is the author of several articles on black abolitionists in nineteenth-century Boston, and he has taught African-American history to a variety of audiences at Florida State University, Murray State University, and Hampton University.

Editorial Statement

This volume is intended to be "user friendly" for students and other general readers. A brief introduction demonstrates how to critically examine a document in African-American history. The documents themselves are chronologically organized in seventeen chapters that correspond to the structure of most survey courses in African-American and U.S. history. These primary sources were selected to convey the breadth of the African-American experience from the Atlantic slave trade to the present. They include letters, speeches, editorials, interviews, memoirs, petitions, poems, songs, and stories by black men and women of all classes in the different regions of the United States. Brief chapter introductions and headnotes place each document in its specific historical context; critical thinking questions aid in examining and evaluating the documents; and bibliographies of related books and articles at the end of each chapter offer avenues for further study.

Most of the documents in this volume are reproduced as they originally appeared, with minor exceptions. Obvious misspellings, printer's errors, and significant punctuation errors have been silently corrected. In a few cases, paragraphing has been silently adjusted for easier reading. Repetitive or extraneous text has been eliminated from some documents; this is indicated by ellipses. Where words have been changed or added to the text to enhance comprehension, they are enclosed in brackets. Finally, in a few documents, antiquated or semi-literate text has been modernized or otherwise corrected to improve readability. These are noted in the source citations as "corrected versions."

Students and instructors who wish to contact the editor with questions, comments, criticisms, or suggestions are urged to write him c/o the History Department, University of Detroit Mercy, 4001 W. McNichols Road, Detroit, MI 48219.

1

Africans in the Atlantic Slave Trade

When Christopher Columbus accidentally "discovered" the Americas in 1492, he opened up new economic opportunities for the rising nation-states of Western Europe. Spain, Portugal, France, the Netherlands, and England quickly undertook to exploit the natural and agricultural resources of this "New World." But the development of gold and silver mines and sugar, coffee, tobacco, rice, and cotton plantations required a large and relatively cheap labor force. After experimenting with enslaved Native Americans and the European poor, the colonizers began to import large numbers of African slaves, who proved to be skilled workers, resistant to many tropical diseases, and readily available. Between 1501 and 1870, nearly twelve million Africans were forcibly loaded aboard ships on the West African coast and taken to the Americas.

A complex transatlantic network developed to procure and transport slaves. West African nations, equipped with firearms by European and American slave traders, warred and conducted kidnapping raids against rival or distant peoples to obtain slaves. The enslaved were then marched overland to the coast, often changing hands several times before being traded to white merchants for firearms, rum, cloth, or other manufactured goods. After several weeks or months of incarceration in coastal forts or stockades, they were loaded on vessels for the long voyage across the Atlantic Ocean. This stage of the trade, known as the Middle Passage, was the most horrific for the slaves. Removed from Africa and consigned to an unknown fate, some lapsed into shock or madness. Others starved themselves or jumped overboard in an attempt to commit suicide. Confined below deck without adequate food, space, ventilation, or sanitary conditions, many suffered from deadly ailments such as dysentery and smallpox. On an average voyage, one out of every six slaves died.

Some ten million African slaves arrived in the Americas during the era of the trade. Although they could be found in every region and economy, the overwhelming number became field hands on sugar plantations in Brazil, on the islands of the Caribbean (such as Haiti, Jamaica, and Barbados), and along the Caribbean rim. Less than 5 percent of the total were landed in British North America, the area that became the eastern United States. But despite this small number, factors such as a more favorable climate, a more balanced ratio of females to males, and somewhat better treatment combined to produce in this region one of the largest African-American populations in the hemisphere.

Venture Smith, Capture and Sale on the Gold Coast

The Atlantic slave trade began with enslavement and exchange on the African continent. This document recounts the capture and sale of Venture Smith in the region known as the Gold Coast (contemporary Ghana) and accurately depicts the warfare conducted by coastal nations against peoples of the interior to procure slaves for the trade. Smith (ca. 1729–1805), originally named Broteer, was the son of a prince of the Dukandarra people (possibly the Denkyira) of the West African interior. Captured at age six, he was sold to an American slave trader, renamed, and taken to Connecticut. He was eventually permitted to purchase his freedom and became a man of some means, owning land, several houses, and at least three slaves. In 1798 Smith published his autobiography, from which the following account is taken.[*]

A message was brought by an inhabitant of the place where I lived the preceding year to my father, that the place had been invaded by a numerous army, from a nation not far distant, furnished with musical instruments, and all kinds of arms then in use; that they were instigated by some white nation who equipped them and sent them to subdue and possess the country; that his nation had made no preparation for war, having been for a long time in profound peace; that they could not defend themselves against such a formidable train of invaders, and must therefore necessarily evacuate their lands to the fierce enemy, and fly to the protection of some chief; and that if he would permit them they would come under his rule and protection when they had to retreat from their own possessions. He was a kind and merciful prince, and therefore consented to these proposals.

He had scarcely returned to his nation with the message, before the whole of his people were obliged to retreat from their country, and come to my father's dominions. He gave them every privilege and all the protection his government could afford. But they had not been there longer than four days before news came to them that the invaders had laid waste their country, and were coming speedily to destroy them in my father's territories. This affrighted them, and therefore they immediately pushed off to the southward, into the unknown countries there, and were never more heard of.

Two days after their retreat, the report turned out to be but too true. A detachment from the enemy came to my father and informed him, that the whole army was encamped not far out of his dominions, and would invade the territory and deprive his people of their liberties and rights, if he did not comply with the following terms. These were to pay them a large sum of money, three hundred fat cattle, and a great number of goats, sheep, asses, &c. My father told the messenger he would comply rather than that

---

[*]From Venture Smith, *A Narrative of the Life and Adventures of Venture, A Native of Africa but Resident about Sixty Years in the United States of America* (New London, Conn., 1798).

his subjects should be deprived of their rights and privileges, which he was not then in circumstances to defend them from so sudden an invasion. Upon turning out those articles, the enemy pledged their faith and honor that they would not attack him. On these he relied and therefore thought it unnecessary to be on his guard against the enemy. But their pledges of faith and honor proved no better than those of other unprincipled hostile nations; for a few days after a certain relation of the king came and informed him, that the enemy who sent terms of accommodation to him and received tribute to their satisfaction, yet meditated an attack upon his subjects by surprise, and that probably they would commence their attack in less than one day, and concluded with advising him, as he was not prepared for war, to order a speedy retreat of his family and subjects. He complied with this advice.

The same night which was fixed upon to retreat, my father and his family set off about the break of day. The king and his two younger wives went in one company, and my mother and her children in another. We left our dwellings in succession, and my father's company went on first. We directed our course for a large shrub plain, some distance off, where we intended to conceal ourselves from the approaching enemy, until we could refresh ourselves a little. But we presently found that our retreat was not secure. For having struck up a little fire for the purpose of cooking victuals, the enemy who happened to be encamped a little distance off, had sent out a scouting party who discovered us by the smoke of the fire, just as we were extinguishing it, and about to eat. As soon as we had finished eating, my father discovered the party, and immediately began to discharge arrows at them. This was what I first saw, and it alarmed both me and the women, who being unable to make any resistance, immediately betook ourselves to the tall thick reeds not far off, and left the old king to fight alone. For some time I beheld him from the reeds defending himself with great courage and firmness, till at last he was obliged to surrender himself into their hands.

They then came to us in the reeds, and the very first salute I had from them was a violent blow on the back part of the head with the fore part of a gun, and at the same time a grasp round the neck. I then had a rope put about my neck, as had all the women in the thicket with me, and was immediately led to my father, who was likewise pinioned and haltered for leading. In this condition, we were all led to the camp. The women and myself being pretty submissive, had tolerable treatment from the enemy, while my father was closely interrogated respecting his money which they knew he must have. But as he gave them no account of it, he was instantly cut and pounded on his body with great inhumanity, that he might be induced by the torture he suffered to make the discovery. All this availed not in the least to make him give up his money, but he despised all the tortures which they inflicted, until the continued exercise and increase of torment, obliged him to sink and expire. He thus died without informing his enemies where his money lay. I saw him while he was thus tortured to death. The shocking scene is to this day fresh in my mind, and I have often been overcome while thinking on it. He was a man of remarkable stature. I should judge as much as six feet and six or seven inches high, two feet across his shoulders, and every way well proportioned. He was a man of remarkable strength and resolution, affable, kind and gentle, ruling with equity and moderation.

The army of the enemy was large, I should suppose consisting of about six thousand men. Their leader was called Baukurre. After destroying the old prince, they decamped and immediately marched towards the sea, lying to the west, taking with them myself and the women prisoners. In the march a scouting party was detached from the main army. To the leader of this party I was made waiter, having to carry his gun, &c. As we were a-scouting we came across a herd of fat cattle, consisting of about thirty in number. These were set upon, and immediately wrested from their keepers, and afterwards converted them into food for the army. The enemy had remarkable success in destroying the country wherever they went. For as far as they had penetrated, they laid the habitations waste and captured the people. The distance they had now brought me was about four hundred miles. All the march I had very hard tasks imposed on me, which I must perform on pain of punishment. I was obliged to carry on my head a large flat stone for grinding our corn, weighing as I should suppose, as much as twenty-five pounds; besides victuals, mat and cooking utensils. Though I was pretty large and stout of my age, yet these burdens were very grievous to me, being only six years and a half old.

We were then come to a place called Malagasco. When we entered the place we could not see the least appearance of either houses or inhabitants, but upon stricter search found, that instead of houses above ground they had dens in the sides of hillocks, contiguous to ponds and streams of water. In these we perceived they had all hid themselves, as I suppose they usually did on such occasions. In order to compel them to surrender, the enemy contrived to smoke them out with faggots. These they put to the entrance of the caves and set them on fire. While they were engaged in this business, to their great surprise some of them were desperately wounded with arrows which fell from above on them. This mystery they soon found out. They perceived that the enemy discharged these arrows through holes on the top of the dens directly into the air. Their weight brought them back, point downwards on their enemies' heads, whilst they were smoking the inhabitants out. The points of the arrows were poisoned, but their enemy had an antidote for it, which they instantly applied to the wounded part. The smoke at last obliged the people to give themselves up. They came out of their caves, first spatting the palms of their hands together, and immediately after extended their arms, crossed at their wrists, ready to be bound and pinioned. I should judge that the dens above mentioned were extended about eight feet horizontally into the earth, six feet in height and as many wide. They were arched over head and lined with earth, which was of the clay kind, and made the surface of their walls firm and smooth.

The invaders then pinioned the prisoners of all ages and sexes indiscriminately, took their flocks and all effects, and moved on their way towards the sea. On the march the prisoners were treated with clemency, on account of their being submissive and humble. Having come to the next tribe, the enemy laid siege and immediately took men, women, children, flocks, and all their valuable effects. They then went on to the next district which was contiguous to the sea, called in Africa, Anamaboo. The enemies' provisions were then almost spent, as well as their strength. The inhabitants knowing what conduct they had pursued, and what were their present intentions, improved the favorable opportunity, attacked them, and took enemy, prisoners, flocks and all their effects. I was then taken a second time. All of us were put into the castle, and kept for market. On a certain time I and other prisoners were put on board a canoe, under our master, and rowed away to a vessel belonging to Rhode Island, commanded by Captain Collingwood, and the mate Thomas Mumford. While we were going to the vessel, our master told us all to appear to the best possible advantage for sale. I was bought on board by one Robertson Mumford, steward of said vessel, for four gallons of rum, and a piece of calico, and called VENTURE, on account of his having purchased me with his own private venture. Thus I came by my name. All the slaves that were bought for that vessel's cargo, were two hundred and sixty.

Olaudah Equiano, The Middle Passage

Those who survived enslavement and the march to the coast faced an even greater ordeal known as the Middle Passage. This document offers a firsthand look at the physical and psychological horrors of that experience through the eyes of a young African named Olaudah Equiano. Born among the Ibo people in what is today eastern Nigeria, Equiano (ca. 1745–1797) was captured and sold into slavery at eleven years of age. He was taken to Barbados, then to Virginia, and renamed Gustavus Vassa. After buying his way out of bondage in 1766, he settled in England and became involved in the campaign against the slave trade. The selection that follows is taken from his autobiography, which was originally published in 1789 to generate public sympathy for that campaign.[*]

The first object which saluted my eyes when I arrived on the coast was the sea, and a slave ship, which was then riding at anchor, and waiting for its cargo. These filled me with astonishment, which was soon converted into terror, which I am yet at a loss to describe, nor the then feelings of my mind. When I was carried on board I was immediately handled, and tossed up, to see if I were sound, by some of the crew; and I was now persuaded that I had got into a world of bad spirits, and that they were going to kill me. Their complexions too differing so much from ours, their long hair, and the language they spoke, which was very different from any I had ever heard, united to confirm me in this belief. Indeed, such were the horrors of my views and fears at the moment, that, if ten thousand worlds had been my own, I would have freely parted with them all to have exchanged my condition with that of the meanest slave in my own country. When I looked round the ship too, and saw a large furnace or copper boiling, and a multitude of black people of every description chained together, every one of our countenances expressing dejection and sorrow, I no longer doubted of my fate; and, quite overpowered with horror and anguish, I fell motionless on the deck and fainted.

When I recovered a little, I found some black people about me, who I believed were some of those who brought me on board, and had been receiving their pay; they talked to

[*]From Olaudah Equiano, *The Interesting Narrative of the Life of Olaudah Equiano or Gustavus Vassa, the African* (New York, 1791).

me in order to cheer me, but all in vain. I asked them if we were not to be eaten by those white men with horrible looks, red faces, and long hair. They told me I was not; and one of the crew brought me small portion of spirituous liquor in a wine-glass; but, being afraid of him, I would not take it out of his hand. One of the blacks therefore took it from him, and gave it to me, and I took a little down my palate, which, instead of reviving me, as they thought it would, threw me into the greatest consternation at the strange feeling it produced having never tasted any such liquor before. Soon after this, the blacks who brought me on board went off, and left me abandoned to despair. I now saw myself deprived of all chance of returning to my native country, or even the least glimpse of hope of gaining the shore, which I now considered as friendly; and I even wished for my former slavery, in preference to my present situation, which was filled with horrors of every kind, still heightened by my ignorance of what I was to undergo.

I was not long suffered to indulge my grief; I was soon put down under the decks, and there I received such a salutation in my nostrils as I had never experienced in my life; so that, with the loathsomeness of the stench, and crying together, I became so sick and low that I was not able to eat, nor had I the least desire to taste any thing. I now wished for the last friend, death, to relieve me; but soon, to my grief, two of the white men offered me eatables; and, on my refusing to eat, one of them held me fast by the hands, and laid me across, I think, the windlass, and tied my feet while the other flogged me severely. I had never experienced any thing of this kind before; and, although not being used to the water, I naturally feared that element the first time I saw it; yet, nevertheless, could I have got over the nettings, I would have jumped over the side; but I could not; and, besides, the crew used to watch us very closely who were not chained down to the decks, lest we should leap into the water: and I have seen some of these poor African prisoners most severely cut for attempting to do so, and hourly whipped for not eating. This indeed was often the case with myself.

In a little time after, amongst the poor chained men, I found some of my own nation, which in a small degree gave ease to my mind. I inquired of them what was to be done with us? They gave me to understand we were to be carried to these white people's country to work for them. I then was a little revived, and thought, if it were no worse than working, my situation was not so desperate; but still I feared I should be put to death, the white people looked and acted, as I thought, in so savage a manner; for I had never seen among any people such instances of brutal cruelty; and this not only shown toward us blacks, but also to some of the whites themselves. One white man in particular I saw, when we were permitted to be on deck, flogged so unmercifully with a large rope near the foremast, that he died in consequence of it; and they tossed him over the side as they would have done a brute. This made me fear these people the more; and I expected nothing less than to be treated in the same manner.

I could not help expressing my fears and apprehensions to some of my countrymen: I asked them if these people had no country, but lived in this hollow place the ship? They told me they did not, but came from a distant one. "Then," said I, "how comes it in all our country we never heard of them?" They told me, because they lived so very far off. I then asked, where were their women? Had they any like themselves? I was told they had. "And why," said I, "do we not see them?" They answered, because they were left behind. I asked how the vessel could go? They told me they could not tell; but that there were cloth put upon the masts by the help of the ropes I saw, and then the vessel went on; and the white men had some spell or magic they put in the water when they liked in order to stop the vessel. I was exceedingly amazed at this account, and really thought they were spirits. I therefore wished much to be from amongst them, for I expected they would sacrifice me: but my wishes were vain; for we were so quartered that it was impossible for any of us to make our escape. While we staid on the coast I was mostly on deck; and one day, to my great astonishment, I saw one of these vessels coming in with the sails up. As soon as the whites saw it, they gave a great shout, at which we were amazed: and the more so as the vessel appeared larger by approaching nearer. At last she came to an anchor in my sight, and when the anchor was let go, I and my countrymen who saw it were lost in astonishment to observe the vessel stop; and were now convinced it was done by magic. Soon after this the other ship got her boats out, and they came on board of us, and the people of both ships seemed very glad to see each other. Several of the strangers also shook hands with us black people, and made motions with their hands, signifying, I suppose, we were to go to their country; but we did not understand them.

At last, when the ship we were in had got in all her cargo, they made ready with many fearful noises, and we were all put under deck, so that we could not see how they managed the vessel. But this disappointment was the least of my sorrow. The stench of the hold while we were on the coast was so intolerably loathsome, that it was dangerous to remain there for any time, and some of us had been permitted to stay on the deck for the fresh air; but now that the whole ship's cargo were confined together, it became absolutely pestilential. The closeness of the place, and the heat of the climate, added to the number in the ship, which was so crowded that each had scarcely room to turn himself, almost suffocated us. This produced copious perspirations, so that the air soon became unfit for respiration, from a variety of loathsome smells, and brought on a sickness amongst the slaves, of which many died, thus falling victims to the improvident avarice, as I may call it, of their purchasers. This wretched situation was again aggravated by the galling of the chains, now become insupportable; and the filth of the necessary tubs, into which the children often fell, and were almost suffocated. The shrieks of the women, and the groans of the dying, rendered the whole scene of horror almost inconceivable. Happily perhaps for myself I was soon reduced so low here that it was thought necessary to keep me almost always on deck; and from my extreme youth I was not put in fetters.

In this situation I expected every hour to share the fate of my companions, some of whom were almost daily brought upon deck at the point of death, which I began to hope would soon put an end to my miseries. Often did I think many of the inhabitants of the deep much more happy than myself; I envied them the freedom they enjoyed, and as often wished I could change my condition for theirs. Every circumstance I met with served only to render my state more painful, and heighten my apprehensions and my opinion of the cruelty of the whites. One day they had taken a number of fishes; and when they had killed and satisfied themselves with as many as they thought fit, to our astonishment who were on the deck, rather than give any of them to us to eat, as we expected, they tossed the remaining fish into the sea again, although we begged and prayed for some as well as we could, but in vain; and some of my countrymen, being pressed by hunger, took an opportunity, when they thought no one saw them, of trying to get a little privately; but they were discovered, and the attempt procured them some very severe floggings.

One day, when we had a smooth sea, and moderate wind, two of my wearied countrymen, who were chained together (I was near them at the time), preferring death to such a life of misery, somehow made through the nettings, and jumped into the sea; immediately another quite dejected fellow, who, on account of his illness, was suffered to be out of irons, also followed their example; and I believe many more would very soon have done the same, if they had not been prevented by the ship's crew, who were instantly alarmed. Those of us that were the most active were in a moment put down under the deck; and there was such a noise and confusion amongst the people of the ship as I never heard before, to stop her, and get the boat out to go after the slaves. However, two of the wretches were drowned, but they got the other, and afterwards flogged him unmercifully, for thus attempting to prefer death to slavery. In this manner we continued to undergo more hardships than I can now relate; hardships which are inseparable from this accursed trade. Many a time we were near suffocation, from the want of fresh air, which we were often without for whole days together. This, and the stench of the necessary tubs, carried off many. . . .

At last, we came in sight of the island of Barbadoes, at which the whites on board gave a great shout, and made many signs of joy to us. We did not know what to think of this; but as the vessel drew nearer, we plainly saw the harbour, and other ships of different kinds and sizes: and we soon anchored amongst them off Bridge Town. Many merchants and planters now came on board, though it was in the evening. They put us in separate parcels, and examined us attentively. They also made us jump, and pointed to the land, signifying we were to go there. We thought by this we should be eaten by these ugly men, as they appeared to us; and, when, soon after we were all put down under the deck again, there was much dread and trembling among us, and nothing but bitter cries to be heard all the night from these apprehensions, insomuch that at last the white people got some old slaves from the land to pacify us. They told us we were not to be eaten, but to work, and were soon to go on land where we should see many of our country people. This report eased us much; and sure enough, soon after we landed, there came to us Africans of all languages.

We were conducted immediately to the merchant's yard, where we were all pent up together like so many sheep in a fold, without regard to sex or age. As every object was new to me, everything I saw filled me with surprise. What struck me at first was, that the houses were built with bricks, in stories, and in every other respect different from those I have seen in Africa: but I was still more astonished in seeing people on horseback. I did not know what this could mean; and indeed I thought these people were full of nothing but magical arts. While I was in this astonishment, one of my fellow prisoners spoke to a countryman of his about the horses, who said they were the same kind they had in their country. I understood them, though they were from a distant part of Africa, and I thought it odd I had not seen any horses there; but afterwards, when I came to converse with different Africans, I found they had many horses amongst them, and much larger than those I then saw. We were not many days in the merchant's custody, before we were sold after their usual manner, which is this: on a signal given (as the beat of a drum), the buyers rush at once into the yard where the slaves are confined, and make choice of the parcel they like best. The noise and clamour with which this is attended, and the eagerness visible in the countenances of the buyers, serve not a little to increase the apprehension of the terrified Africans, who may well be supposed to consider them as the ministers of that destruction to which they think themselves devoted. In this manner, without scruple, are relations and friends separated, most of them never to see each other again. I remember in the vessel in which I was brought over, in the men's apartment, there were several brothers who, in the sale, were sold in different lots; and it was very moving on this occasion to see and hear their cries at parting.

O, ye nominal Christians! might not an African ask you, learned you this from your God? who says unto you, Do unto all men as you would men should do unto you. Is it not enough that we are torn from our country and friends to toil for your luxury and lust of gain? Must every tender feeling be likewise sacrificed to your avarice? Are the dearest friends and relations, now rendered more dear by their separation from their kindred, still to be parted from each other, and thus preventing from cheering the gloom of slavery with the small comfort of being together, and mingling their sufferings and sorrows? Why are parents to love their children, brothers their sisters, or husbands their wives? Surely this is a new refinement in cruelty, which, while it has no advantage to atone for it, thus aggravates distress, and adds fresh horrors even to the wretchedness of slavery.

Asking Questions of the Documents

1. What impact did the Atlantic slave trade have on the nations of the West African interior?

2. What role did Europeans and Americans play in the Atlantic slave trade? What role did Africans play?

3. What physical and psychological horrors faced Venture Smith during his enslavement, movement to the coast, and exchange with European traders?

4. What conditions faced Olaudah Equiano in the Middle Passage? How did he respond to this experience? How do you think you would have responded?

5. Both Smith and Equiano were children at the time of their enslavement and transport to the Americas. They wrote about these experiences decades later. What might explain their ability to remember these experiences in such vivid detail?

6. Compare the emotional tone of Smith and Equiano's narratives. What factors in their lives after slavery might explain this difference?

For Further Reading

Curtin, Philip D. *The Atlantic Slave Trade: A Census*. Madison, Wisc.: University of Wisconsin Press, 1969.

———. "Epidemiology and the Slave Trade." *Political Science Quarterly* 83 (June 1968): 190-216.

Littlefield, Daniel F. *Rice and Slaves: Ethnicity and the Slave Trade in Colonial South Carolina*. Baton Rouge, La.: Louisiana State University Press, 1981.

Rawley, James A. *The Transatlantic Slave Trade: A History*. New York: W. W. Norton and Company, 1981.

Reynolds, Edward. *Stand the Storm: A History of the Transatlantic Slave Trade*. London: Allison and Busby, Ltd., 1985.

Williams, Eric. *Capitalism and Slavery*. Chapel Hill, N.C.: University of North Carolina Press, 1944.

2

Becoming African American:
The Colonial Experience

The first African slaves in British North America were landed in 1619 at Jamestown, Virginia. For a few decades, Africans in the colony were treated much like European indentured servants. Many obtained their freedom after several years of bound service, acquired land, voted, and testified in court. But the growing demand for workers, especially in the tobacco and rice fields of the plantation South, led to the statutory recognition of African slavery in Virginia and most other colonies by the 1660s. The labor of African slaves became a vital element of the colonial economy, and thousands were imported annually during the eighteenth century. By the time the U.S. Congress outlawed American involvement in the Atlantic slave trade in 1808, nearly half a million Africans had been brought into what was then the eastern United States.

Colonial America became the crucible in which a new and distinct African-American culture developed. This involved three overlapping processes. First, the hundreds of African societies represented in the Middle Passage merged their languages, religions, music, folktales, and other cultural practices into generalized African cultural forms. Second, contact with European colonists (and, to a lesser extent, Native Americans) supplied additional cultural influences. Third, the experience of bondage prompted African slaves to shape their culture to meet the day-to-day needs of an oppressed people.

The pace, nature, and degree of culture change varied by region. In the lowcountry rice districts of Georgia and the Carolinas, most slaves worked somewhat independently on large plantations with only a few whites. In some coastal areas of South Carolina, slaves constituted 90 percent of the population. Here, where their primary contact was with other Africans, slaves maintained a significant continuity with African culture. This was most evident in the Gullah language and culture that emerged on the sea islands of the region. In the tobacco colonies of the Chesapeake, such as Virginia and Maryland, slaves constituted a large minority (nearly 40 percent) of the population. Living in slave quarters and working in gangs in the fields, they held on to major elements of their African culture. But they also interacted frequently with whites, adopting some European ways at the same time that whites were being "Africanized." This pattern of transculturation quickened as a result of the wave of mid-eighteenth-century religious revivalism known as the Great Awakening, which resulted in the conversion of large numbers of African slaves to Christianity for the first time. In the northern colonies of Pennsylvania, New Jersey, New York, and New England, most slaves were farmworkers, urban craftsmen, and domestic servants. They constituted a small minority of the population (less than 5 percent), often lived in the homes of their masters, and worked closely with whites. Most acculturated quickly, adopting Christianity and the English language and abandoning much of their African culture. African slaves in all three regions saw themselves and their culture molded and transformed into patterns that were definably African-American by the end of the colonial era.

Olaudah Equiano, Culture Shock

African slaves found colonial America to be a strange new world. While their bodies slowly adapted to a different physical environment, their minds continuously encountered cultural ways that seemed odious, wondrous, confusing, or bizarre. Their new surroundings, whether thriving seaports or isolated plantations, were often a babble of frightening and unintelligible sights and sounds. Slaves expressed surprise at the language, dress, houses, technology, music, gestures, and religion of their white masters. Those from the oral cultures of West African villages were amazed and disconcerted by the phenomenon of literacy—what some called the "talking book." The young Olaudah Equiano provides evidence of the "culture shock" faced by newly imported African slaves as he recounts his travels from Barbados to Virginia to England during his first year out of Africa.[*]

I now totally lost the small remains of comfort I had enjoyed in conversing with my countrymen; the women too, who used to wash and take care of me, were all gone different ways, and I never saw one of them afterwards.

I stayed in this island [Barbados] for a few days; I believe it could not be above a fortnight; when I, and some few more slaves, who were not saleable among the rest, from very much fretting, were shipped off in a sloop for North America. On the Passage we were better treated than when coming from Africa, and we had plenty of rice and fat pork. We were landed up a river a good way from the sea, about Virginia country, where we saw a few of our native Africans, and not one soul who could talk to me. I was a few weeks weeding grass and gathering stones in a plantation; and at last all my companions were distributed different ways, and only myself was left. I was now exceedingly miserable, and thought myself worse off than any of the rest of my companions; for they

---

[*] Olaudah Equiano, *The Interesting Narrative of the Life of Olaudah Equiano or Gustavus Vassa, the African* (New York, 1791).

could talk to each other, but I had no person to speak to that I could understand. In this state I was constantly grieving and pining, and wishing for death rather than anything else.

While I was in this plantation, the gentleman to whom I supposed the estate belonged, being unwell, I was one day sent for to his dwelling-house to fan him. When I came into the room where he was, I was very much affrighted at some things I saw, and the more so, as I had seen a black woman slave as I came through the house, who was cooking the dinner, and the poor creature was cruelly loaded with various kinds of iron machines; she had one particularly on her head, which locked her mouth so fast that she could scarcely speak, and could not eat nor drink. I was much astonished and shocked at this contrivance, which I afterwards learned was called the iron muzzle. Soon after I had a fan put into my hand, to fan the gentleman while he slept; and so I did indeed with great fear. While he was fast asleep I indulged myself a great deal in looking about the room, which to me appeared very fine and curious. The first object that engaged my attention was a watch, which hung on the chimney, and was going. I was quite surprised at the noise it made, and was afraid it would tell the gentleman anything I might do amiss; and when I immediately after observed a picture hanging in the room, which appeared constantly to look at me, I was still more affrighted, having never seen such things as these before. At one time I thought it was something relative to magic; and not seeing it move, I thought it might be some way the whites had to keep their great men when they died, and offer them libations, as we used to do our friendly spirits. In this state of anxiety I remained till my master awoke, when I was dismissed out of the room, to my no small satisfaction and relief; for I thought that these people were all made up of wonders. In this place I was called JACOB. . . .

I had been some time in this miserable, forlorn, and such dejected state, without having anyone to talk to, which made my life a burden, when the kind and unknown hand of the Creator (who in every deed leads the blind in a way they know not) now began to appear, to my comfort; for one day, the captain of a merchant ship, called the *Industrious Bee*, came on some business to my master's house. This gentleman, whose name was Michael Henry Pascal, was a lieutenant in the Royal Navy, but now commanded this trading ship, which was somewhere in the confines of the country many miles off.

While he was at master's house, it happened that he saw me, and liked me so well that he made a purchase of me. I think I have often heard him say he gave thirty or forty pounds sterling for me; but I do not remember which. However, he meant me for a present to some of his friends in England; and I was sent accordingly from the house of my master (one Mr. Campbell) to the place where the ship lay. I was conducted on horseback by an elderly black man, a mode of travelling which appeared very odd to me. When I arrived, I was carried on board a fine large ship, loaded with tobacco, &c., and just ready to sail for England.

I now thought my condition much mended; having sails to lie on, and plenty of good victuals to eat; and everybody on board used me very kindly, quite contrary to what I had seen of any white people before; I therefore began to think that they were not all of the same disposition. A few days after I was on board we sailed for England. I was still at a loss to conjecture my destiny. By this time, however, I could smatter a little imperfect English; and I wanted to know as well as I could where we were going. Some of the people of the ship used to tell me they were going to carry me back to my own country, and this made me very happy. I was quite rejoiced at the idea of going back; and thought if I could get home what wonders I should have to tell. But I was reserved for another fate, an was soon undeceived when we came within sight of the English coast.

While I was on board of this ship, my captain and master named me GUSTAVUS VASSA. I at that time began to understand him a little, and refused to be called so, and told him, as well as I could, that I would be called JACOB; but he said I should not, and still called me Gustavus. And when I refused to answer to my new name, which at first I did, it gained me many a cuff; so at length I submitted, and by it I have been known ever since.

The ship had a very long passage. . . . However, all my alarms began to subside when we got sight of land; and at last the ship reached Falmouth, after a passage of thirteen weeks. Every heart on board seemed gladdened on our reaching the shore, and none more than mine. The captain immediately went on shore, and sent on board some fresh provisions, which we wanted very much. We made good use of them, and our famine was turned into feasting, almost without ending. It was about the beginning of the spring 1757, when I arrived in England, and I was nearly twelve years of age at that time. I was very much struck with the buildings and the pavement of the streets in Falmouth; and, indeed, every object I saw filled me with fresh surprise.

One morning, when I got upon deck, I perceived it covered all over with the snow that fell over night. As I had never seen anything of the kind before, I thought it was salt; so I immediately ran down to the mate, and desired him, as well as I could, to come and see how somebody in the night had thrown salt all over the deck. He, knowing what it was, desired me to bring some of it down to him.

Accordingly I took up a handful of it, which I found very cold indeed; and when I brought it to him he desired me to taste it. I did so, and was surprised above measure. I then asked him what it was; he told me it was snow, but I could not by any means understand him. He asked me if we had no such thing in my country; I told him "No." I then asked him the use of it, and who made it; he told me a great man in the heavens, called God. But here again I was to all intents and purposes at a loss to understand him; and the more so, when a little after I saw the air filled with it, in a heavy shower, which fell down on the same day.

After this I went to church; and having never been at such a place before, I was again amazed at seeing and hearing the service. I asked all I could about it, and they gave me to understand it was "worshipping God, who made us and all things." I was still at a great loss, and soon got into an endless field of inquiries, as well as I was able to speak and ask about things. However, my dear little [white] friend Dick used to be my best interpreter; for I could make free with him and he always instructed me with pleasure. And from what I could understand by him of this God, and in seeing that these white people did not sell one another as we did, I was much pleased; and in this I thought that they were much happier than we Africans. I was astonished at the wisdom of the white people in all things which I beheld; but I was greatly amazed at their not sacrificing, nor making any offerings, and at their eating with unwashen hands, and touching the dead. I also could not help remarking the particular slenderness of their women, which I did not at first like; and I thought them not so modest and shamefaced as the African women.

I had often seen my master and Dick employed in reading; and I had a great curiosity to talk to the books, as I thought they did; and so to learn how all things had a beginning. For that purpose I have often taken up a book, and talked to it, and then put my ears to it, when alone, in hopes it would answer me; and I have been very much concerned when I found it remaining silent.

Charles Ball, African Culture in the Lowcountry

Acculturation occurred slowly among African slaves in the plantation South. Religion offers an especially useful index to the pace and degree of culture change. Africans were not welcomed into the religious fellowship of whites until the mid-eighteenth century. Masters were usually indifferent or reluctant to convert their slaves, fearing that it might prove subversive to good discipline. This began to change with the Great Awakening. Where slaves were thinly dispersed among whites, many were converted. But on plantations where contact with whites was slight, worship and belief continued to hold close to remembered ways, whether Islam or one of a variety of African traditional religions. This is documented by slave autobiographer Charles Ball (1780–), who was raised on tobacco plantations in Maryland and sold as a young man to the South Carolina lowcountry, where he worked in the rice swamps and newly emerging cotton fields. He fled north to freedom in the early 1830s and settled in rural Pennsylvania. There he told his story to a white Quaker, who published it as *Slavery in the United States* (1836). The following account, taken from Ball's narrative, describes the religious life of a community of slaves in the South Carolina lowcountry about 1800 and their masters' lack of concern for their spiritual welfare.[*]

At the time I first went to Carolina, there were a great many African slaves in the country, and they continued to come in for several years afterwards. I became intimately acquainted with some of these men. Many of them believed there were several gods; some of whom were good, and others evil, and they prayed as much to the latter as to the former. I knew several who must have been, from what I have since learned, Mahomedans [Muslims]; though at that time, I had never heard of the religion of

---

[*] Charles Ball, *Slavery in the United States: A Narrative of the Life and Adventures of Charles Ball, A Black Man* (Lewistown, Pa., 1836).

Mahomed. There was one man, on this plantation, who prayed five times every day, always turning his face to the east, when in the performance of his devotion.

There is, in general, very little sense of religious obligation, or duty, amongst the slaves on the cotton plantations; and Christianity cannot be, with propriety, called the religion of these people. They are universally subject to the grossest and most abject superstition; and uniformly believe in witch-craft, conjuration [conjuring], and the agency of evil spirits in the affairs of human life. . . .

They have not the slightest religious regard for the Sabbath day, and their masters make no efforts to impress them with the least respect for this sacred institution. My first Sunday on this plantation was but a prelude to all that followed; and I shall here give an account of it. At the time I rose . . . a large number of the men, as well as some of the women, had already quitted the quarter, and gone about the business of the day. That is, they had gone to work for wages for themselves—in this manner: our overseer had, about two miles off a field of near twenty acres, planted in cotton, on his own account. He was the owner of this land; but as he had no slaves, he was obliged to hire people to work it for him, or let it lie waste. . . . About twenty of our people went to work for him today, for which he gave them fifty cents each. Several of the others, perhaps forty in all, went out through the neighbourhood to work for other planters.

On every plantation, with which I ever had any acquaintance, the people are allowed to make patches, as they are called—that is, gardens—in some remote and unprofitable part of the estate, generally in the woods, in which they plant corn, potatoes, pumpkins, melons, etc. for themselves. These patches they must cultivate on Sunday, or let them go uncultivated. I think, that on this estate, there were about thirty of these patches, cleared in the woods; and fenced—some with rails, and others with brush—the property of the various families. The vegetables that grow in these patches, were always consumed in the families of the owners [of the patches]; and the money that was earned by hiring out, was spent in various ways; sometimes for clothes, sometimes for better food than was allowed by the overseer, and sometimes for rum; but those who drank rum, had to do it by stealth.

By the time the sun was up an hour . . . our quarter was nearly as quiet and clear of inhabitants, as it had been at the same period on the previous day. As I had nothing to do for myself, I went with Lydia, whose husband was still sick, to help her work in her patch, which was about a mile and a half from our dwelling. We took with us some bread, and a large bucket of water; and worked all day. She had onions, cabbages, cucumbers, melons, and many other things in her garden. In the evening, as we returned home, we were joined by the man who prayed five times a day; and at the going down of the sun, he stopped and prayed aloud in our hearing, in a language I did not understand.
. . .

I must here observe, that when the slaves go out to work for wages on Sunday, their employers never flog them; and so far as I know never give them abusive language. I have often hired myself to work on Sunday, and have been employed in this way by more than fifty persons, not one of whom ever insulted or mistreated me in any way. . . . The practice of working on Sunday, is so universal among slaves on the cotton plantations, that the immorality of the matter is never spoken of.

John Marrant, The Impact of the Great Awakening

The Great Awakening proved to be a major vehicle for the acculturation of African slaves. This wave of religious revivalism swept the length of colonial America from the 1730s through the 1760s, stirring seaports from Boston to Savannah and even reaching into the plantation districts of the rural South, especially in the Chesapeake. It brought thousands of new converts, including many African slaves, to Christianity for the first time. They were moved by the enthusiastic preaching and worship, the emphasis on an emotional conversion rather than theological knowledge, and the relative equality that existed in the new evangelical churches that emerged from the Awakening. George Whitefield, the Awakening's leading evangelist, regularly spoke to racially mixed congregations. The following account by John Marrant, a free black, tells of his dramatic conversion by Whitefield in Charleston in late 1769 or early 1770. Marrant (1755–1791), who had worked as a carpenter and a musician in the city, became a missionary and prosetylized among Native Americans in the South and black communities in Nova Scotia and Massachusetts before settling in England.[*]

One evening I was sent for in a very particular manner to go and play [the French-horn] to some Gentlemen, which I agreed to do, and was on my way to fulfil my promise; and passing by a large meeting house I saw many lights in it, and crowds of people going in. I enquired what it meant, and was answered by my companion that a crazy man was hallooing there; this raised my curiosity to go in, that I might hear what he was halllooing about. He persuaded me not to go in, but in vain. He then said, "If you will do one thing I will go in with you." I asked him what that was? He replied, "Blow the French-horn among them." I liked the proposal well enough, but expressed my fears of being beaten for disturbing them; but upon his promising to stand by me and defend me, I agreed. So we went, and with much difficulty got within the doors.

I was pushing the people to make room, to get the horn off my shoulder to blow it, just as Mr. Whitefield was naming his text, and looking round, as I thought, directly upon me, and pointing with his finger, he uttered these words, "PREPARE TO MEET THY GOD O ISRAEL." The Lord accompanied the word with such power, that I was struck to the ground, and lay both speechless and senseless near half an hour. When I was come a little to, I found two men attending me, and a woman throwing water in my face, and holding a smelling-bottle to my nose; and when something more recovered, every word I heard from the minister was like a parcel of swords thrust in to me, and what added to my distress, I thought I saw the devil on every side of me. I was

---

[*] John Marrant, *A Narrative of the Lord's Wonderful Dealings with John Marrant, A Black, (Now Going to Preach the Gospel in Nova-Scotia) Born in New-York, in North-America* (London, [1785]).

constrained in the bitterness of my spirit to halloo out in the midst of the congregation, which disturbing them, they took me away; but finding I could neither walk nor stand, they carried me as far as the vestry, and there I remained till the service was over.

When the people were dismissed Mr. Whitefield came into the vestry, and being told of my condition he came immediately, and the first word he said to me was, "JESUS CHRIST HAS GOT THEE AT LAST." He asked where I lived, intending to come and see me the next day; but recollecting he was to leave the town the next morning, he said he could not come himself, but would send another minister; he desired them to get me home, and then taking his leave of me, I saw him no more. When I reached my sister's house, being carried by two men, she was very uneasy to see me in so distressed a condition. She got me to bed, and sent for a doctor, who came immediately, and after looking at me, he went home, and sent me a bottle of mixture, and desired her to give me a spoonful every two hours; but I could not take any thing the doctor sent, nor indeed keep in bed; this distressed my sister very much, and she cried out, "The lad will surely die." She sent for two other doctors, but no medicine they prescribed could I take. No, no; it may be asked, a wounded spirit who can cure? as well as who can bear? In this distress of soul I continued for three days without any food, only a little water now and then.

On the fourth day, the minister Mr. Whitefield had desired to visit me came to see me, and being directed upstairs, when he entered the room, I thought he made my distress much worse. He wanted to take hold of my hand, but I durst not give it to him. He insisted upon taking hold of it, and then I got away from him on the other side of the bed; but being very weak I fell down, and before I could recover he came to me and took me by the hand, and lifted me up, and after a few words desired to go to prayer. So he fell upon his knees, and pulled me down also; after he had spent some time in prayer he rose up, and asked me how I did now; I answered, much worse; he then said, "Come, we will have the old thing over again," and so we kneeled down a second time, and after he had prayed earnestly we got up, and he said again, "How do you do now"; I replied worse and worse, and asked him if he intended to kill me? "No, no, said he, you are worth a thousand dead men, let us try the old thing over again," and so falling upon our knees, he continued in prayer a considerable time, and near the close of his prayer, the Lord was pleased to set my soul at perfect liberty, and being filled with joy I began to praise the Lord immediately; my sorrows were turned into peace, and joy, and love. The minister said, "How is it now?" I answered, all is well, all happy. He then took his leave of me; but called every day for several days afterwards, and the last time he said, "Hold fast that thou hast already obtained, 'till Jesus Christ come." I now read the Scriptures very much.

Asking Questions of the Documents

1. What aspects of European culture were most confusing and troublesome to Olaudah Equiano? Why? How did he react? Do you think his reactions were reasonable?

2. Why were slaves in the South Carolina lowcountry able to retain their African religious beliefs and practices for so long? Why might that become more difficult

after the 1730s? after 1808? What does Charles Ball's account suggest about his own religious persuasion?

3. Why did the revivalism of the Great Awakening appeal to African slaves? How might conversion to Christianity affect nonreligious aspects of slave culture?

4. Describe the conversion process experienced by John Marrant. What behavior changes did it produce? What connection does Marrant's account suggest between conversion to Christianity and the desire for literacy among the slaves? What are the cultural implications of this connection?

For Further Reading

Berlin, Ira. "Time, Space, and the Evolution of Afro-American Society on British Mainland North America." *American Historical Review* 85 (February 1980): 44-78.

Huggins, Nathan I. *Black Odyssey: The Afro-American Ordeal in Slavery.* New York: Random House, 1977. See Chapter 2 on the "Afro-Americanization" process.

Piersen, William D. *Black Yankees: The Development of an Afro-American Subculture in Eighteenth-Century New England.* Amherst, Mass.: University of Massachusetts Press, 1988.

Sobel, Mechal. *The World They Made Together: Black and White Values in Eighteenth-Century Virginia.* Princeton, N.J.: Princeton University Press, 1987.

Wood, Peter H. *Black Majority: Negroes in Colonial South Carolina from 1670 through the Stono Rebellion.* New York: W. W. Norton and Company, 1974.

Wright, Donald R. *African Americans in the Colonial Era: From African Origins through the American Revolution.* Arlington Heights, Ill.: Harlan Davidson, Inc., 1990.

3

Slavery, Race, and the American Revolution

The coming of the American Revolution prompted many colonists—black and white—to openly question the morality of slavery for the first time. Between 1763 and 1776, as white Americans moved to sever their relationship with the mother country of Britain, slavery too became a concern of pamphlets, sermons, and legislative debates. Black bondage seemed inconsistent with colonial arguments for political liberty, which rested upon a natural rights philosophy that embraced the equality and the inalienable rights of all humankind.

The rising political and philosophical challenge to slavery stirred white and black Americans alike. Calls for gradual emancipation and the abolition of the Atlantic slave trade struck a responsive chord among whites in the North, where slaves comprised less than 5 percent of the population. Even in the Chesapeake, where half of all African Americans lived, slaveholders publicly discussed emancipation and hundreds privately freed (or manumitted) their slaves. Although rarely affected by revenue stamps, sugar duties, or boycotts against tea, African Americans were also politicized by the rhetoric of revolution. Whether speaking with "jack tars" (white workers) on the streets of colonial ports or eavesdropping on the dinner table conversations of their masters, they increasingly imbibed the ideology of natural rights. This frequently led to action. Slaves from Virginia to New England flooded local courts and legislatures with petitions for freedom. Thousands made personal declarations of independence by running away.

When war finally broke out between America and Britain in 1775, African Americans hoped that the struggle would bring slavery to an end. Yet they were divided as to which side would best accomplish that objective. White colonists spoke of liberty and equality but held slaves. The British promised freedom to all slaves who flocked to their banner but were often characterized as tyrants. As a result, slaves and free blacks fought for both sides. Some five thousand eventually joined the American forces, fighting valiantly in major battles from Lexington and Concord to Yorktown. Tens of thousands of slaves fled to the British lines. A few of these even shouldered arms for the king in Virginia and the Carolinas. At the conclusion of the conflict, many runaway slaves left with other Loyalists for the British colonies of Nova Scotia, Florida, and Jamaica.

After the Revolution, some proponents of political liberty feared that challenges to slavery and other institutions might lead too far in the direction of social revolution in the new United States. A conservative reaction set in. Defenders of the status quo began to construct a coherent racist ideology for the first time, questioning both the equality and humanity of African Americans. Even though slavery was declining in the North, the Constitutional Convention of 1787 did nothing to challenge the institution elsewhere. As the eighteenth century ended, the practice of black bondage remained firmly entrenched throughout the plantation South.

Phillis Wheatley, "Our Modern Egyptians"

African Americans enthusiastically embraced the natural rights philosophy that undergirded the American Revolution. The incompatibility of slavery with this ideology of human equality and inalienable rights is clearly stated in the following letter from Phillis Wheatley to Rev. Samson Occom, a Native American clergyman with whom she corresponded. Born in Africa, Wheatley (ca. 1754–1784), was enslaved and brought to Boston at age seven. There she became the house servant of a sympathetic Quaker couple, from whom she obtained her surname. They encouraged her interest in learning and her flair for poetry, even sending her in 1773 to England, where she published a book of poems. An advocate of emancipation during the struggle for American independence, Wheatley finally received her own freedom in 1778.[*]

February 11, 1774

Rev'd and honor'd Sir,

I have this Day received your obliging kind Epistle, and am greatly satisfied with your Reasons respecting the Negroes, and think highly reasonable what you offer in Vindication of their natural Rights. Those that invade them cannot be insensible that the divine Light is chasing away the thick Darkness which broods over the Land of Africa; and the Chaos which has reign'd so long, is converting into beautiful Order, and reveals more and more clearly, the glorious Dispensation of civil and religious Liberty, which are so inseparably united, that there is little or no Enjoyment of one without the other. Otherwise, perhaps, the Israelites had been less solicitous for their Freedom from Egyptian Slavery; I don't say they would have been contented without it. By no Means, for in every human Breast, God has implanted a Principle, which we call Love of

---

[*] *Boston News-Letter* (Massachusetts Gazette), 24 March 1774.

Freedom; it is impatient of Oppression, and pants for Deliverance. And by the leave of our modern Egyptians, I will assert that the same principle lives in us. God grant Deliverance in his own Way and Time, and get him honor upon all those whose Avarice impels them to countenance and help forward the Calamities of their fellow Creatures. This I desire not for their Hurt, but to convince them of the strange Absurdity of their Conduct whose Words and Actions are so diametrically opposite. How well the cry for Liberty, and the reverse Disposition for the exercise of oppressive Power over others agree, I humbly think it does not require the Penetration of a Philosopher to determine.

Phillis Wheatley

A Petition for Freedom in Massachusetts

The coming of the American Revolution raised the hopes of African Americans that slavery would finally be abolished. As a result, slaves throughout the Chesapeake and the North petitioned local courts and new state legislatures for an end to bondage. This practice was especially prevalent in Massachusetts, where petitions first reached the legislature in 1773 and continued throughout the rest of the decade. Some petitioners asked for the immediate abolition of slavery, others for the gradual beginning of the process, and a few for transportation to the African continent. The following petition from eight Boston blacks drew upon the natural rights philosophy in arguing for the passage of a gradual emancipation act in the state.*

To the Honorable Legislature of the State of Massachusetts Bay, January 13, 1777:

The petition of a great number of blacks detained in a state of slavery in the bowels of a free & Christian country humbly sheweth that your petitioners apprehend we have in common with all other men a natural and unalienable right to that freedom which the Great Parent of the Universe hath bestowed equally on all mankind, and which they have never forfeited by any compact or agreement whatever. But they were unjustly dragged by the hand of cruel power from their dearest friends and some of them even torn from the embraces of their tender parents—from a populous, pleasant, and plentiful country and in violation of laws of nature and nations—and, in defiance of all the tender feelings of humanity, brought here to be sold like beasts of burthen & like them condemned to slavery for life among a people professing the mild religion of Jesus—a people not insensible of the secrets of rational beings nor without spirit to resent the

---

* Corrected version of the original petition reprinted in Massachusetts Historical Society, *Collections*, 5th ser., Vol. 3 (Boston, 1877), 436-37.

unjust endeavours of others to reduce them to a state of bondage and subjection. Your honours need not to be informed that a life of slavery like that of your petitioners, deprived of every social privilege, of every thing requisite to render life tolerable, is far worse than nonexistence.

In imitation of the laudable example of the good people of these states, your petitioners have long and patiently waited the event of petition after petition by them presented to the legislative body of this state and cannot but with grief reflect that their success hath been but too similar. They cannot but express their astonishment that it has never been considered that every principle from which Americans have acted in the course of their unhappy difficulties with Great Britain pleads stronger than a thousand arguments in favour of your petitioners. They therefore humbly beseech your honours to give this petition its due weight & consideration & cause an act of the legislature to be passed whereby they may be restored to the enjoyments of that which is the natural right of all men—and their children who were born in this land of liberty may not be held as slaves after they arrive at the age of twenty one years. So may the inhabitants of this state, no longer chargeable with the inconsistency of acting themselves the part which they condemn and oppose in others, be prospered in their present glorious struggle for liberty and have those blessings to them, &c.

Lancaster Hill
Peter Bess
Brister Slenser
Prince Hall
Jack Pierpont
Nero Funelo
Newport Sumner
Job Look

Benjamin Banneker, Challenging the Racial Views of a Founding Father

A coherent racist ideology was first constructed in the wake of the American Revolution. Even though moved by natural rights philosophy to challenge the institution of slavery, white Americans remained uncomfortable with the social and economic effects of emancipation. This dichotomy appeared in the thinking of many of the Founding Fathers, especially Thomas Jefferson. Among the earliest to question the morality of slavery, he owned some 150 slaves until his death. The leading American exponent of the natural rights philosophy, he nevertheless believed that blacks were permanently inferior—both mentally and morally—to whites. African Americans raised their voices to challenge this ideology. One of the most articulate was Benjamin

Banneker (1731–1806), a free black from Maryland. Considered to be one of the leading American men of science, he predicted a solar eclipse, published reliable almanacs each year from 1791 to 1802, manufactured the first American clock, and helped design the street pattern in the District of Columbia. In the following letter to Jefferson, Banneker subtly exposes the contradictions in the Founding Father's thinking on race.*

Maryland, Baltimore County
Near Ellicott's Lower Mills

August 19th, 1791

Thomas Jefferson
Secretary of State

Sir,

I am fully sensible of the greatness of that freedom which I take with you on the present occasion; a liberty which Seemed to me Scarcely allowable, when I reflected on that distinguished, and dignifyed station in which you Stand; and the almost general prejudice and prepossession which is so previlent in the world against those of my complexion.

I suppose it is a truth too well attested to you, to need a proof here, that we are a race of Beings who have long laboured under the abuse and censure of the world, that we have been looked upon with an eye of contempt, and that we have long been considered rather as brutish than human, and Scarcely capable of mental endowments.

Sir, I hope I may Safely admit, in consequence of that report which hath reached me, that you are a man far less inflexible in Sentiments of this nature, than many others; that you are measurably friendly and well disposed towards us, and that you are willing and ready to Lend your aid and assistance to our relief from those many distresses and numerous calamaties to which we are reduced.

Now, Sir, if this is founded in truth, I apprehend you will readily embrace every opportunity to eradicate that train of absurd and false ideas and opinions which so generally prevail with respect to us, and that your Sentiments are concurrent with mine, which are that one universal Father hath given being to us all, and that he hath not only made us all of one flesh, but that he hath also without partiality afforded us all the Same Sensations, and endued us all with the same faculties, and that however variable we may be in Society or religion, however diversified in Situation or colour, we are all of the Same Family, and Stand in the Same relation to him.

Sir, if these are the Sentiments of which you are fully persuaded, I hope you cannot but acknowledge, that it is the indispensible duty of those who maintain for themselves the rights of human nature, and who profess the obligations of Christiantity, to extend their power and influence to the relief of every part of the human race, from whatever

---

* Copy of a *Letter from Benjamin Banneker to the Secretary of State, with His Answer* (Philadelphia, 1792).

burthen or oppression they may unjustly labour under; and this I apprehend a full conviction of the truth and obligation of these principles should lead all to.

Sir, I have long been convinced, that if your love for your Selves and for those inesteemable laws which preserve to you the rights of human nature, was founded on Sincerity, you could not but be Solicitous, that every Individual of whatsoever rank or distinction, might with you equally enjoy the blessings thereof, neither could you rest Satisfyed, short of the most active diffusion of your exertions, in order to their promotion from any State of degradation, to which the unjustifyable cruelty and barbarism of men may have reduced them.

Sir, I freely and Chearfully acknowledge, that I am of the African race, and, in that colour which is natural to them of the deepest dye*; and it is under a Sense of the most profound gratitude to the Supreme Ruler of the universe, that I now confess to you, that I am not under that state of tyrannical thraldom, and inhuman captivity, to which too many of my brethren are doomed; but that I have abundantly tasted of the fruition of those blessings which proceed from that free and unequalled liberty with which you are favoured and which I hope you will willingly allow you have received from the immediate Hand of that Being from whom proceeedeth every good and perfect gift.

Sir, Suffer me to recall to your mind that time in which the Arms and tyranny of the British Crown were exerted with every powerful effort, in order to reduce you to a State of Servitude; look back I entreat you on the variety of dangers to which you were exposed, reflect on that time in which every human aid appeared unavailable, and in which even hope and fortitude wore the aspect of inability to the Conflict, and you cannot but be led to a Serious and grateful Sense of your miraculous and providential preservation; You cannot but acknowledge, that the present freedom and tranquillity which you enjoy you have mercifully received, and that it is the peculiar blessing of Heaven.

This, Sir, was a time in which you clearly saw into the injustice of a State of Slavery, and in which you had just apprehensions of the horrors of its condition, it was now Sir, that your abhorrence was so excited, that you publickly held forth this true and invaluable doctrine, which is worthy to be recorded and remembered in all Succeeding ages. "We hold these truths to be Self evident, that all men are created equal, and that they are endowed by their creator with certain inalienable rights, that amongst these are life, liberty, and the pursuit of happiness."

Here, Sir, was a time in which your tender feelings for yourselves engaged you thus to declare, you were then impressed with proper ideas of the great valuation of liberty, and the free possession of those blessings to which you were entitled by nature; but Sir how pitiable it is to reflect, that altho you were so fully convinced of the benevolence of the Father of mankind, and of his equal and impartial distribution of those rights and privileges which he had conferred upon them, that you should at the Same time counteract his mercies, in detaining by fraud and violence so numerous a part of my brethren under groaning captivity and cruel oppression, that you should at the Same time be found guilty of that most criminal act, which you professedly detested in others, with respect to yourselves.

---

* My Father was brought here a Slave from Africa.

Sir, I suppose that your knowledge of the situation of my brethren is too extensive to need a recital here; neither shall I presume to prescribe methods by which they may be relived, otherwise than by recommending to you, and all others, to wean yourselves from those narrow prejudices which you have imbibed with respect to them, and as Job proposed to his friends "Put your Souls in their Souls' stead," thus shall your hearts be enlarged with kindness and benevolence toward them, and thus shall you need neither the direction of myself or others in what manner to proceed herein.

And now, Sir, altho my Sympathy and affection for my brethren hath caused my enlargement thus far, I ardently hope that your candour and generosity will plead with you in my behalf, when I make known to you, that it was not originally my design; but that having taken up my pen in order to direct to you a present, a copy of an Almanack which I have calculated for the Succeeding year, I was unexpectedly and unavoidably led thereto.

This calculation, Sir, is the production of my arduous study, in this advanced Stage of life; for having long had unbounded desires to become Acquainted with the Secrets of nature, I have had to gratify my curiosity herein thro my own assiduous application to Astronomical Study, in which I need not to recount to you the many difficulties and disadvantages which I have had to encounter. . . .

And now Sir, I Shall conclude and Subscribe my Self with the most profound respect,

Your most Obedient and humble Servant

Benjamin Banneker

Asking Questions of the Documents

1. What was the natural rights philosophy? How did Phillis Wheatley and the eight black petitioners from Boston use this argument to challenge the morality of slavery?

2. What did the Boston petitioners ask the Massachusetts legislature to do in order to be consistent with the natural rights philosophy? Why might they have urged this approach rather than the immediate abolition of slavery?

3. What strategies does Benjamin Banneker use to expose the contradictions in Thomas Jefferson's thinking on race? Are they effective?

4. Why would Banneker be an especially effective opponent of the racist ideology of Jefferson and other Founding Fathers? Why do you think he sent Jefferson a copy of his almanac?

For Further Reading

Berlin, Ira, and Ronald Hoffman, eds. *Slavery and Freedom in the Age of the American Revolution.* Charlottesville, Va.: University of Virginia Press, 1983.

Finkelman, Paul. *Slavery and the Founders: Race and Liberty in the Age of Jefferson.* London: M. E. Sharpe, 1996.

Frey, Sylvia. *Water from the Rock: Black Resistance in a Revolutionary Age.* Princeton, N.J.: Princeton University Press, 1991.

Kaplan, Sidney. *The Black Presence in the Era of the American Revolution, 1770-1800.* Rev. ed. Amherst, Mass.: University of Massachusetts Press, 1989.

Nash, Gary B. *Race and Revolution.* Madison, Wisc.: Madison House, 1991.

Quarles, Benjamin. *The Negro in the American Revolution.* Chapel Hill, N.C.: University of North Carolina Press, 1961.

Wood, Peter H. "'The Dream Deferred': Black Freedom Struggles on the Eve of White Independence." In *In Resistance: Studies in African, Caribbean, and Afro-American History*, ed. Gary Y. Okihiro, 166-87. Amherst, Mass.: University of Massachusetts Press, 1986.

Zilversmit, Arthur. *The First Emancipation: The Abolition of Slavery in the North.* Chicago: University of Chicago Press, 1967.

4

Free Black Communities in the New Nation

Free black communities developed throughout the United States in the wake of the American Revolution. There had been only a few thousand free blacks in colonial America. But the free black population expanded dramatically in the decades following independence. This was the result of four factors. First, thousands of slaves were emancipated by the British as a war measure or gained their freedom in return for fighting on the American side. Second, northern state legislatures and courts, animated by the ideology of human equality and natural rights, mandated gradual emancipation for slaves within their jurisdictions. Third, hundreds of slaveowners in the Chesapeake, similarly inspired by the rhetoric of revolution, personally freed (or manumitted) their slaves. Finally, several thousand French-speaking mulattoes migrated from the Caribbean to the United States during the Haitian Revolution. From the first federal census of 1790 until the beginning of the Civil War, free blacks constituted about 10 percent of the African-American population in the United States. Slightly more than half lived in the South.

Freedom did not mean equality with whites. A matrix of laws and customs subjected free blacks—whether living in the North or the South—to discriminatory treatment. For this reason, historians haved termed them "quasi-free" or "slaves without masters." So-called black laws restricted the civil liberties of free blacks throughout the nation. In many areas of the South, they could not learn to read and write, travel or associate freely, or engage in certain trades. Arkansas even enacted a law in 1859 requiring all free blacks to leave the state. Things were little better in the North. Several states prohibited them from voting, serving on juries, testifying in court cases involving whites, or becoming residents. Everywhere, free blacks were consigned to the economic margins and excluded from or segregated within the dominant social institutions—schools, churches, theaters, streetcars, and the like. Racial slurs and stereotypes hounded them on city streets, in minstrel shows, and in the popular press.

A majority of free blacks congregated in urban areas, where they formed hundreds of independent institutions to resist discriminatory treatment and to serve their social, economic, intellectual, and religious needs. Churches were the earliest and most important. But they were soon followed by schools, libraries, reading rooms, and forums for literary discussion and debate; lodges; burial and insurance societies; associations to aid the ill and indigent; asylums for orphans and the aged; and moral reform organizations. Rich and vibrant free black communities developed in Boston, New York City, Philadelphia, Baltimore, Washington, D.C., Charleston, New Orleans, and dozens of other American cities. After 1827 an independent black press publicized the concerns and accomplishments of these communities. But their successes frequently made them targets for white mob violence.

Faced with unequal and abusive treatment from whites, some free blacks considered abandoning the United States for a more hospitable place. They received encouragement and support from the American Colonization Society, which was founded in 1816 to finance the expatriation of free blacks and to spur the voluntary emancipation of southern slaves. The largely white organization established the colony of Liberia on the west coast of Africa in 1822 as a site for African-American settlement. But the colonization movement ultimately gained few free black converts. Although ten thousand African Americans left for Liberia before the Civil War, only four thousand of these were free blacks—less than 1 percent of the free black population.

Maria W. Stewart, A Little Better than Slavery

Free blacks were victimized by discriminatory laws and customs that kept them on the social and economic margins. The causes and effects of such treatment are considered in the following excerpt from a speech by Maria W. Stewart (1803–1879), a Boston free black. After her husband's death in 1829, Stewart embarked on a brief career as an antislavery activist, feminist, and crusader for free black rights. She defied social convention by becoming the first black woman to speak from a public platform before American audiences. Her unconventional behavior stirred such hostility that in 1833 she abandoned public speaking and left Boston.*

I have heard much respecting the horrors of slavery; but may Heaven forbid that the generality of my color throughout these United States should experience any more of its horrors than to be a servant of servants, or hewers of wood and drawers of water! Tell us no more of southern slavery; for with few exceptions, although I may be very erroneous in my opinion, yet I consider our condition but little better than that. . . . After all, methinks there are no chains so galling as those that bind the soul, and exclude it from the vast field of useful and scientific knowledge. . . .

I have asked several individuals of my sex, who transact business for themselves, if providing our girls were to give them the most satisfactory references, they would not be

---

* Maria W. Stewart, "Lecture Delivered at the Franklin Hall, Boston, September 21, 1832," in *Productions of Mrs. Maria W. Stewart* (Boston, 1835).

willing to grant them an equal opportunity with others? Their reply has been—for their own part, they had no objection; but as it was not the custom, were they to take them into their employ, they would be in danger of losing the public patronage.

And such is the powerful force of prejudice. Let our girls possess whatever amiable qualities of soul they may; let their characters be fair and spotless as innocence itself; let their natural taste and ingenuity be what they may; it is impossible for scarce an individual of them to rise above the condition of servants. Ah! why is this cruel and unfeeling distinction? Is it merely because God has made our complexion to vary? . . . O, horrible idea, indeed! To possess noble souls aspiring after high and honorable acquirements, yet confined by the chains of ignorance and poverty to lives of continual drudgery and toil. . . .

I observed a piece . . . a few months since, stating that the colonizationists had published a work respecting us, asserting that we were lazy and idle. I confute them on that point. Take us generally as a people, we are neither lazy nor idle: and considering how little we have to excite or stimulate us, I am almost astonished that there are so many industrious and ambitious ones to be found; although I acknowledge, with extreme sorrow, that there are some who never were and never will be serviceable to society. And have you not a similar class among yourselves?

Again it was asserted that we were "a ragged set, crying for liberty." I reply to it, the whites have so long and so loudly proclaimed the theme of equal rights and privileges, that our souls have caught the flame also, ragged as we are. As far as our merit deserves, we feel a common desire to rise above the condition of servants and drudges. I have learnt, by bitter experience, that continual hard labor deadens the energies of the soul, and benumbs the faculties of the mind; the ideas become confined, the mind barren, and, like the scorching sands of Arabia, produces nothing: or like the uncultivated soil, brings forth thorns and thistles.

Again, continual and hard labor irritates our tempers and sours our dispositions; the whole system becomes worn out with toil and fatigue; nature herself becomes almost exhausted, and we care but little whether we live or die. It is true, that the free people of color throughout these United States are neither bought nor sold, nor under the lash of the cruel driver; many obtain a comfortable support; but few, if any, have an opportunity of becoming rich and independent; and the enjoyments we most pursue are as unprofitable to us as the spider's web or the floating bubbles that vanish into air. As servants, we are respected; but let us presume to aspire any higher, our employer regards us no longer. . . .

Most of our color have dragged out a miserable existence of servitude from the cradle to the grave. And what literary acquirement can be made, or useful knowledge derived, from either maps, books, or charts, by those who continually drudge from Monday morning until Sunday noon? . . . I am also one of the wretched and miserable daughters of the descendants of fallen Africa. Do you ask, why are you wretched and miserable? I reply, look at many of the most worthy and most interesting of us doomed to spend our lives in gentlemen's kitchens. Look at our young men, smart, active, and energetic, with souls filled with ambitious fire; if they look forward, alas! What are their prospects? They can be nothing but the humblest laborers, on account of their dark complexions; hence many of them lose their ambition, and become worthless. Look at our middle-aged men, clad in their rusty plaids and coats; in winter, every cent they earn goes to buy their wood and pay their rents; the poor wives also toil beyond their strength, to help support their families. Look at our aged sires, whose heads are whitened with the frosts of seventy winters, with their old wood-saws on their backs. Alas, what keeps us so? Prejudice, ignorance and poverty.

Richard Allen, The Rise of African-American Churches

Free blacks formed a variety of institutions to fight the effects of prejudice and to serve the social, cultural, and economic needs of their growing communities. Churches were the earliest and most important of these institutions. In most cases, they functioned not only as places of worship but housed schools and hosted political meetings, concerts, debates, and the gatherings of benevolent and moral reform organizations. Beginning in 1787, thousands of free blacks in the North and the Chesapeake abandoned white sanctuaries to establish separate Methodist, Baptist, Presbyterian, and Episcopal congregations. The reason for the rise of these churches is explained in the following account from the autobiography of black clergyman Richard Allen. Raised in slavery in Delaware, Allen (1760–1831) bought his freedom at age seventeen and settled in Philadelphia, where in 1792 he and Absalom Jones led free black parishioners out of the largely white St. George's Methodist Church. Many of these separatists soon organized as the Bethel African Methodist Church, with Allen as their pastor. In 1816 he called together Bethel and several other black Methodist congregations to create the African Methodist Episcopal denomination—the earliest distinctly black religious body.[*]

A number of us usually attended St. George's church in Fourth street; and when the colored people began to get numerous in attending the church, they moved us from the seats we usually sat on, and placed us around the wall, and on Sabbath morning, we went to the church and the sexton stood at the door, and told us to go in the gallery. He told us to go, and we would see where to sit. We expected to take the seats over the ones we formerly occupied below, not knowing any better. We took those seats. Meeting had begun, and they were nearly done singing, and just as we got to the seats, the elder said, "Let us pray." We had not been long upon our knees before I heard considerable scuffling and low talking. I raised my head up and saw one of the trustees, H__M__, having hold of the Rev. Absalom Jones, pulling him up off his knees, and saying, "You must get up—you must not kneel here." Mr. Jones replied, "Wait until prayer is over."

[*] Richard Allen, *The Life Experiences and Gospel Labors of the Rt. Rev. Richard Allen* (Philadelphia, 1833).

Mr. H__M__ said "No, you must get up now, or I will call for aid and force you away." Mr. Jones said, "Wait until prayer is over, and I will get up and trouble you no more." With that he beckoned to one of the other trustees, Mr. L___ S___ to come to his assistance. He came, and went to William White to pull him up. By this time prayer was over, and we all went out of the church in a body, and they were no more plagued with us in the church. . . . We then hired a store-room, and held worship by ourselves. Here we were pursued with threats of being disowned, and read publicly out of meeting if we did continue worship in the place we had hired; but we believed the Lord would be our friend. We got subscription papers out to raise money to build the house of the Lord. . . .

I bought an old frame that had been formerly occupied as a blacksmith shop, . . . and hauled it on the lot in Sixth near Lombard street, that had formerly been taken for the Church of England. I employed carpenters to repair the old frame, and fit it for a place of worship. In July 1794, Bishop Asbury being in town I solicited him to open the church for us which he accepted. . . . The house was called Bethel, agreeable to the prayer that was made . . . that it might be a bethel to the gathering in of thousands of souls. My dear Lord was with us, so that there were many hearty "amens" echoed through the house. This house of worship has been favored with the awakening of many souls, and I trust they are in the Kingdom, both white and colored.

Our warfare and troubles now began afresh. Mr. C__ proposed that we should make over the church to the Conference. This we objected to, he asserted that we could not be Methodists unless we did, we told him he might deny us their name, but they could not deny us a seat in Heaven. Finding that he could not prevail with us so to do, he observed that we had better be incorporated, then we would get any legacies that were left for us, if not, we could not. We agreed to be incorporated. He offered to draw the incorporation himself, that it would save us the trouble of paying for to get it drawn. We cheerfully submitted to his proposed plan. He drew the incorporation, but incorporated our church under the Conference; our property was then all consigned to the Conference for the present bishops, elders, ministers, etc., that belonged to the white Conference, and our property was gone. Being ignorant of incorporations we cheerfully agreed thereto. We labored about ten years under this incorporation, until James Smith was appointed to take the charge in Philadelphia; he soon waked us up by demanding the keys and books of the church, and forbid us holding any meetings except by orders from him; these propositions we told him we could not agree to. He observed he was elder, appointed to the charge, and unless we submitted to him, he would read us all out of meeting. We told him the house was ours, we had bought it, and paid for it. He said he would let us know it was not ours, it belonged to the Conference; we took counsel on it; counsel informed us we had been taken in; according to the incorporation it belonged to the white connection. We asked him if it couldn't be altered; he told us if two-thirds of the society agreed to have it altered, it could be altered. . . . I called the society together and laid it before them. My dear Lord was with us. It was unanimously agreed to, by both male and female. We had another incorporation drawn that took the church from the Conference. . . .

About this time, our colored friends in Baltimore were treated in a similar manner by the white preachers and trustees, and many of them driven away who were disposed to seek a place of worship. . . . Many of the colored people in other places were in a situation nearly like those of Philadelphia and Baltimore, which induced us, in April

1816, to call a general meeting, by way of Conference. Delegates from Baltimore and other places . . . met those of Philadelphia, and taking into consideration their grievances, . . . it was resolved: "That the people of Philadelphia, Baltimore, etc., etc., should become one body, under the name of the African Methodist Episcopal Church." We deemed it expedient to have a form of discipline, whereby we may guide our people in the fear of God, in the unity of the Spirit, and in the bonds of peace, and preserve us from that spiritual despotism which we have so recently experienced.

Samuel Cornish, An Independent Press

Second only to the church in importance as an institution in free black communities was the African-American press. At least seventeen black newspapers were published before the Civil War. They spoke out for emancipation and equality, addressed subjects neglected or superficially treated by white journals, countered racial slurs and stereotypes in the broader culture, and linked together dozens of free black communities. The first African-American newspaper, *Freedom's Journal*, was founded in New York City in 1827 by free blacks Samuel Cornish and John B. Russwurm. Cornish (ca. 1796-1858), a Presbyterian clergyman, would be the most important figure in the African-American press over the next two decades. In the following editorial, which appeared in the *Journal*'s first issue, he explains to readers the purposes and objectives of his new venture.[*]

The noble objects which we have in view by the publication of this Journal . . . encourage us to come boldly before an enlightened publick. . . . We should advertise to the world our motives by which we are actuated, and the objects which we contemplate.

We wish to plead our own cause. Too long have others spoken for us. Too long has the publick been deceived by misrepresentations, in things which concern us dearly, though in the estimation of some mere trifles; for though there are many in society who exercise towards us benevolent feelings; still (with sorrow we confess it) there are those who make it their business to enlarge upon the least trifle, which tends to the discredit of any person of colour; and pronounce anathemas and denounce our whole body for the misconduct of this guilty one. We are aware that there are many instances of vice among us, but we avow that it is because no one has taught its subjects to be virtuous; many instances of poverty, because no sufficient efforts accommodated to minds contracted by slavery, and deprived of early education have been made, to teach them how to husband their hard earnings, and to secure to themselves comfort.

---

[*] *Freedom's Journal* (New York), 16 March 1827.

Education being an object of the highest importance to the welfare of society, we shall endeavour to present just and adequate views of it, and to urge upon our brethren the necessity and expediency of training their children, while young, to habits of industry, and thus forming them for becoming useful members of society. It is surely time that we should awake from this lethargy of years, and make a concentrated effort for the education of our youth. We form a spoke in the human wheel and it is necessary that we should understand our [de]pendence on the different parts, and theirs on us, in order to perform our part with propriety.

Though not desiring of dictating, we shall feel it our incumbent duty to dwell occasionally upon the general principles and rules of economy. The world has grown too enlightened, to estimate any man's character by his personal appearance. Though all men acknowledge the excellency of Franklin's maxims, yet comparatively few practise upon them. We may deplore when it is too late, the neglect of these self-evidents truths, but it avails little to mourn. Ours will be the task of admonishing our brethren on these points.

The civil rights of a people being of the greatest value, it shall ever be our duty to vindicate our brethren, when oppressed; and to lay the case before the publick. We shall also urge upon our brethren (who are qualified by the laws of the various states), the expendiency of using their elective franchise; and of making independent use of the same. We wish them not to become the tools of party.

And as much time is frequently lost, and wrong principles instilled, by the perusal of works of trivial importance, we shall consider it a part of our duty to recommend to our young readers, such authors as will not only enlarge their stock of useful knowledge, but such as will also serve to stimulate them to higher attainments in science.

We trust also, that through the columns of the FREEDOM'S JOURNAL, many practical pieces, having for their bases, the improvement of our brethren, will be presented to them, from the pens of many of our respected friends, who have kindly promised their assistance.

It is our earnest wish to make our Journal a medium of intercourse between our brethren in the different states of this great confederacy: that through its columns an expression of our sentiments, on many interesting subjects which concern us, may be offered to the publick: that plans which apparently are beneficial may be candidly discussed and properly weighed; if worthy, receive our cordial approbation; if not, our marked disapprobation.

Useful knowledge of every kind, and everything that relates to Africa, shall find a ready admission in our columns; and as that vast continent becomes daily more known, we trust that many things will come to light, proving that the natives of it are neither so ignorant nor stupid as they have generally supposed to be.

And while these important subjects shall occupy the columns of the FREEDOM'S JOURNAL, we would not be unmindful of our brethren who are still in the iron fetters of bondage. They are our kindred by all the times of nature; and though but little can be effected by us, still let our sympathies be poured forth, and our prayers in their behalf, ascend to Him who is able to succour them.

From the press and the pulpit we have suffered much by being incorrectly represented. Men whom we equally love and admire have not hesitated to represent us disadvantageously, without becoming personally acquainted with the true state of things, nor discerning between virtue and vice among us. The virtuous part of our people feel themselves sorely aggrieved under the existing state of things—they are not appreciated.

Our vices and our degradation are ever arrayed against us, but our virtues are passed by unnoticed. And what is still more lamentable, our friends, to whom we concede all the principles of humanity and religion, from these very causes seem to have fallen into the current of popular feeling and are imperceptibly floating on the stream— actually living in the practice of prejudice, while they abjure it in theory, and feel it not in their hearts. Is it not very desirable that such should know more of our actual condition; and of our efforts and feelings, that in forming or advocating plans for our amelioration, they may do it more understandingly? In the spirit of candor and humility we intend by a simple representation of facts to lay our case before the publick, with a view to arrest the progress of prejudice, and to shield ourselves against the consequent evils. We wish to conciliate all and to irritate none, yet we must be firm and unwavering in our principles, and perservering in our efforts.

John B. Russwurm, Colonization Endorsed

The African colonization movement divided free black communities. A minority advocated the Liberian alternative as the only hope for improving their existence. The most prominent black colonizationist was John B. Russwurm (1799–1851), the second black to earn an American college degree when he graduated in 1826 from Bowdoin College. He left *Freedom's Journal* in 1829, accepted an appointment from the Maryland Colonization Society, and sailed for Liberia, where he eventually served as governor of the Maryland-in-Liberia settlement. In the following editorial, he explains his reasons for endorsing colonization.

Free Blacks go back to Africa.

We feel proud in announcing . . . ourselves . . . ready to embrace the first convenient opportunity to embark for the shores of Africa. . . .

The subject of Colonization is certainly important, as having a great bearing on that of slavery: for it must be evident that the universal emancipation so ardently desired by *us* & by all our friends can never take place unless some door is opened whereby the emancipated may be removed, as fast as they drop their galling chains, to some other land beside the free states; for it is a fact, that prejudices now in our part of the country, are so high, that it is often the remark of liberal men from the south, that their free people are treated better than we are in the boasted free states of the north. If the free states have passed no law as yet forbidding the emigration of free persons of colour into their limits; it is no reason that they will not, as soon as they find themselves a little

---

Freedom's Journal (New York), 14 March 1829.

more burdened. We will suppose that a general law of emancipation should be promulgated in the state of Virginia, under the existing statutes which require every emancipated slave to leave the state, would not the other states, in order to shield themselves from the evils of having so many thousands of ignorant beings thrown upon them be obliged in self-defense to pass prohibitory laws? . . . If no good whatever arose from the establishment of colonies, the fact that they remove all obstacles in the way of emancipation should gain for them the support and good wishes of every friend of humanity, & of every enlightened man of colour. It is true, that no such laws at present are in force to our knowledge, but who can foretell how soon before they may, without waiting for the period of a general emancipation in any of the slaveholding states.

Our wiseacres may talk as much as they please upon . . . our future standing in society, but it does not alter the case in the least; it does not improve our situation in the least; but it is calculated rather to stay the exertions of those who are really willing to make some efforts to improve their own present conditions. We are considered a distinct people, in the midst of the millions around us, and in the most favorable parts of the country; and it matters not from what cause this sentence has been passed upon us; the fiat has gone forth and should each of us live to the age of Methuselah, at the end of the thousand years, we should be exactly in our present situation: a proscribed race, however unjustly—a degraded people, deprived of all the rights of freemen and in the eyes of the community, a race who had no lot or portion with them.

We hope that none of our readers will from our remarks think that we approve in the least of the present prejudices in the way of the man of colour; far from it, we deplore them as much as any man; but they are not of our creating, and they are not in our power to remove. . . . It will never be in our power to remove or overcome them. . . .

Sensible then, as all are of the disadvantages under which we at present labour, can any consider it a mark of folly, for us to cast our eyes upon some other portion of the globe where all these inconveniences are removed—where the Man of Colour freed from the fetters and prejudice and degradation, under which he labours in this land, may walk forth in all the majesty of his creation—a Free Man! It was, we believe, the remark of [an Englishman], while on the African coast, that the natives whom he saw were a fine athletic race, walking fearlessly as if sensible of their important station as men, and quite different from the thousands of their brethren whom he had seen in the West Indies and the United States; and never was a truer remark made, if we are to credit all other travellers on that Continent, who have likewise born testimony to the same fact.

Peter Williams Jr., Colonization Rejected

The vast majority of free blacks rejected the African colonization movement. The views of Peter Williams Jr., a black Episcopal priest in New York City, were representative of their thoughts on the subject. Although Williams (ca. 1780–1840) had initially encouraged Russwurm and others to go to Liberia, he became an outspoken critic of colonization by 1830. He explains his reasons for that stance in the following document from that year, a Fourth of July sermon to his congregation. Williams spent his final decade toiling in the American antislavery movement.[*]

Though delivered from the fetters of slavery, we are oppressed by an unreasonable, unrighteous, and cruel prejudice, which aims at nothing less than the forcing away of all the free coloured people of the United States to the distant shores of Africa. Far be it from me to impeach the motives of every member of the African Colonization Society. The civilizing and Christianizing of that vast continent, and the extirpation of the abominable traffic in slaves (which notwithstanding all the laws passed for its suppression is still carried on in all its horrors), are no doubt the principal motives which induce many to give it their support.

But there are those, and those who are most active and most influential in its cause, who hesitate not to say that they wish to rid the country of the free coloured population, and there is sufficient reason to believe, that with many, this is the principal motive for supporting that society; and that whether Africa is civilized or not, and whether the Slave Trade be suppressed or not, they would wish to see the free coloured people removed from this country to Africa.

Africa could certainly be brought into a state of civil and religious improvement without sending all the free people of colour in the United States there.

How inconsistent are those who say that Africa will be benefited by the removal of the free people of colour of the United States there, while they say they are *the most vile and degraded* people in the world. If we are as vile and degraded as they represent us, and they wish the Africans to be rendered a virtuous, enlightened, and happy people, they should not *think* of sending *us* among them, lest we should make them worse instead of better. . . . Those who say *we* are the most vile people in the world would send us to Africa to improve the character and condition of the natives. Such arguments would not be listened to for a moment were not the minds of the community strangely warped by prejudice. . . .

[*] *Emancipator* (Boston), 22 April 1834.

Much has been said by the Colonizationists about improving the character and condition of the people of colour of this country by sending them to Africa. This is more inconsistent still. We are to be improved by being sent far from civilized society. This is a novel mode of improvement. What is there in the burning sun, the arid plains, and barbarous customs of Africa, that is so peculiarly favourable to our improvement! What hinders our improving here, where schools and colleges abound, where the gospel is preached at every corner, and where all the arts and sciences are verging fast to perfection? Nothing, nothing but prejudice. It requires no large expenditures, no hazardous enterprises to raise the people of colour in the United States to as highly improved a state as any class of the community. All that is necessary is that those who profess to be anxious for it should lay aside their prejudices and act toward them as they do by others.

We are NATIVES of this country, we ask only to be treated as well as FOREIGNERS. Not a few of our fathers suffered and bled to purchase its independence; we ask only to be treated as well as those who fought against it. We have toiled to cultivate it, and to raise it to its present prosperous condition; we ask only to share equal privileges with those who come from distant lands, to enjoy the fruits of our labour. Let those moderate requests be granted, and we need not to go to Africa nor anywhere else to be improved and happy. We cannot but doubt the purity of the motives of those persons who deny us these requests, and would send us to Africa to gain what they might give us at home.

But they say the prejudices of the country against us are invincible; and as they cannot be conquered, it is better that we should be removed beyond their influence. . . . The African Colonization Society is a numerous and influential body. Would they lay aside their *own* prejudices, much of the burden would be at once removed. . . . But, alas! The course which they have pursued has an opposite tendency. By the *scandalous misrepresentations* which they are continually giving of our character and conduct we have sustained much injury, and have reason to apprehend much more. . . .

They profess to have no other object in view than the colonizing of the free people of colour on the coast of Africa, with their *own consent*; but if our homes are made so uncomfortable that we cannot continue in them, or . . . we are driven from them, and no other door is open to receive us but Africa, our removal there will be anything but voluntary. It is very certain that very few free people of colour *wish* to go to that *land*. The Colonization Society *know* this, and yet they do certainly calculate that in time they will have us all removed there. How can this be effected but by making our situation worse here, and closing every other door against us?

Asking Questions of the Documents

1. Why does Maria W. Stewart argue that the condition of free blacks was "but a little better than" slavery? What were the effects of discriminatory treatment on the free black psyche? What caused this discriminatory treatment of free blacks?

2. What prompted free blacks to form independent African-American churches? What role did Rev. Richard Allen play in this process?

3. Why was it necessary to create an independent African-American press? What subjects did Samuel Cornish plan to discuss in *Freedom's Journal*? What did he hope that the newspaper would accomplish?

4. Contrast the views and arguments of John B. Russwurm and Peter Williams Jr. on the African colonization movement. How do they differ in their characterizations of African peoples and cultures? in their opinion of the possibility of improving race relations in the United States? What did Williams see as the real motives animating white colonizationists?

For Further Reading

Berlin, Ira. *Slaves without Masters: The Free Negro in the Antebellum South*. New York: Pantheon, 1974.

Curry, Leonard P. *The Free Black in Urban America, 1800-1850: The Shadow of the Dream*. Chicago: University of Chicago Press, 1981.

George, Carol V. R. *Segregated Sabbaths: Richard Allen and the Emergence of Independent Black Churches, 1760–1840*. New York: Oxford University Press, 1973.

Hutton, Frankie. *The Early Black Press in America, 1827–1860*. Westport, Conn.: Greenwood Press, 1993.

Litwack, Leon F. *North of Slavery: The Negro in the Free States, 1790–1860*. Chicago: University of Chicago Press, 1961.

Miller, Floyd J. *The Search for a Black Nationality: Black Colonization and Emigration, 1787–1863*. Urbana, Ill.: University of Illinois Press, 1975.

Staudenraus, Philip J. *The African Colonization Movement, 1816–1865*. New York: Columbia University Press, 1961.

5

Antebellum Slavery: Testimony from the Quarters

Slavery expanded at an even faster pace than the free black population after 1776. This growth occurred in only one region. Black bondage had existed throughout the United States at the moment of independence but it quickly became the South's "peculiar institution." Although thousands of African Americans were emancipated in the wake of the American Revolution, the slave population increased eightfold to four million, all in the South, by 1860.

The growth of slavery followed the emergence of cotton as a major cash crop in the South. In 1793, Eli Whitney invented a device known as the cotton gin, which easily and quickly separated the seeds from the fibers of the cotton plant. Southern planters soon turned to cotton production to meet the emerging demand for raw cotton in the textile factories of England and the North. After the War of 1812, they carved millions of acres of additional cotton lands out of the developing states of Alabama, Mississippi, Louisiana, Arkansas, and eastern Texas—an area collectively called the Cotton Kingdom. The South, which had grown a mere four thousand bales of cotton in 1790, produced four and a half million bales in 1860, the year before the Civil War.

The expansion of cotton production greatly increased the demand for slaves in the South. Planters encouraged the development of slave families, the primary sources of the swelling slave population. They also created an internal slave trade that carried hundreds of thousands of slaves from the older plantation districts of the Chesapeake and the lowcountry to the emerging Cotton Kingdom. In an experience reminiscent of the Middle Passage, slaves were torn away from family and friends and marched overland or taken by ship to Mobile, New Orleans, Natchez, or other cities, where they were resold to masters in the newer plantation districts.

Although some slaves became house servants, artisans, or factory workers, most worked as field hands on the farms and plantations of the antebellum (or pre-Civil War) South. They labored from dawn until dusk, planting, cultivating, or harvesting cotton or other cash crops, such as tobacco, rice, sugar, or hemp. It was a cruel existence. Most field hands worked long hours under grueling conditions, ate a monotonous and often inadequate diet of corn and pork, wore ill-fitting hand-me-down clothes, and slept in dark and poorly heated and ventilated cabins. Those who failed to meet their masters' expectations for their work or behavior, or who tried to escape, were severely punished.

This usually took the form of whipping, although being sold away from family and friends was a frequent and probably even crueler punishment.

After sundown or on Sundays, field hands spent most of their time in the quarters, the collection of cabins that housed slaves on southern farms and plantations. Here they created a culture that helped ease the pain of slavery, including a distinctive religion, music, and folklore. Freedom and resistance were major themes of the culture of the quarters. These found expression in the behavior of the slaves, most of whom chose to resist slavery in covert ways. They slowed down their work, feigned ignorance or illness, broke tools, abused work animals, destroyed crops, or stole food. But thousands sought freedom by fleeing to fugitive (or maroon) communities in swamps or mountainous districts, to the frontier, or to the North. A few even planned outright revolt. Historians have identified sixty-five slave conspiracies or rebellions in the United States between 1790 and the Civil War.

This chapter presents firsthand accounts of the world of antebellum slaves. The documents that follow—whether interviews, autobiographies, songs, or folktales—offer valuable testimony from the quarters about their work, culture, and treatment. They include the voices of well-known bondsmen Solomon Northup, Frederick Douglass, and Nat Turner; ordinary slaves Louisa Picquet, Peter Randolph, and David Holmes; and the generations of anonymous slaves who produced the spirituals and the Tar Baby tale.

Solomon Northup, Life and Labor on a Cotton Plantation

The life of a slave revolved around his or her work routine. For field hands, this meant long hours under a hot sun, with little rest and nourishment. It also meant constant fear of being punished when their work (or other behavior) failed to meet white expectations. The following document offers a firsthand account of slave life and labor in the Cotton Kingdom. It was written by Solomon Northup (1808–1863), a free black from New York State, who was kidnapped in 1841 and sold into slavery; he worked for the next twelve years on cotton plantations in the Red River region of central Louisiana. After being located, released, and returned to his family in 1853, he published an autobiography of his life in slavery to generate support for the antislavery movement. This selection is taken from that volume.[*]

The hands are required to be in the cotton field as soon as it is light in the morning, and, with the exception of ten or fifteen minutes, which is given them at noon to swallow their allowance of cold bacon, they are not permitted to be a moment idle until it is too dark to see, and when the moon is full, they oftentimes labor until the middle of

---

[*] Solomon Northup, *Twelve Years a Slave: Narrative of Solomon Northup* (Auburn, N.Y., 1853).

the night. They do not dare to stop even at dinner time, nor return to the quarters, however late it be, until the order to halt is given by the driver.

The day's work over in the field, the baskets are "toted," or in other words, carried to the gin-house, where the cotton is weighed. No matter how fatigued and weary he may be—no matter how much he longs for sleep and rest—a slave never approaches the gin-house with his basket of cotton but with fear. If it falls short in weight—if he has not performed the full task appointed him, he knows that he must suffer. And if he has exceeded it by ten or twenty pounds, in all probability his master will measure the next day's task accordingly. So, whether he has too little or too much, his approach to the gin-house is always with fear and trembling. Most frequently they have too little, and therefore it is they who are not anxious to leave the field. After weighing, follow the whippings; and then the baskets are carried to the cotton house, and their contents stored away like hay, all hands being sent in to tramp it down. If the cotton is not dry, instead of taking it to the gin-house at once, it is laid upon platforms, two feet high, and some three times as wide, covered with boards or plank, with narrow walks running between them.

This done, the labor of the day is not yet ended, by any means. Each one must then attend to his respective chores. One feeds the mules, another the swine—another cuts the wood, and so forth; besides, the packing is all done by candle light. Finally, at a late hour, they reach the quarters, sleepy and overcome with the long day's toil. Then a fire must be kindled in the cabin, the corn ground in the small hand-mill, and supper, and dinner for the next day in the field, prepared. All that is allowed them is corn and bacon, which is given out at the corncrib and the smoke-house every Sunday morning. Each one receives, as his weekly allowance, three and a half pounds of bacon, and corn enough to make a peck of meal. That is all—no tea, coffee, sugar, and with the exception of a very scanty sprinkling now and then, no salt . . . .

An hour before daylight the horn is blown. Then the slaves arouse, prepare their breakfast, fill a gourd with water, in another deposit their dinner of cold bacon and corn cake, and hurry to the field again. It is an offense invariably followed by a flogging, to be found at the quarters after daybreak. Then the fears and labors of another day begin; and until its close there is no such thing as rest.

Frederick Douglass, Whipping Slaves

The fear of punishment was one of the few incentives a slave had to work hard and be obedient. Masters employed a wide variety of coercive measures to motivate and control their slaves; whippings were the most common punishments. These were often public, ritualized acts in front of the assembled community of slaves. In the following document, Frederick Douglass recounts the range of real and imagined infractions that could cause a slave to be whipped. After growing up in bondage in eastern Maryland, Douglass (1818–1895) escaped in 1838 to Massachusetts. He was quickly drawn into the abolitionist crusade and became a leading antislavery speaker, the author of two best-selling autobiographies of his slave experiences, and the editor of several antislavery journals. Even after slavery ended, he remained the most prominent spokeman for African-American interests until his death.[*]

It would astonish one, unaccustomed to a slaveholding life, to see with what wonderful ease a slaveholder can find things of which to make occasion to whip a slave. A mere look, word, or motion—a mistake, accident, or want of power—are all matters for which a slave may be whipped at any time. Does a slave look dissatisfied? It is said, he has the devil in him, and it must be whipped out. Does he speak loudly when spoken to by his master? Then he is getting high-minded, and should be taken down a button-hole lower. Does he forget to pull off his hat at the approach of a white person? Then he is wanting in reverence, and should be whipped for it. Does he ever venture to vindicate his conduct, when censured for it? Then he is guilty of impudence—one of the greatest crimes of which a slave can be guilty. Does he ever venture to suggest a different mode of doing things from that pointed out by his master? He is indeed presumptuous, and getting above himself; and nothing less than a flogging will do for him. Does he, while plowing, break a plough—or, while hoeing, break a hoe? It is owing to his carelessness, and for it a slave must always be whipped.

Louisa Picquet, The Experiences of a Female Slave

Slaves especially feared being sold away from family and friends. But in the antebellum South, hundreds of thousands of families were separated by the internal slave trade. In the interview below, Louisa Picquet, a light-skinned former slave, recounts her experiences in the trade and tells of the particular dangers faced by female slaves. After working as a slave in Georgia and Alabama, Picquet (ca. 1827–?) was sold to John Williams, who forced her into concubinage in New Orleans. After his death in 1848, she was freed and settled with her children in Ohio. She was interviewed by Hiram Mattison, a white abolitionist clergyman, in 1860.[†]

---

[*] Frederick Douglass, *Narrative of the Life of Frederick Douglass, An American Slave, Written by Himself* (Boston, 1845).

[†] Mattison, *Louisa Picquet, the Octoroon: Or Inside Views of Southern Domestic Life* (Boston, 1861).

Q: How did you say you come to be sold?

A: Well, you see, Mr. Cook [my master] made great parties, and go off to watering-places, and get in debt, and had to break up, and then he took us to Mobile, and hired the most of us out, so the men he owe could not find us, and sell us for the debt. Then, after a while, the sheriff came from Georgia after Mr. Cook's debts, and found us all, and took us to auction, and sold us. My mother and brother was sold to Texas, and I was sold to New Orleans.

Q: How old were you, then?

A: Well, I don't know exactly, but the auctioneer said I wasn't quite fourteen. I didn't know myself.

Q: How old was your brother?

A: I suppose he was about two months old. He was little bit of baby.

Q: Where were you sold?

A: In the city of Mobile. . . . They put all the men in one room, and all the women in another; and then whoever want to buy come and examine, and ask you whole lot of questions. They began to take the clothes off me, and a gentleman said they needn't do that, and told them to take me out. He said he knew I was a virtuous girl, and he'd buy me, anyhow. He didn't strip me, only just under my shoulders.

Q: Were there others there white like you?

A: Oh yes, plenty of them. There was only Lucy of our lot, but others!

Q: Were others stripped and examined?

A: Well, not quite naked, but just [the] same.

Q: You say the gentleman told them to "take you out." What did he mean by that?

A: Why, take me out of the *room* where the women and girls were kept; where they examine them—out where the auctioneer sold us. . . . At the market, where the block is.

Q: What block?

A: My! Don't you know? The stand, where we have to get up.

Q: Did *you* get up on the stand?

A: Why, of course; we all have to get up to be seen.

Q: What else do you remember about it?

A: Well, they first begin at upward of six hundred for me, and then bid some fifty more, and some twenty-five more, and that way.

Q: Do you remember any thing the auctioneer said about you when he sold you?

A: Well, he said he could not recommend me for any thing else only that I was a good-lookin' girl, and a good nurse, and kind and affectionate to children; but I was never used to any hard work. He told them they could see that. My hair was quite short, and the auctioneer spoke about it, but said, "You see it good quality, and give it a little time, it will grow out again." You see Mr. Cook had my hair cut off. My hair grew fast, and look so much better than Mr. Cook's daughter, and he fancy I had better hair than his daughter, and so he had it cut off to make a difference.

Q: Well, how did they sell you and your mother? That is, which was sold first?

A: Mother was put up the first of our folks. She was sold for [a] splendid cook, and Mr. Horton, from Texas, bought her and the baby, my brother. Then Henry, the carriage-driver, was put up, and Mr. Horton bought him, and then two field-hands, Jim and Mary. The women there tend mills and drive ox wagons, and plough, just like men. Then I was sold next. Mr. Horton run me up to fourteen hundred dollars. He wanted I should go with my mother. Then someone said "fifty." Then Mr. Williams allowed that he did not care what they bid, he was going to have me anyhow. Then he bid fifteen hundred. Mr. Horton said 'twas no use to bid anymore, and I was sold to Mr. Williams. I went right to New Orleans then.

Q: Who was Mr. Williams?

A: I didn't know then, only he lived in New Orleans. Him and his wife had parted, some way—he had three children, boys. When I was going away I heard someone cryin' and prayin' the Lord to go with her only daughter, and protect me. I felt pretty bad then, but hadn't no time only to say good-bye. . . . It seems fresh in my memory when I think of it—no longer than yesterday. Mother was right on her knees, with her hands up, prayin' to the Lord for me. She didn't care who saw her, the people all lookin' at her. I often thought her prayers followed me, for I never could forget her. Whenever I wanted any thing real bad after that, my mother was always sure to appear to me in a dream that night, and have plenty to give me, always.

Q: Have you never seen her since?

A: No, never since that time. I went to New Orleans, and she went to Texas. So I understood.

Q: Well, how was it with you after Mr. Williams bought you?. . .

A: Mr. Williams told me what he bought me for, soon as we started for New Orleans. He said he was getting old, and when he saw me he thought he'd buy me, and end his days with me. He said if I behave myself he'd treat me well; but, if not, he'd whip me almost to death.

Q: How old was he?

A: He was over forty; I guess pretty near fifty. He was grayheaded. That's the reason he was always so jealous. He never let me go out anywhere. . . .

Q: Had you any children while in New Orleans?

A: Yes, I had four.

Q: Who was their father?

A: Mr. Williams.

Q: Was it known that he was living with you?

A: Everybody knew I was housekeeper, but he never let on that he was the father of my children. I did all the work in his house—nobody there but me and the children.

Q: What children?

A: My children and his. You see he had three sons.

Q: How old were his children when you went there?

A: I guess the youngest was nine years old. When he had company, gentlemen folks, he took them to the hotel. He never have no gentlemen company home. Sometimes he would come and knock, if he stay out later than usual time; and if I did not let him in in a minute, when I would be asleep, he'd come in and take the light, and look under the bed, and in the wardrobe, and all over, and then ask me why I did not let him in sooner. I did not know what it meant till I learnt his ways.

Q: Were your children mulattoes?

A: No, sir! They were all white. They look just like him. The neighbors all see that. After a while he got so disagreeable that I told him, one day, I wished he would sell me, or "put me in his pocket"—that's the way we say—because I had no peace at all. I rather die than live that way.

Peter Randolph, Culture and Religion in the Quarters

Slaves created a distinctive culture in the quarters. The product of both African and European sources, as well as the experience of bondage, it helped slaves survive and resist the "peculiar institution." Religion was a key element of this culture. Whites used Christianity to socialize slaves to work hard, be honest and obedient, and accept their situation. But slaves forged a faith more suited to their needs. Meeting secretly in the swamps, woods, brush arbors, and slave cabins of southern farms and plantations, they created a variation of the Christianity they had received—one that helped them endure slavery and often preached the value of freedom and the virtues of resistance. Historians call this the "invisible institution." In the following document excerpted from his autobiography, Peter Randolph describes the varied religious experiences of antebellum slaves. Born in slavery in Virginia, Randolph (1825-?) was manumitted in 1847 upon the death of his owner. He became an antislavery speaker and itinerant Baptist clergyman in Canada and the North, before returning to Virginia after the Civil War.[*]

Many say the Negroes receive religious education—that Sabbath worship is instituted for them as for others, and were it not for slavery, they would die in their sins—that really, the institution of slavery is a benevolent missionary enterprise. Yes, they are preached to, and I will give my readers some faint glimpses of these preachers, and their doctrines and practices. . . . The prominent preaching to the slave is, "'Servants, obey your masters.' Do not steal or lie, for this is very wrong. Such conduct is sinning against the Holy Ghost, and is base ingratitude to your kind masters, who feed, clothe, and protect you." All Gospel, my readers! It is great policy to build a church for the "dear slave," and allow him the wondrous privilige of such holy instruction! . . .

---

[*] Peter Randolph, *Sketches of Slave Life: Or, Illustrations of the Peculiar Institution* (Boston, 1855).

On the Sabbath, after doing their morning work, and breakfast over (such as it was), that portion of the slaves who belong to the church ask of the overseer permission to attend meeting. If he is in the mood to grant their request, he writes them a pass, as follows: "Permit the bearer to pass and repass to ___, this evening, unmolested." Should a pass not be granted, the slave lies down, and sleeps for the day—the only way to drown his sorrow and disappointment.

Others of the slaves, who do not belong to the church, spend their Sabbath in playing with marbles, and other games, for each other's food, etc. Some occupy the time in dancing to the music of the banjo, made out of a large gourd. This is continued till the after part of the day, when they separate, and gather wood for their log-cabin fires for the ensuing week.

Not being allowed to hold meetings on the plantation, the slaves assemble in the swamps, out of reach of the patrols. They have an understanding among themselves as to the time and place of getting together. This is often done by the first one arriving breaking from the trees, and bending them in the direction of the selected spot. Arrangements are then made for conducting the exercises. They first ask each other how they feel, the state of their minds, etc. The male members then select a certain space, in separate groups, for their division of the meeting. Preaching in order, by the brethren; then praying and singing all round, until they generally feel quite happy. The speaker usually commences by calling himself unworthy, and talks very slowly, until, feeling the spirit, he grows excited, and in a short time, there fall to the ground twenty or thirty men and women under its influence. Enlightened people call it excitement; but I wish the same was felt by everybody, so far as they are sincere.

The slave forgets all his sufferings, except to remind others of the trials during the past week, exclaiming: "Thank God, I shall not live here always!" Then they pass from one to another, shaking hands, and bidding each other farewell, promising, should they meet no more on earth, to strive and meet in heaven, where all is joy, happiness, and liberty. As they separate, they sing a parting hymn of praise.

Sometimes the slaves meet in an old log-cabin, when they find it necessary to keep a watch. If discovered, they escape, if possible; but those who are caught often get whipped. Some are willing to be punished thus for Jesus' sake. Most of the songs used in worship are composed by the slaves themselves, and describe their own sufferings.

Spirituals

Spirituals are among the most renowned examples of the culture and religion of the quarters. Created by the slaves for use in their worship services, these songs also conveyed a social message. One historian has labelled them "the slave's description and criticism of his environment." The following spirituals, three of the best known, suggest the multiple meanings of these plaintive texts.[*]

Go Down, Moses

When Israel was in Egypt's land,
Let my people go,
Oppressed so hard they could not stand,
Let my people go.

Go down Moses,
Way down in Egypt land,
Tell ole Pharaoh,
Let my people go.

Thus saith the Lord, bold Moses said,
Let my people go,
If not I'll smite your first-born dead,
Let my people go.

Go down Moses,
Way down in Egypt land,
Tell ole Pharaoh,
Let my people go.

No more shall they in bondage toil,
Let my people go,
Let them come out with Egypt's spoil,
Let my people go.

Go down Moses,
Way down in Egypt land,
Tell ole Pharaoh,
Let my people go.

---

[*] Theodore F. Seward, comp., *Jubilee Songs: As Sung by the Jubilee Singers, of Fisk University, Nashville, Tenn., under the Auspices of the American Missionary Association* (New York, 1872).

Steal Away to Jesus

Steal away, steal away, steal away to Jesus!
Steal away, steal away home,
I ain't got long to stay here.

My Lord, He calls me, He calls me by the thunder,
The trumpet sounds within-a my soul,
I ain't got long to stay here.

· Steal away, steal away, steal away to Jesus!
Steal away, steal away home,
I ain't got long to stay here.

My Lord, He calls me, He calls me by the lightning,
The trumpet sounds within-a my soul,
I ain't got long to stay here.

Steal away, steal away, steal away to Jesus!
Steal away, steal away home.
I ain't got long to stay here.

Didn't My Lord Deliver Daniel

Didn't my Lord deliver Daniel,
    deliver Daniel, deliver Daniel,
Didn't my Lord deliver Daniel,
An' why not every man.

He delivered Daniel from the lion's den,
Jonah from the belly of the whale,
An' the Hebrew chillun from the fiery furnace,
An' why not every man.

Didn't my Lord deliver Daniel,
    deliver Daniel, deliver Daniel,
Didn't my Lord deliver Daniel,
An' why not every man.

The moon run down in a purple stream,
The sun forbear to shine,
An' every star disappear,
King Jesus shall-a be mine.

The win' blows eas' an' the win' blows wes',
It blows like the judg-a-ment day,

An' ev'ry po' soul that never did pray'll
Be glad to pray that day.

Didn't my Lord deliver Daniel,
    deliver Daniel, deliver Daniel,
Didn't my Lord deliver Daniel,
An' why not every man.

The Tar Baby Tale

Folktales were used both to entertain and to educate in the quarters. As in Africa, slaves used stories about animals to teach moral lessons. But they also used these tales to instruct younger slaves in the skills needed to survive and resist the "peculiar institution." Among their favorites were those about Brer Fox (who represented the master) and Brer Rabbit (who represented the slaves). These were collected by journalist Joel Chandler Harris in his "Uncle Remus" stories after the Civil War. The following retelling of the Tar Baby tale, which was passed down by generations of slaves, suggests the instructional value of these folktales.*

One day Brer Fox went to work and got some tar, and mixed it with some turpentine, and fixed up a contraption that he called a Tar Baby. He took this Tar Baby and he set her in the big road, and then he lay off in the bushes to see what the news was going to be. And he didn't have to wait long, either, 'cause by and by came Brer Rabbit pacin' down the road—lippity-clippity, clippity-lippity—just as sassy as a jaybird. Brer Fox, he lay low. Brer Rabbit came prancin' along till he spied the Tar Baby, and then he fetched up on his hind legs like he was astonished. The Tar Baby, she sat there, and Brer Fox, he lay low.

"Mornin'!" said Brer Rabbit—"nice weather this mornin'."

Tar Baby didn't say nothin', and Brer Fox, he lay low. "How do your symptoms seem to be?" said Brer Rabbit. Brer Fox, he winked his eye slowly, and lay low, and the Tar Baby, she didn't say nothin'.

"How you come on, then? Are you deaf?" said Brer Rabbit. "'Cause if you are, I can holler louder."

Tar Baby stayed still, and Brer Fox, he lay low.

"You are stuck up, that's what you are," said Brer Rabbit, "and I'm going to cure you, that's what I'm going to do."

---

* Corrected version of the original tale published in Joel Chandler Harris, *Uncle Remus: His Songs and Sayings* (New York, 1880).

Brer Fox, he sort of chuckled in his stomach, but Tar Baby didn't say nothin'.

"I'm going to teach you how to talk to respectable folks if it's my last act," said Brer Rabbit. "If you don't take off that hat and tell me howdy, I'm going to bust you wide open."

Tar Baby stayed still, and Brer Fox, he lay low.

Brer Rabbit kept on askin' him, and the Tar Baby, she kept on sayin' nothin', till finally Brer Rabbit drew back with his fist, and blip, he hit the side of her head. His fist stuck and he couldn't pull loose. The tar held him. But Tar Baby, she stayed still, and Brer Fox, he lay low.

"If you don't let me loose, I'll knock you again," said Brer Rabbit, and with that he fetched her a swipe with the other hand, and that stuck. Tar Baby, she didn't say nothin', and Brer Fox, he lay low.

"Turn me loose, before I kick the stuffing out of you," said Brer Rabbit, but the Tar Baby, she didn't say nothin'. She did hold on, and then Brer Rabbit lost the use of his feet in the same way. Brer Fox, he lay low. Then Brer Rabbit squalled out that if the Tar Baby didn't turn him loose, he'd butt her. And then he butted, and his head got stuck. Then Brer Fox, he sauntered forth, lookin' just as innocent as one of your mammy's mockingbirds.

"Howdy, Brer Rabbit," said Brer Fox, "you look sort of stuck up this morning," and he rolled on the ground and laughed and laughed until he could laugh no more. By and by he up and said, "Well, I expect I've got you this time, Brer Rabbit. You've been runnin' around here sassin' after me a mighty long time, but I expect you've come to the end of the row. You've been cuttin' your capers and bouncin' around in this neighborhood till you've come to believe yourself the boss of the whole gang. And then you are always somewhere you have no business. Who ask you to come and strike up an acquaintance with this Tar Baby? And who stuck you there where you are? Nobody in the round world. You just stuck and jammed yourself on that Tar Baby without waitin' for an invite, and there you are, and there you'll stay till I fix a brushpile and fires her up, 'cause I'm going to barbecue you this day, sure."

Then Brer Rabbit talked mighty humble. "I don't care what you do with me, Brer Fox," he said, "just so you don't fling me in that briar patch. Roast me, Brer Fox, but don't fling me in that briar patch."

"Its so much trouble to kindle a fire," said Brer Fox, "that I expect I'll have to hang you."

"Hang me just as high as you please, Brer Fox," said Brer Rabbit, "but for the Lord's sake don't fling me in that briar patch."

"I ain't got no string," said Brer Fox, "and now I expect I'll have to drown you."

"Drown me just as deep as you please, Brer Fox," said Brer Rabbit, "but don't fling me in that briar patch."

"There ain't no water near," said Brer Fox, "and now I expect I'll have to skin you."

"Skin me, Brer Fox," said Brer Rabbit, "snatch out my eyeballs, tear out my ears by the roots, and cut off my legs, but please, Brer Fox, don't fling me in that briar patch."

'Cause Brer Fox wanted to hurt Brer Rabbit as bad as he could, he caught him by the hind legs and slung him right in the middle of the briar patch. There was a considerable flutter where Brer Rabbit struck the bushes, and Brer Fox sort of hung around to see what was going to happen. By and by he heard somebody call him, and way up on the hill he saw Brer Rabbit sittin' cross-legged on a chinquapin log combin' the pitch out of his hair with a chip. Then Brer Fox knew that he'd been tricked. Brer Rabbit was itchin' to fling back some of his sass, and he hollered out: "Bred and born in a briar patch, Brer Fox—bred and born in a briar patch!" And with that he skipped away.

David Holmes, Escaping from Slavery

The culture of the quarters taught the value of freedom and the virtue of resistance. Although slaves usually chose to resist in covert ways, thousands attempted to escape from bondage. Some hid in nearby woods or swamps, or set out for the frontier. But once slavery ended in the North, that region became the favorite destination of runaway slaves. However, they were not even safe there. Masters often sent slave catchers northward to track down and return escaped slaves. After the Fugitive Slave Act of 1850 put the U.S. government in the business of capturing runaways, many sought the safer climes of Canada. In the following excerpt from an interview, David Holmes (1824–?), a Virginia slave, recounts his flight across the western part of that state, over the Ohio River, and through Ohio, Pennsylvania, and New York to Quebec. He describes the free blacks, Quakers, and other abolitionists—collectively known as the Underground Railroad—who protected and transported him in his flight across the North. Holmes eventually reached England, where he was interviewed in 1853 by Louis A. Chamerovzow, a leading British abolitionist.[*]

Young master . . . said I looked as though I should like to run off, but I'd better not, or he'd send the hounds after me. One day another planter came, and master and he had a talk about me. I overheard them. Master's friend said I looked likely to run off, and the best thing he could do with Jack—that was me—would be to send him down the river: that's down South. I got a fright then, and when I got home I told the old woman and the old man about it. I used to call them mother and father. They were very good to me, and nursed me when I was sick and couldn't work. We had a good deal of talk, and I said I thought I should run. But I didn't quite make up my mind. Three or four days after, young *missus* came in. It was late in the evening, after we had done work and gone home. She told me I was sold, and I was going to be took way, so I'd better make off, or else I should be sent down South. When she was gone, the old woman began to get me ready for a start. She gave me a big corn-loaf she had just got baked, and a little rum

---

[*] *Anti-Slavery Reporter* (London), 1 February 1853.

and tobacco, and when all was quite still she and the old man set me outside, and told me to run for it. We cried a great deal, but we couldn't stop long about it. I got clear off the plantation and made for the woods.

I wanted to go towards Canada. I didn't know much about the way, but I went by the North Star. Heard about that from an old man, a slave, who had gone off a good many times; but he never had the luck to get right away. He used to point out the North Star to me, and tell me that if any man followed that, it would bring him into the north country, where the people were free: and that if a slave could get there he would be free.

I walked and ran all night, and in the morning I got to the woods. I walked on and ran all day. I wanted to get a good start, so I wouldn't stop to rest. I guided myself in the day by guess, and went on till a good piece after dark. Then I got up a tree and had a sleep. Can't say how long I slept, but I was so stiff when I woke, I could scarce get down. The soreness went off after awhile, and I got along well. I went on this way for thirteen days. My bread lasted nine days, and when that was gone I went two days with a drink of water. Then I got near a potato-patch, and I went in and took a lot. I ate some raw, and stowed away as many more as I could. They would have lasted me three or four days, perhaps five; but on the thirteenth day I came in sight of a town. I didn't much like to go in, in the daytime, so I hid about.

At last I made up my mind to go in. There was a good many people, and they looked very hard at me. I went on till I came to a river and a bridge. As I was staring about, I saw a coloured man down by the waterside, so I went up to him and asked him the name of the place. I can't remember it nohow, now. He asked me where I wanted to go, so I told him I was making for the North. He asked me if I would let him ferry me over the river, then I needn't go through the town. So I got into his boat, and we went off. . . . I was just going to tell him where I came from, when he shut me up. He said he didn't want to know anything about me. If I was going North and hadn't got any friends, he would tell me where to go. When we got over the river, he showed me a broad road, and told me to keep straight down that road about six miles, till I came to a large white house on the left. He said he hoped I should get to my friends, and then he shook hands with me, and went away quite quick.

I followed the road, and found the white house. It had a green gate and there was a white gentleman in the garden. I stood at the gate, looking over. I didn't much like going in. Presently the gentleman asked me if I wouldn't come in. I said I'd have a drink of water. He said I'd better come in, so I went. He took me into a little parlour, where there were three [Quaker] ladies. . . . I think they called themselves abolitionists. . . . I stayed in that house all day. They asked me if I was escaping. I told them I was, and was going to tell 'em more, but they said they didn't want to know any more. As soon as it was dusk, they put me into a wagon, and we travelled all night till a little before daybreak, when we got to another house. The people here were not Quakers. I stayed here all day till after dark, then went away again in a two-horse wagon, and got to another house before day. I had to stop here five days. There had been a grand fuss about some slaves that had got away on this track, so I was obliged to keep close. On the fifth night I started once more, on horseback. A man went with me on another horse, and he got me on safe to another house as day broke. I remained here two days. They said the dogs were out. The second night they set me off again in a wagon, and we went through a town, till we got to another house, on a farm, kept by some more abolitionists. I rested here till next night. Before I started, the gentleman gave me the coat and pantaloons I've got on. He told me I might travel now in the daytime. . . . [Eventually, I came] to a place they called Quebec.

The Confessions of Nat Turner

Some slaves struck back violently against slavery. On at least sixty-five occasions, they conspired to revolt against their masters. The most famous of these insurrections was led by Nat Turner (1800–1831), a slave preacher, in Southampton County, Virginia. A religious vision had persuaded him that he was to spark a bloody struggle to free his people. On 22 August 1831, Turner and his followers began their revolt. For nearly two days, they moved from plantation to plantation, killing some sixty whites, including Turner's master, Joseph Travis. The revolt was soon crushed and, after hiding out for two months, Turner was apprehended and hanged. But these events generated widespread hysteria among whites throughout the South, leading to the execution of dozens of blacks and the imposition of more restrictive slave codes. In the following selection, Turner explains his motives, recounts much of the violence, and suggests the link between slave religion and slave revolt. It is excerpted from an interview conducted by attorney Thomas R. Gray while Turner was awaiting execution.*

Sir—You have asked me to give a history of the motives which induced me to undertake the late insurrection. . . .

I had [a] revelation, which fully confirmed me in the impression that I was ordained for some great purpose. . . . And about this time I had a vision—and I saw white spirits and black spirits engaged in battle, and the sun was darkened—the thunder rolled in the Heavens, and blood flowed in streams. . . . And on the 12th of May, 1828, I heard a loud noise in the heavens, and the Spirit instantly appeared to me and said the Serpent was loosened, and Christ had laid down the yoke he had borne for the sins of men, and that I should take it on and fight against the Serpent, for the time was fast approaching when the first should be last and the last should be first. . . . And by signs in the heavens that it would make known to me when I should commence the great work—and until the first sign appeared, I should conceal it from the knowledge of men. And on the appearance of the sign (the eclipse of the sun last February), I should arise and prepare myself, and slay my enemies with their own weapons. And immediately on the sign

---

* Thomas R. Gray, *The Confessions of Nat Turner, the Leader of the Late Insurrection in Southamton, Va.* (Baltimore, 1831).

appearing in the heavens, the seal was removed from my lips, and I communicated the great work laid out for me to do, to four in whom I had the greatest confidence (Henry, Hark, Nelson, and Sam). . . .

On Saturday evening, the 20th of August, it was agreed between Henry, Hark, and myself, to prepare a dinner the next day for the men we expected and then to concert a plan, as we had not yet determined on any. . . . It was quickly agreed we should commence at home on that night, and until we had armed and equipped ourselves, and gathered sufficient force, neither age nor sex was to be spared (which was invariably adhered to). . . .

Hark went to the door [of my master's house] with an axe, for the purpose of breaking it open, as we knew we were strong enough to murder the family, if they were awakened by the noise; but reflecting that it might create an alarm in the neighborhood, we determined to enter the house secretly, and murder them whilst sleeping. Hark got a ladder and set it against the chimney, on which I ascended, and hoisting a window, entered and came downstairs, unbarred the door, and removed the guns from their places. It was then observed that I must spill the first blood. On which, armed with a hatchet, and accompanied by Will, I entered my master's chamber. It being dark, I could not give a death blow; the hatchet glanced from his head, he sprang from the bed and called his wife. It was his last word; Will laid him dead, with a blow of his axe, and Mrs. Travis shared the same fate, as she lay in bed. The murder of this family, five in number, was the work of a moment; not one of them awoke. There was a little infant sleeping in a cradle, that was forgotten, until we had left the house and gone some distance, when Henry and Will returned and killed it. We got here four guns that would shoot and several old muskets, with a pound or two of powder.

We remained some time at the barn, where we paraded. I formed them in a line as soldiers, and . . . marched them off to Mr. Salathul Francis', about six hundred yards distant. Sam and Will went to the door and knocked.

Mr. Francis asked who was there, Sam replied it was him, and he had a letter for him, on which he got up and came to the door; they immediately seized him, and dragging him out a little from the door, he was dispatched by repeated blows on the head; there was no other white person in the family. We started from there for Mrs. Reese's, maintaining the most perfect silence on our march, where finding the door unlocked, we entered, and murdered Mrs. Reese in her bed, while sleeping. Her son awoke, but it was only to sleep the sleep of death; he had only time to say who is that, and he was no more. From Mrs. Reese's, we went to Mrs. Turner's, a mile distant, which we reached about sunrise on Monday morning. Henry, Austin, and Sam went to the still, where, finding Mr. Peebles, Austin shot him, and the rest of us went to the house; as we approached, the family discovered us, and shut the door. Vain hope! Will, with one stroke of his axe, opened it, and we entered and found Mrs. Turner and Mrs. Newsome in the middle of a room, almost frightened to death. Will immediately killed Mrs. Turner, with one blow of his axe. I took Mrs. Newsome by the hand, and with the sword I had when I was apprehended, I struck her several blows over the head, but not being able to kill her, as the sword was dull. Will, turning around, and discovering it, dispatched her also.

A general destruction of property and search for money and ammunition always succeeded the murders. . . . 'Twas my object to carry terror and devastation wherever we went. . . . Our number amounted [in time] to fifty or sixty, all mounted and armed with guns, axes, swords, and clubs.

Asking Questions of the Documents

1. Describe the work and treatment of slaves on farms and plantations in the antebellum South.

2. Why were slaves whipped? What psychological effect might a whipping have on a slave? Why do you think slaves were usually whipped in front of the assembled community of slaves?

3. Why was Louisa Picquet sold by her master? What other reasons might cause a slave to be sold? Describe how such sales took place. What psychological effect might being sold have on a slave? Why? Why was Picquet bought by John Williams? What does that suggest about the particular dangers faced by female slaves?

4. What was the role of religion in the culture of the quarters? What three different slave religious experiences does Peter Randolph describe? How did religion help the slaves endure bondage?

5. What underlying meanings can you find in the three spirituals provided? Why have spirituals been called "the slave's description and criticism of his environment"? Is it accurate to call the spirituals a form of resistance? Why?

6. What lessons might a young slave learn from the Tar Baby tale? Why would slaves identify with Brer Rabbit and identify their masters with Brer Fox? Masters often spread tar on fences to catch slaves who sneaked into fields or orchards to steal food. Does this add to your understanding of the tale?

7. What prompted David Holmes to escape from slavery? What other reasons might cause slaves to run away? How did Holmes escape from the South? Why did he go on to Canada? What kind of assistance did he receive from abolitionists in the North? Would you have helped a runaway slave? Why? What do you think Holmes's emotions might have been during his flight to freedom?

8. What prompted Nat Turner to organize his slave revolt? What does this suggest about the connection between slave religion and slave revolt? Was slave revolt a reasonable response to slavery?

For Further Reading

Blassingame, John W. *The Slave Community: Plantation Life in the Antebellum South.* Rev. ed. New York: Oxford University Press, 1979.

Genovese, Eugene D. *Roll, Jordan, Roll: The World the Slaves Made.* New York: Pantheon, 1972.

Levine, Lawrence W. *Black Culture and Black Consciousness: Afro-American Folk Thought from Slavery to Freedom.* New York: Oxford University Press, 1977.

Oates, Stephen B. *The Fires of Jubilee: Nat Turner's Fierce Rebellion.* New York: Harper and Row Publishers, 1975.

Raboteau, Albert J. *Slave Religion: The "Invisible Institution" in the Antebellum South.* New York: Oxford University Press, 1978.

Webber, Thomas L. *Deep Like the Rivers: Education in the Slave Quarter Community, 1831–1865.* New York: W. W. Norton and Company, 1978.

White, Deborah Gray. *Ar'nt I a Woman?: Female Slaves in the Plantation South.* New York: W. W. Norton and Company, 1985.

6

Black Abolitionists

Slaves had always resisted their masters, but organized opposition to slavery (known as abolitionism) first emerged among free blacks and fugitive slaves in the 1820s, largely in response to the rise of the African colonization movement and the spread of slavery in the South. With the conversion of thousands of northern whites to militant abolitionism in the 1830s, this antislavery movement became interracial in nature. Working together, black and white abolitionists tried to end slavery through moral suasion—spoken or published appeals to the consciences of individual white Americans, slaveholders and nonslaveholders alike, designed to convince them that it was an evil which must be immediately abolished.

Black abolitionists, especially former slaves, were vital to the credibility of this crusade. Like their white colleagues, they understood the importance of public opinion to a successful campaign for emancipation. This meant competing with proslavery apologists, who argued that slaves were contented, well treated, and in need of the civilizing and Christianizing influence that the "peculiar institution" supposedly provided. The most convincing abolitionists were the hundreds of former slaves, including Frederick Douglass and Lewis G. Clarke, who lectured before antislavery audiences in meeting halls and churches throughout the North and abroad. Dozens of others published autobiographical accounts of their experiences in slavery, carrying the antislavery message into the homes of white Americans. They exposed the brutality of bondage—the toil, deprivation, torture, rape, and forced separation of slave families—effectively refuting proslavery myths of the kind master and the contented slave.

Even as black and white abolitionists worked together within the movement and shared common assumptions about the evil of slavery, each brought with them unique perspectives. Blacks viewed the institution through the lens of personal experience. Few white abolitionists had encountered slavery firsthand; as a result, they looked at the institution in relatively abstract terms. Many white abolitionists sought to end slavery through moral suasion or political action; blacks took a less doctrinaire approach, embracing a wide variety of antislavery tactics, including violence. These differences prompted black abolitionists to work more independently of their white colleagues in the 1840s and 1850s.

Events of the 1850s left many black abolitionists in a mood of despair. After three decades of organized struggle against slavery, they could point to little progress. Even the federal government seemed to have fallen into proslavery hands. The Fugitive Slave

Act of 1850 put the nation in the business of capturing and returning fugitive slaves; the Kansas-Nebraska Act (1854) reopened vast western territories to the expansion of slavery; and in *Dred Scott v. Sanford* (1857), the U.S. Supreme Court denied black claims to American citizenship. Federal complicity with proslavery forces prompted some black abolitionists to consider abandoning the United States. They explored emigration alternatives, hoping to create an independent black nation in Africa, Latin America, or the Caribbean; Haiti, looked especially promising by the end of the decade. However, the coming of the Civil War in 1861 renewed African-American hopes for slavery's end.

David Walker, An Antislavery Appeal

[handwritten: He believe that we should be treated as citizen also.]

[handwritten margin note: I could die ... I could die (I)]

Organized black abolitionist activity first emerged among free blacks and fugitive slaves in the urban North during the 1820s. The most prominent of these early black abolitionists was David Walker (ca. 1797–1830) of Boston, who had been born and reared free in North Carolina. In his famous and controversial *Appeal*, which was first published in 1829, he denounced slavery, colonization, and American racial practices; hinted at the efficacy and likelihood of slave insurrection; and attempted to stir up antislavery sentiment among other informed members of his race. This volume was circulated secretly in the South, provoking fear and threats of reprisal on the part of slaveholders.* *[handwritten: 1829 die (don't know how)]*

[handwritten: 1831 Turner went killing whites]

God will not suffer us always to be oppressed. Our sufferings will come to an *end*, in spite of all the Americans this side of *eternity.* . . . The whites want slaves, and want us for their slaves, but some of them will curse the day they ever saw us. As true as the sun ever shone in its meridian splendor, my colour will root some of them out of the very face of the earth. They shall have enough of making slaves of, and butchering, and murdering us in the manner which they have. . . .

Ignorance and treachery one against the other—a grovelling, servile, and abject submission to the lash of tyrants, we see plainly, my brethren, are not the natural elements of the blacks, as the Americans try to make us believe; but these are the misfortunes which God has suffered our fathers to be enveloped in for many ages, no doubt in consequence of their disobedience to their Maker, and which do, indeed, reign at this time among us, almost to the destruction of all other principles: for I must truly say that ignorance, the mother of treachery and deceit!!, gnaws into our very vitals. Ignorance, as it now exists among us, produces a state of things, oh my Lord! too

---

* *David Walker's Appeal in Four Articles; Together with a Preamble, to the Coloured Citizens of the World*, 3d ed. (Boston, 1830).

horrible to present to the world. Any man who is curious to see the full force of ignorance developed among the coloured people of the United States of America, has only to go into the southern and western states of this confederacy, where, if he is not a tyrant, but has the feelings of a human being, who can feel for a fellow creature, he may see enough to make his very heart bleed! He may see there, a son take his mother, who bore almost the pains of death to give him birth, and by the comand of a tyrant, strip her as naked as she came into the world, and apply the cowhide to her, until she falls a victim to death in the road! He may see a husband take his dear wife, not infrequently in a pregnant state, and perhaps far advanced, and beat her for an unmerciful wretch, until his infant falls a lifeless lump at his feet! . . .

The whites have had us under them for more than three centuries, murdering us and treating us like brutes. . . . They do not know, indeed, that there is an unconquerable disposition in the breasts of the blacks, which, when it is fully awakened and put in motion, will be subdued, only with the destruction of the animal existence. Get the blacks started, and if you do not have a gang of tigers and lions to deal with, I am a deceiver of the blacks and of the whites. . . .

If you commence, make sure work—do not trifle, for they will not trifle with you—they want us for their slaves, and think nothing of murdering us in order to subject us to that wretched condition—therefore, if there is an *attempt* made by us, kill or be killed. Now, I ask you, had you not rather be killed than to be a slave to a tyrant, who takes the life of your mother, wife, and dear little children? Look upon your mother, wife and children, and answer God almighty; and believe this, that it is no more harm for you to kill a man, who is trying to kill you, than it is for you to take a drink of water when thirsty; in fact, the man who will stand still and let another murder him, is worse than an infidel, and, if he has common sense, ought not to be pitied. . . .

Men of colour, who are also of sense, for you particularly is my APPEAL designed. Our more ignorant brethren are not able to penetrate its value. I call upon you therefore to cast your eyes upon the wretchedness of your brethren, and to do your utmost to enlighten them—*go to work and enlighten your brethren*! Let the Lord see you doing what you can to rescue them and yourselves from degradation. Do any of you say that you and your family are free and happy, and what have you to do with the wretched slaves and other people? So can I say, for I enjoy as much freedom as any of you, if I am not quite as well off as the best of you. Look into our freedom and happiness, and see of what kind they are composed!! They are of the very lowest kind—they are the very *dregs*!—they are the most servile and abject kind, that ever a people was in possession of! If any of you wish to know how FREE you are, let one of you start and go through the southern and western states of this country, and unless you travel as a slave to a white man (a servant is a *slave* to the man he serves) or have your free papers (which if you are not careful they will get from you), if they do not take you up and put you in jail, and if you cannot give good evidence of your freedom, sell you into eternal slavery, I am not a living man. . . . And yet some of you have the hardihood to say you are free and happy! . . . Your full glory and happiness, as well as all other coloured people under Heaven, shall never be fully consummated, but with the *entire emancipation of your enslaved brethren all over the world.*

Lewis G. Clarke, The Testimony of a Former Slave

Former slaves offered firsthand evidence of the claims of the antislavery movement. Through lecture tours and published autobiographies, they testified to the brutality of bondage and effectively countered proslavery myths of the kind master and the contented slave. Both the eloquent language of a Frederick Douglass and the halting ramblings of an unlettered fugitive helped establish the credibility of the movement. The following document, drawn from an October 1842 speech by Lewis G. Clarke in Brooklyn, personalizes the antislavery message, exposing the evils of slavery in his native Kentucky, long considered to have a relatively mild form of the institution. Clarke (1815–1897), the son of a white man and a mulatto slave woman, had fled from bondage only one year before. He became a prominent antislavery lecturer and coauthored a slave autobiography that reached thousands of readers in the United States and abroad. He returned to Kentucky after the Civil War.[*]

Kentucky is the best of the slave States, . . . but the masters manage to fix things pretty much to their own liking. . . . The law gives him full swing, and he don't fail to use his privilege, I can tell you. . . . I can't tell these respectable people as much as I would like to, but think for a minute how you would like to have *your* sisters, and *your* wives, and *your* daughters, completely, totally, and altogether in the power of a master. You can picture to yourselves a little how you would feel; but oh, if I could *tell* you! A slave woman ain't allowed to respect herself, if she would. I had a pretty sister; she was whiter than I am, for she took more after her father. When she was sixteen years old, her master sent for her. When he sent for her again, she cried, and did not want to go. She told her mother her troubles, and she tried to encourage her to be decent, and hold up her head above such things, if she could. Her master was so mad, to think she complained to her mother, that he sold her right off to Louisiana; and we heard afterward that she died there of hard usage.

Now, who would like to be a slave, even if there was nothing bad about it but such treatment of his sisters and daughters? But there's a worse thing yet about slavery, the worst thing in the whole lot, though it's all bad. . . . I mean the patter rollers [patrols]. I suppose you know they have *patter rollers* to go round o' nights, to see that the slaves are all in, and not planning any mischief? . . . They hire these patter rollers, and they have to take the meanest fellows above ground; and because they are so mortal sure the slaves don't *want* their freedom, they have to put all power into their hands, to do with the niggers jest as they like. If a slave don't open his door to them, at any time of night, they break it down. They steal his money, if they can find it, and act just as they please with his wives and daughters. If a husband dares to say a word, or even look as if he

---

[*] *Signal of Liberty* (Ann Arbor, Mich.), 23 January 1843.

wasn't quite satisfied, they tie him up and give him thirty-nine lashes. If there's any likely young girls in a slave's hut, they're mighty apt to have business there, especially if they think any colored young man takes a fancy to any of 'em. Maybe he'll get a pass from his master, and go to see the young girl for a few hours. [If] the patter rollers break in and find him, they'll abuse the girl as bad as they can on purpose to provoke him. If he looks cross, they'll give him a flogging, tear up his pass, turn him out of doors, and then take him up and whip him for being out without a pass. If the slave says they tore it up, they swear he lies, and nine times out of ten the master won't come out agin 'em, for they say it won't *do* to let the niggers suppose they may complain of the patter rollers; they must be taught that it's their business to obey 'em in everything; and the patter roller knows that very well. Oh how often I've seen the poor girls sob and cry, when there's been such goings on! Maybe you think, because they're slaves, they ain't got no feeling and no shame! A woman's being a slave don't stop her genteel ideas; that is, according to their way, and as far as they *can*. They know they must submit to their masters; besides, their masters, maybe, dress 'em up, and make 'em little presents, and give 'em more priviliges, while the whim lasts; but that ain't like having a parcel of low, dirty, swearing, drunk patter rollers let loose among 'em, like so many hogs. This breaks down their spirits dreadfully, and makes 'em wish they were dead.

Now, who among you would like to have *your* wives, and daughters, and sisters, in *such* a situation? This is what every slave in all of these States is exposed to. Yet folks go from these parts down to Kentucky, and come back, and say the slaves have enough to eat and drink, and they are very happy, and they wouldn't mind it much to be slaves themselves. I'd like to have 'em to try it; it would teach them a little more than they know now.

Henry Highland Garnet, Let Your Motto Be Resistance

Black abolitionists frequently differed from their white colleagues on tactical questions. While many white abolitionists sought to end slavery by moral suasion alone, black activists embraced a wide variety of means, including violence. A leading advocate of slave insurrection was Henry Highland Garnet (1815–1882) of New York City, a Presbyterian clergyman. His most famous statement of this position was an 1843 speech before the National Convention of Colored Citizens in Buffalo, from which the following document is excerpted. It provoked considerable controversy, and he was verbally attacked by white abolitionists and some leaders of his own race.

Garnet supported black emigration to Africa before the Civil War and in 1881 was named U.S. ambassador to Liberia.[*]

Brethren and Fellow Citizens:

Your brethren of the north, east, and west have been accustomed to meet together in National Conventions, to sympathize with each other, and to weep over your unhappy condition. In these meetings, we have addressed all classes of the free, but we have never, until this time, sent a word of consolation and advice to you. We have been contented in sitting still and mourning over your sorrows, earnestly hoping that before this day your sacred liberties would have been restored. But we have hoped in vain. Years have rolled on, and tens of thousands have been borne on streams of blood, and tears, to the shores of eternity. While you have been oppressed, we have also been partakers with you; nor can we be free while you are enslaved. We therefore, write to you as being bound with you. . . .

SLAVERY! How much misery is comprehended in that single word. What mind is there that does not shrink from its direful effects? Unless the image of God is obliterated from the soul, all men cherish the love of Liberty. The nice, discerning political economist does not regard the sacred right more than the untutored African who roams in the wilds of Congo. Nor has the one more right to the full enjoyment of his freedom than the other. In every man's mind the good seeds of liberty are planted, and he who brings his fellow down so low as to make him contented with a condition of slavery, commits the highest crime against God and man. Brethren, your oppressors aim to do this. They endeavor to make you as much like brutes as possible. When they have blinded the eyes of your mind—when they have embittered the sweet waters of life—when they have shut out the light which shines from the word of God—then, and not till then, has American Slavery done its perfect work.

TO SUCH DEGRADATION, IT IS SINFUL IN THE EXTREME FOR YOU TO MAKE VOLUNTARY SUBMISSION. The divine commandments, you are in duty bound to reverence and obey. If you do not obey them, you will surely meet with the displeasure of the Almighty. He requires you to love him supremely, and your neighbor as yourself—to keep the Sabbath day holy—to search the Scriptures—and to bring up your children with respect for his laws, and to worship no other God but him. But slavery sets all these at naught, and hurls defiance in the face of Jehovah. The forlorn condition in which you are placed does not destroy your moral obligation to God. You are not certain of heaven because you suffer yourselves to remain in a state of slavery, where you cannot obey the commandments of the Sovereign of the universe. If the ignorance of slavery is a passport to heaven, then it is a blessing, and no curse, and you should rather desire its perpetuity than its abolition. God will not receive slavery, nor ignorance, nor any other state of mind, for love and obedience to him. Your condition does not absolve you from your moral obligation. The diabolical injustice by which your liberties are cloven down, NEITHER GOD, NOR ANGELS, NOR JUST MEN COMMAND YOU TO SUFFER FOR A SINGLE MOMENT. THEREFORE, IT IS

---

[*] Henry Highland Garnet, *Walker's Appeal, with a Brief Sketch of His Life* (New York, 1848); *Weekly Anglo-African* (New York), 28 March 1863.

YOUR SOLEMN AND IMPERATIVE DUTY TO USE EVERY MEANS, BOTH MORAL, INTELLECTUAL, AND PHYSICAL, THAT PROMISE SUCCESS. If a band of heathen men should attempt to enslave a race of Christians, and to place their children under the influence of some false religion, surely heaven would frown upon the men who would not resist such aggression, even to death. If, on the other hand, a band of Christians should attempt to enslave a race of heathen men, and to entail slavery upon them, and to keep them in heathenism in the midst of Christianity, the God of heaven would smile upon every effort which the injured might make to disenthrall themselves.

Brethren, it is as wrong for your lordly oppressors to keep you in slavery as it was for the man thief to steal our ancestors from the coast of Africa. You should, therefore, now use the same manner of resistance as would have been just in our ancestors, when the bloody footprints of the first remorseless soul thief was placed upon the shores of our fatherland. The humblest peasant is as free in the sight of God as the proudest monarch that ever swayed a sceptre. Liberty is a spirit sent out from God and, like its great Author, is no respecter of persons.

Brethren, the time has come when you must act for yourselves. It is an old and true saying that, "if hereditary bondsmen would be free, they must themselves strike the blow." You can plead your own cause, and do the work of emancipation better than any other. The nations of the old world are moving in the great cause of universal freedom, and some of them at least will, ere long, do you justice. The combined powers of Europe have placed their broad seal of disapprobation upon the African slave trade. But in the slaveholding parts of the United States, the trade is as brisk as ever. They buy and sell you as if you were brute beasts. The North has done much—her opinion of slavery in the abstract is known. But in regard to the South, we adopt the opinion of the *New York Evangelist*—"We have advanced so far, that the cause apparently waits for a more effectual door to be thrown open than has been yet." We are about to point out to you that more effectual door. Look around you, and behold the bosoms of your loving wives beating with untold agonies! Hear the cries of your poor children! Remember the stripes your fathers bore. Think of the torture and disgrace of your noble mothers. Think of your wretched sisters, loving virtue and purity, as they are driven into concubinage and are exposed to the unbridled lusts of incarnate devils. Think of the undying glory that hangs around the ancient name of Africa—and forget not that you are native-born American citizens, and as such, you are justly entitled to the rights that are granted to the freest. Think how many tears you have poured out upon the soil which you have cultivated with unrequited toil and enriched with your blood; and then go to your lordly enslavers and tell them plainly that you ARE DETERMINED TO BE FREE. Appeal to their sense of justice, and tell them that they have no more right to oppress you than you have to enslave them. Entreat them to remove the grievous burdens which they have imposed upon you, and to remunerate you for your labor. Promise them renewed diligence in the cultivation of the soil, if they will render you an equivalent for your services. Point them to the increase in happiness and prosperity in the British West-Indies since the act of Emancipation. Tell them in language which they cannot misunderstand of the exceeding sinfulness of slavery, and of a future judgment, and of the righteous retributions of an indignant God. Inform them that all you desire is FREEDOM, and that nothing else will suffice. Do this, and forever after cease to toil for the heartless tyrants, who give you no other reward but stripes and abuse. If they then commence the work of death, they, and not you, will be responsible for the consequences. You had far better all die—*die immediately*—than live slaves, and entail your wretchedness upon your posterity. If you would be free in this generation, here is your only hope. However much you and all of us may desire it, there is not much hope of redemption without the shedding of blood. If you must bleed, let it all come at once—rather *die freemen, than live to be slaves*. It is impossible, like the children of Israel, to make a grand exodus from the land of bondage. . . . In the name of the merciful God, and by all that life is worth, let it no longer be a debatable question whether it is better to choose LIBERTY OR DEATH. . . .

Brethren arise, arise! Strike for your lives and liberties. Now is the day and the hour. Let every slave throughout the land do this, and the days of slavery are numbered. You cannot be more oppressed than you have been—you cannot suffer greater cruelties than you have already. RATHER DIE FREEMEN, THAN LIVE TO BE SLAVES. Remember that you are THREE MILLIONS!

It is in your power to torment the God-cursed slaveholders, that they will be glad to let you go free. If the scale was turned, and black men were the masters and white men the slaves, every destructive agent and element would be employed to lay the oppressor low. Danger and death would hang over their heads day and night. Yes, the tyrants would meet with plagues more terrible than those of Pharaoh. But you are a patient people. You act as though you were made for the special use of these devils. You act as though your daughters were born to pamper the lusts of your masters and overseers. And worse than all, you tamely submit, while your lords tear your wives from your embraces and defile them before your eyes. In the name of God, we ask, are you men? Where is the blood of your fathers? Has it all run out of your veins? Awake, awake; millions of voices are calling you! Your dead fathers speak to you from their graves. Heaven, as with a voice of thunder, calls on you to arise from the dust.

Let your motto be RESISTANCE, RESISTANCE, RESISTANCE! No oppressed people have ever secured their liberty without resistance. What kind of resistance you had better make, you must decide by the circumstances that surround you, and according to the suggestion of expediency. Brethren, adieu! Trust in the living God. Labor for the peace of the human race, and remember that you are three millions.

Sojourner Truth, Women's Rights

The antislavery movement brought expanded roles and responsibilities to African-American women. Dozens penned autobiographies of their lives in bondage, lectured, wrote editorials, or raised funds for the cause. In time, many came to see slavery as a metaphor for their own plight as women. Some, such as Sojourner Truth (ca. 1797–1883), a prominent lecturer throughout the North in the 1840s and 1850s, moved easily between abolitionism and feminism. This speech, given before an 1851 women's rights convention in Akron, Ohio, was her most powerful feminist statement.[*]

I am [for] woman's rights. I have as much muscle as any man, and can do as much work as any man. I have plowed and reaped and husked and chopped and mowed, and can any man do more than that? I have heard much about the sexes being equal; I can carry as much as any man, and can eat as much too, if I can get it. I am as strong as any man that is now. As for intellect, all I can say is, if woman have a pint and man a quart—why can't she have her little pint full? You need not be afraid to give us our rights for fear we will take too much, for we can't take more than our pint'll hold. The poor men seem to be all in confusion, and don't know what to do. Why children, if you have woman's rights, give it to her and you will feel better. You will have your own rights, and they won't be so much trouble. I can't read, but I can hear. I have heard the bible and have learned that Eve caused man to sin. Well if woman upset the world, do give her a chance to set it right side up again. The lady [preceding me] has spoken about Jesus, how he never spurned woman from him, and she was right. When Lazarus died, Mary and Martha came to him with faith and love and besought him to raise their brother. And Jesus wept—and Lazarus came forth. And how came Jesus into the world? Through God who created him and woman who bore him. Man, where is your part? But the women are coming up, blessed be God, and a few of the men are coming up with them. But man is in a tight place; the poor slave is on him, woman is coming on him, and he is surely between a hawk and a buzzard.

Martin R. Delany, A Call for Emigration

Events of the 1850s prompted some black abolitionists to consider emigrating to a more hospitable place. Martin R. Delany (1812–1885) of Pittsburgh, a physician and antislavery editor, emerged as the leading spokesman for this sentiment. His *Condition, Elevation, Emigration and Destiny of the Colored People of the United States* (1852), which explored alternatives in Africa, Latin America, and the Caribbean, struck a responsive chord among many free blacks and stimulated a growing emigration movement. The following document is part of his conclusion to that volume. In 1859 Delany visited the Niger Valley in Africa and made plans to establish a settlement there for American blacks. When Reconstruction ended after the Civil War,

---

[*] *Anti-Slavery Bugle* (Salem, Oh.), 21 June 1851.

threatening the newly won rights of African Americans, he promoted another African settlement venture.[*]

The time has now fully arrived when the colored race is called upon by all the ties of common humanity, and all the claims of consummate justice, to go forward and take their position, and do battle in the struggle now being made for the redemption of the world. Our cause is a just one; the greatest at present that elicits the attention of the world. For if there is a remedy, that remedy is now at hand. God himself, as assuredly as he rules the destinies of nations and entereth measures into the "hearts of men," has presented these measures to us. Our race is to be redeemed; it is a great and glorious work, and we are the instrumentalities by which it is to be done. But we must go from among our oppressors; it never can be done by staying among them. God has, as certain as he has ever designed anything, designed this great portion of the New World for us, the colored races; and as certain as we stubborn our hearts, and stiffen our necks against it, his protecting arm and fostering care will be withdrawn from us.

Shall we be told that we can live nowhere, but under the will of our oppressors; that this (the United States) is the country most favorable to our improvement and progress? Are we incapable of self-government, and making such improvements for ourselves as we delight to enjoy after American white men have made them for themselves? No, it is not true. Neither is it true that the United States is the best country for our improvement. That country is the best in which our manhood can be best developed.

Asking Questions of the Documents

1. What, according to David Walker, kept free blacks from fighting against slavery before the 1820s? What did he suggest would happen once they began fighting? Why? Toward whom did Walker direct his *Appeal*?

2. What did Lewis G. Clarke believe to be the most evil features of American slavery? Do you think his speech would have been effective in persuading white audiences in the North and abroad of the evils of the institution? Why?

3. How did Henry Highland Garnet attempt to convince slaves to revolt? Why would his speech be controversial, both within and beyond the antislavery movement? Compare and contrast its tone and content to that of Walker's *Appeal*.

4. Why did a feminist ideology develop among black women in the antislavery movement? What arguments did Sojourner Truth make in favor of women's rights?

5. What prompted the rise of emigration sentiment among black abolitionists in the 1850s? What arguments did Martin R. Delany make in favor of African-American migration beyond the United States?

---

[*] Martin R. Delany, *The Condition, Elevation, Emigration and Destiny of the Colored People of the United States* (Philadelphia, 1852).

For Further Reading

Andrews, William L. *To Tell a Free Story: The First Century of Afro-American Autobiography, 1760-1865*. Urbana, Ill.: University of Illinois Press, 1986.

Blackett, R. J. M. *Building an Antislavery Wall: Black Americans in the Atlantic Abolitionist Movement, 1830-1860*. Baton Rouge, La.: Louisiana State University Press, 1983.

Miller, Floyd J. *The Search for a Black Nationality: Black Colonization and Emigration, 1787-1863*. Urbana, Ill.: University of Illinois Press, 1975.

Pease, Jane H., and William H. Pease. *They Who Would Be Free: Blacks' Search for Freedom, 1830-1861*. New York: Atheneum, 1974.

Quarles, Benjamin. *Black Abolitionists*. New York: Oxford University Press, 1969.

Stewart, James Brewer. *Holy Warriors: The Abolitionists and American Slavery*. New York: Hill and Wang, 1976.

Yee, Shirley J. *Black Women Abolitionists: A Study in Activism, 1828-1860*. Knoxvile, Tenn.: University of Tennesee Press, 1992.

- The teach themself how to be good abolitionist.
-

7

The Emancipation Experience

The Civil War, which began in 1861 after the secession of eleven slave states, not only divided the nation; it brought the death of slavery in the South. At first, President Abraham Lincoln insisted that federal forces were merely fighting to restore the Union. But African Americans sensed in the struggle an opportunity to gain their freedom. Black leaders pressed Lincoln to adopt emancipation as a war goal. And as Union forces advanced on the periphery of the Confederacy, hundreds of thousands of slaves— eventually defined as contrabands by the Lincoln government—escaped to the freedom and safety of Union lines. In January 1863 Lincoln responded by announcing the Emancipation Proclamation, which declared free all slaves in areas then in rebellion against the United States. After two years of fighting, emancipation had become Union policy.

Committed to emancipation and desperate for additional manpower on the battlefield, the Lincoln government soon welcomed the contributions of African Americans to the war effort. Black leaders urged and personally recruited both contrabands and free blacks to fight in the Union forces. Some 180,000 blacks eventually enlisted and served in the Union army. With the exception of a few light-skinned blacks who surreptitiously fought in white regiments, recruits were organized in all-black units under white officers. There, despite promises of equality, they received less pay and endured worse conditions than white soldiers. But they fought valiantly in hundreds of battles and skirmishes throughout the South. Another thirty thousand blacks joined the Union navy. All together, African Americans represented one-tenth of all U.S. military personnel in the conflict. Thousands of other African Americans worked for the Union army as scouts, teamsters, nurses, cooks, and laborers, or became missionaries, teachers, and relief workers in the contraband camps filling up behind Union lines.

The final defeat of the Confederacy in mid-1865, and the ratification of the Thirteenth Amendment at the close of that year, signalled the end of black bondage in the United States. Four million slaves became free men and women for the first time. They jubilantly celebrated their new status on the plantations and in the cities and contraband camps of the South. Many traversed the roads of the South looking for family and friends, seeking new employment opportunities, or simply testing the limits of their newly gained freedom. Emancipation was a reality after two and a half centuries of African-American life. Now both blacks and the nation would have to define what that freedom meant.

William Summerson, Fleeing to Union Lines

Contrabands pressed the Lincoln government on the question of emancipation by fleeing in large numbers to Union lines. This occurred from the very beginning of the war. In the following document, William Summerson (1839–?), a South Carolina slave, recounts his 1862 flight to the Union naval blockade along the Atlantic coast. Summerson, who had worked on a steamer operating between Charleston and the mouth of the St. Johns River in Florida before the war, was a clerk in a store operated by his master in Charleston. After the war threatened to separate him from his wife, he devised an ingenious escape. Union naval officials then forwarded Summerson and his wife to the contraband camps at Port Royal in the South Carolina Sea Islands.[*]

Ever since I knew enough to know right from wrong, I have wanted to get my freedom, but there was no way of escape. Slavery walled me in. While I was in Charleston, in March 1862, I was married. The May following, my wife was to be carried back into the country, and I might never see her again; so I hid her from the last of April until we escaped together. She was hidden with some of my friends, and as the slaves escaped so constantly to the blockade, no one searched for her. At 12 o'clock on Friday, June 13, my mistress sent down to the store for me, and told me to go down to lawyer Porter, in Broad Street. He was brother to my mistress. He said to me, "William, would you rather go into the country with your mistress or be sold?" A great agony came over me, for I should have to leave my wife, and might never see her face again. I told him I would rather go with my mistress, and he said, "No, you cannot go with your mistress; you must be sold."

Then he took me to the Court-House to have some traders estimate my value. One said I was worth $1,000, another $1,100. He then told me he would give me till the next day to find a man to buy me. I could not find anyone to buy me, and he knew I could not. This was only a form, to make me submit. While I was in the Court-House, and the traders were examining me, I lifted my heart to the Almighty, and besought him to make a way for me to escape. After I left the Court-House, I went back to the store, and that night, the last that was left me, as I prayed and groaned before the Almighty, He put a plan into my head which carried me safely to freedom.

The plan was this: I had a friend, also a slave, who came from the country three times a week with vegetables. The place was called Sanandros [St. Andrew's] Parish; it

[*] *National Anti-Slavery Standard* (New York), 27 December 1862.

was about seven miles from Charleston. I thought after he had disposed of his load, I would get him to put me in a rice barrel and take me back in his wagon. This was the only way I could get out of the city. The days on which he came in were Monday, Thursday, and Saturday. He had a pass for the wagon. I saw him on Saturday morning. I was to be sold that afternoon, and we made the agreement. I left the store at 12 o'clock that day, and went to the place where I had agreed to meet him, and hid under a piazza. He drove up to the piazza, and I got into the barrel, and he headed me up, and I was put into the wagon, and he drove away.

After we drove through the city we came to the new bridge over the Ashley River. There were fifty pickets stationed by this bridge. One read the pass at the bridge, and we passed on. Every half mile for seven miles we met a rebel picket, who stopped the wagon, read the pass, and had the right to search the wagon. I took my clothes, and a picture of John Brown, which I had kept with my few treasures, in the barrel with me. We left Charleston at 6 p.m., and reached the plantation at 10 p.m. I got out at 10:30 p.m.; so I was in the barrel four hours and a half. This driver went back to the city, and was to bring my wife in the same way. She was taken to a stable, and put in a barrel and headed up. He took her through the city as he did me, but the mule had worked all the day before, and would not draw well, so they had to stop and rest, which made it at midnight when she got there. She got into the barrel at 4 p.m., so she was eight hours and a half therein.

On the road one of the rebels got into the wagon and sat on the barrel she was in, and rode half a mile in that way, and only the power of the Almighty kept the barrel from breaking and bringing her to light. After she got there, she could not move, and was drenched with perspiration. We fanned her, and finally managed to restore her. We staid there till Wednesday, 12:30 midnight. We walked three miles through a swamp, with the water up to our knees. After we got to this point, we had to cross a railroad bridge about fifty feet high. We walked across on the sleepers. It was about half a mile long, and was on the Charleston and Savannah railroad. About a quarter of a mile beyond was a boat that my friend, the driver of the vegetable wagon, had brought for me. I found a man there who wanted to escape, but did not dare venture; but I persuaded him to go with us. We then started.

We had fifteen miles to go before we could get to the Federal blockade, and on the way we had to pass a rebel gunboat and a fort. I meant to wait till the tide fell, so that the gunboat would go back into the Cut where she lay at low water, but I did not see her till I got close upon her, and heard the men talking, and looked up and saw them on the deck. I kept close to the marsh, so they might not see me, and managed to get round the point. About a mile and a half above this point was the fort which I had to pass. I passed the fort in the same way as I passed the boat. After I got a litle beyond, I crossed on to the same shore that she was, and after I got a little way along the shore, day broke as clear as could be. I looked back and could not see the fort, and I knew I was out of their reach.

About two hours and a half later we reached the Federal gunboats in the Stono River. When I got in sight of the Union boats, I raised a white flag, and when I came near, they cheered me, and pointed to the flagship Pawnee. There I had the pleasure of a breakfast of hot coffee, ham, nice butter, and all under the American flag—all strange things in Charleston. There I gave the Almighty praise and glory for delivering me so far. On board the Pawnee I told the Captain about Charleston harbor, and how the vessels run the blockade, and the next day but one they took two vessels from the information I gave them.

Frederick Douglass, "Men of Color, To Arms"

After the Emancipation Proclamation and the decision of the Lincoln government to enlist black troops, African Americans had an unprecedented opportunity to overthrow the institution of slavery. Black leaders urged both contrabands and free blacks to join the Union forces and actively recruited for black regiments. Frederick Douglass was a leading recruiter for the Massachusetts 54th Colored Infantry, the first unit organized among African Americans in the North. In the following editorial, which appeared in his own monthly magazine and soon became a recruiting flyer, he outlined for the men of his race the reasons they should enlist.*

When the first rebel cannon shattered the walls of Sumter and drove away its starving garrison, I predicted that the war then and there inaugurated would not be fought out entirely by white men. Every month's experience during these dreary years has confirmed that opi nion. A war undertaken and brazenly carried on for the perpetual enslavement of colored men, calls logically and loudly for colored men to help suppress it. Only a moderate share of sagacity was needed to see that the arm of the slave was the best defense against the arm of the slaveholder. Hence with every reverse to the national arms, with every exulting shout of victory raised by the slaveholding rebels, I have implored the imperiled nation to unchain against her foes, her powerful black hand. Slowly and reluctanty that appeal is beginning to be heeded. Stop not now to complain that it was not heeded sooner. It may or may not have been best that it should not. This is not the time to discuss that question. Leave it to the future. When the war is over, the country is saved, peace is established, and the black man's rights are secured, as they will be, history with an impartial hand will dispose of that and sundry other questions. Action! Action! not criticism, is the plain duty of this hour. Words are now useful only as they stimulate to blows. The office of speech now is only to point out when, where, and how to strike to the best advantage. There is no time to delay. The tide is at its flood that leads on to fortune. From East to West, from North to South, the sky is written all over, "Now or never."

Liberty won by white men would lose half its luster. "Who would be free themselves must strike the blow." "Better even die free, than to live slaves." This is the sentiment of every brave colored man amongst us. There are weak and cowardly men in all nations.

---

* *Douglass' Monthly* (Rochester, N.Y.), March 1863.

We have them amongst us. They tell you this is the "white man's war"; that you will be "no better off after than before the war"; that the getting of you into the army is to "sacrifice you on the first opportunity." Believe them not; cowards themselves, they do not wish to have their cowardice shamed by your brave example. Leave them to their timidity, or to whatever motive may hold them back. I have not thought lightly of the words I am now addressing you. The counsel I give comes of close observation of the great struggle now in progress, and of the deep conviction that this is your hour and mine. In good earnest then, and after the best deliberation, I now for the first time during this war feel at liberty to call and counsel you to arms. By every consideration which binds you to your enslaved fellow-countrymen, and the peace and welfare of your country; by every aspiration which you cherish for the freedom and equality of yourselves and your children; by all the ties of blood and identity which make us one with the brave black men now fighting our battles in Louisiana and in South Carolina, I urge you to fly to arms, and smite with death the power that would bury the government and your liberty in the same hopeless grave. . . . We can get at the throat of treason and slavery through the State of Massachusetts. She was first in the war of independence; first to break the chains of her slaves; first to make the black man equal before the law; first to admit colored citizens to her common schools, and she was first to answer with her blood the alarm cry of the nation, when its capital was menaced by rebels. . . . I need not add more.

Massachusetts now welcomes you to arms as soldiers. She has but a small colored population from which to recruit. She has full leave of the general government to send one regiment to the war, and she has undertaken to do it. Go quickly and help fill up the first colored regiment from the North. I am authorized to assure you that you will receive the same wages, the same rations, the same equipments, the same protection, the same treatment, and the same bounty, secured to the white soldiers. You will be led by able and skillful officers, men who will take especial pride in your efficiency and success. They will be quick to accord to you all the honor you shall merit by your valor, and see that your rights and feelings are respected by other soldiers. I have assured myself on these points, and can speak with authority. More than twenty years of unswerving devotion to our common cause may give me some humble claim to be trusted at this momentous crisis. I will not argue. To do so implies hesitation and doubt, and you do not hesitate. You do not doubt. The day dawns; the morning star is bright upon the horizon! The iron gate of our prison stands half open. One gallant rush from the North will fling it wide open, while four millions of our brothers and sisters shall march out into liberty. The chance is now given you to end in a day the bondage of centuries, and to rise in one bound from social degradation to the plane of common equality with all other varieties of men. Remember Denmark Vesey of Charleston; remember Nathaniel Turner of Southampton; remember Shields Green and [John] Copeland, who followed noble John Brown, and fell as glorious martyrs for the cause of the slave. Remember that in a contest with oppression, the Almighty has no attribute which can take sides with oppressors. The case is before you. This is our golden opportunity. Let us accept it, and forever wipe out the dark reproaches unsparingly hurled against us by our enemies. Let us win for ourselves the gratitude of the country, and the best blessings of our posterity through all time.

Meunomennie L. Maimi, The Meaning of the War

African-American soldiers viewed the Civil War as nothing less than a conflict between slavery and freedom. They believed that their participation would help to bring about the death of the "peculiar institution." This perspective is poignantly articulated in the following letter from Meunomennie L. Maimi (1835–?), a light-skinned Connecticut black serving in the 20th Connecticut Volunteers in Virginia, to his wife at home. In 1863 Maimi transferred to the all-black Massachusetts 54th Colored Infantry.

> Buckingham Legion, Co. I 20th Regt., C.V.
> Camp near Stafford C. H.

March 1863

My Dear Wife:

When I wrote you the last letter I was quite sick, and did not know as I should ever be able to write you again; but I am better now and write to relieve your mind, in case you might worry too much about me. When I wrote my last letter, I did not expect to write another; but some good news which I received and the kind usage of a few friends, who came to my hut and did what was needed for me, have saved you your husband, and I am enabled to write again. There is one thing your selfish love for your husband has made you forget, and that is, that he is naturally a soldier, and in time of war, and particularly in times like the present, a good soldier has something else to do besides enjoying himself at home with his family. I shall come, if permitted to go home, but as soon as my health will admit, I will return to duty.

Do you know or think what the end of this war is to decide? It is to decide whether we are to have freedom to all or slavery to all. If the Southern Confederacy succeeds, then you may bid farewell to all liberty thereafter and either be driven to a foreign land or held in slavery here. If our government succeeds, then your and our race will be free. The government has torn down the only barrier that existed against us as a people. When slavery passes away, the prejudices that belonged to it must follow. The government calls for the colored man's help and, if he is not a fool, he will give it. . . .

[Slaveholders] are my enemies, my flag's enemies, the flag I was born under, have suffered so much under—the enemies to God and our government. It is they who have struck down the flag which so long has defended their institutions before they left our Union. It has by them been cast to the earth and trampled under foot, because it professed to be the flag of liberty and freedom, although it was only liberty for the white man. . . . They tore that flag from its staff and in its place put their rebel rag, and swore by it that freedom should die. But they shall find that it cannot die, that its black sons as

ly Anglo-African (New York), 18 April 1863

well as its loyal white sons are faithful, and will shed the last drop of blood in defense of the starry banner that is to be the emblem of freedom to all, whether black or white. . . .

I do not blame you altogether for what you said about returning home, as it was cowardly in me to complain to you of . . . bad usage. I forgive you, as it was prompted by your too-selfish love for your husband. But I want you to remember hereafter that you are a soldier's wife, a warrior's bride—one who has not a single drop of cowardly blood in his veins, and who will not desert his flag, or country, or his brother in bonds, not even for his dearly beloved wife, the friend of his bosom. Ponder this well; take the right sense of it and be proud that you have such a man for a husband. What is money but trash? And is trash to be compared to a country's and my own liberty? If the government gets so poor, before the war ends, that it cannot pay but $10 per month and no bounties, I will take that and fight on. That will buy bread for you and my poor old grandmother. If I return at all, let me come back to your arms a free man, of a free country and a free flag, and my brothers free, or else let me rest in death on the battlefield, with my face to the slaveholders, a continual reproach and curse unto him, as long as the world shall stand or a slaveholder breathe. This from your soldier-husband.

M. L. Maimi

Susie King Taylor, Life in Camp

African-American women contributed to the Union war effort in a variety of ways. Many stayed home and raised families alone, while their husbands and sons enlisted in the Union army. Free black women's organizations in the North raised funds and collected supplies for black regiments and the contraband camps in the South. Some assisted Union regiments as nurses, cooks, laundresses, teachers, and in other ways. Susie King Taylor (1848–1912), a literate Georgia contraband, travelled with the First South Carolina Volunteers (later renamed the 33rd U.S. Colored Troops), a regiment of former slaves, from 1862 until the end of the war. In the following excerpt from her autobiography, she recounts the rhythms of camp life and the horrors of the battlefield as she experienced them along the South Carolina coast.[*]

I was enrolled as company laundress, but I did very little of it, because I was always busy doing other things through camp, and was employed all the time doing something for the officers and comrades. . . . I learned to handle a musket very well while in the

---

[*] Susie King Taylor, *Reminiscences of My Life in Camp with the 33rd United States Colored Troops* (Boston, 1902).

regiment and could shoot straight and often hit the target. I assisted in cleaning the guns and used to fire them off, to see if the cartridges were dry, before cleaning and re-loading, each day. I thought this was great fun. I was also able to take a gun apart and put it together again. . . . I often got my own meals and would fix some dishes for the noncommissioned officers also. . . .

About the first of June 1864, the regiment was ordered to Folly Island, staying there until the latter part of the month, when it was ordered to Morris Island. We landed on Morris Island between June and July 1864. This island was a narrow strip of sandy soil, nothing growing on it but a few bushes and shrubs. The camp was one mile from the boat landing, called Pawnell Landing. . . .

The regiment under Colonel Trowbridge did garrison duty, but they had troublesome times from Fort Gregg, on James Island, for the rebels would throw a shell over on our island every now and then. Finally orders were received for the boys to prepare to take Fort Gregg, each man to take 150 rounds of cartridges, canteens of water, hardtack, and salt beef. This order was sent three days prior to starting, to allow them to be in readiness. I helped as many as I could to pack haversacks and cartridge boxes.

The fourth day, about five o'clock in the afternoon, the call was sounded, and I heard the first sergeant say, "Fall in, boys, fall in," and they were not long obeying the command. Each company marched out of its street, in front of their colonel's headquarters, where they rested for half an hour, as it was not dark enough, and they did not want the enemy to have a chance to spy their movements. At the end of this time the line was formed with the 103rd New York (white) in the rear, and off they started, eager to get to work. It was quite dark by the time they reached Pawnell Landing. I have never forgotten the goodbyes of that day, as they left camp. Colonel Trowbridge said to me as he left, "Good-by, Mrs. King, take care of yourself if you don't see us again." I went with them as far as the landing, and watched them until they got out of sight, and then I returned to the camp. There was no one at camp but those left on picket and a few disabled soldiers, and one woman, a friend of mine, Mary Shaw, and it was lonesome and sad, now that the boys were gone, some never to return.

Mary Shaw shared my tent that night, and we went to bed, but not to sleep, for the fleas nearly ate us alive. We caught a few, but it did seem, now that the men were gone, that every flea in camp had located my tent, and caused us to vacate. Sleep being out of the question, we sat up the remainder of the night.

About four o'clock, July 2, the charge was made. The firing could be plainly heard in camp. I hastened down to the landing and remained there until eight o'clock that morning. When the wounded arrived, or rather began to arrive, the first one brought in was Samuel Anderson of our company. He was badly wounded. Then others of our boys, some with their legs off, arm gone, foot off, and wounds of all kinds imaginable. They had to wade through creeks and marshes, as they were discovered by the enemy and shelled very badly. A number of the men were lost, some got fastened in the mud and had to cut the legs of their pants, to free themselves. The 103rd New York suffered the most, as their men were very badly wounded.

My work now began. I gave assistance to try to alleviate their sufferings, I asked the doctor at the hospital what I could get for them to eat. They wanted soup, but that I could not get; but I had a few cans of condensed milk and some turtle eggs, so I thought

I would try to make some custard. I had doubts as to my success, for cooking with turtle eggs was something new to me, but the adage has it, "Nothing ventured, nothing done," so I made a venture and the result was a very delicious custard. This I carried to the men, who enjoyed it very much. My services were given at all times for the comfort of these men. I was on hand to assist whenever needed.

Charlotte Forten, Teaching the Contrabands on the Sea Islands

Hundreds of free blacks from the North went South during the Civil War to work as missionaries, teachers, and relief workers in the contraband camps of the South. They hoped to prepare these former slaves for their new role as free men and women. In the following document, Charlotte Forten describes her experiences in a contraband school at Port Royal on the South Carolina Sea Islands. Forten (1837–1912), a member of a famous family of black abolitionists in Philadelphia, was well educated and had taught in the integrated schools of Salem, Massachusetts, before going South. Although she found the task of teaching the contrabands—both young and old—demanding, she was encouraged by their desire to obtain the education which had been denied them in slavery.[*]

The first day at school was rather trying. Most of my children were very small, and consequently restless. Some were too young to learn the alphabet. These little ones were brought to school because the older children—in whose care their parents leave them while at work—could not come without them. We were therefore willing to have them come, although they seemed to have discovered the secret of perpetual motion, and tried one's patience sadly. But after some days of positive, though not severe treatment, order was brought out of chaos, and I found but little difficulty in managing and quieting the tiniest and most restless spirits. I never before saw children so eager to learn, although I had had several years' experience in New England schools. Coming to school is a constant delight and recreation to them. They come here as other children go to play. The older ones, during the summer, work in the fields from early morning until eleven or twelve o'clock, and then come into school, after their hard toil in the hot sun, as bright and anxious to learn as ever.

Of course, there are some stupid ones, but these are the minority. The majority learn with wonderful rapidity. Many of the grown people are desirous of learning to read. It is wonderful how a people who have been so long crushed to the earth, so imbruted as these have been—and they are said to be among the most degraded negroes of the

South—can have so great a desire for knowledge, and such a capacity for attaining it. One cannot believe that the haughty Anglo-Saxon race, after centuries of such an experience as these people have had, would be very much superior to them. And one's indignation increases against those who, North as well as South, taunt the colored race with inferiority while they themselves use every means in their power to crush and degrade them, denying them every right and privilege, closing against them every avenue of elevation and improvement. Were they, under such circumstances, intellectual and refined, they would certainly be vastly superior to any other race that ever existed.

After the lessons, we used to talk freely to the children, often giving them slight sketches of the great and good men. Before teaching them the "John Brown" song, which they learned to sing with great spirit, [another teacher] told them the story of the brave old man who had died for them. I told them about Toussaint [L'Ouverture], thinking it well they should know what one of their own color had done for his race. They listened attentively, and seemed to understand. We found it rather hard to keep their attention in school. It is not strange, as they have been so entirely unused to intellectual concentration. It is necessary to interest them every moment, in order to keep their thoughts from wandering. Teaching here is consequently far more fatiguing than at the North. In the church, we had of course but one room in which to hear all the children; and to make one's self heard, when there were often as many as a hundred and forty reciting at once, it was necessary to tax the lungs very severely. . . .

The tiniest children are delighted to get a book in their hands. Many of them already know their letters. The parents are eager to have them learn. They sometimes said to me, "Do, Miss, let de chil'en learn everting dey can. *We* nebber hab no chance to learn nuttin', but we wants de chil'en to learn." They are willing to make many sacrifices that their children may attend school. One old woman, who had a large family of children and grandchildren, came regularly to school in the winter, and took her seat among the little ones. She was at least sixty years old. Another woman—who had one of the best faces I ever saw—came daily, and brought her baby in her arms. It happened to be one of the best babies in the world, a perfect little "model of deportment," and allowed its mother to pursue her studies without interruption.

Felix Haywood, The Death of Slavery

For a majority of southern blacks, the end of slavery came with the final defeat of the Confederacy. In the following document, Felix Haywood (ca. 1845–?), a Texas slave, describes the reaction of slaves in his community as Union soldiers liberated their plantations in mid-1865. Haywood became a cowboy on the plains of central Texas after the Civil War. The following recollections are from an interview in the 1930s.*

The end of the war, it come just like that—like you snap your fingers. . . . How did we know it! Hallelujah broke out—

Abe Lincoln freed the nigger
With the gun and the trigger;
And I ain't going to get whipped any more. I got my ticket,
Leaving the thicket
And I'm a-heading for the Golden Shore!

Soldiers, all of a sudden, was everywhere—coming in bunches, crossing and walking and riding. Everyone was a-singing. We was all walking on golden clouds. Hallelujah!

Union forever,
Hurrah, boys, hurrah!
Although I may be poor,
I'll never be a slave—
Shouting the battle cry of freedom.

Everybody went wild. We all felt like heroes, and nobody had made us that way but ourselves. We was free. Just like that, we was free. . . . Right off colored folks started on the move. They seemed to want to get closer to freedom, so they'd know what it was—like it was a place. . . . We knowed freedom was on us, but we didn't know what was to come.

---

* B. A. Botkin, ed., *Lay My Burden Down: A Folk History of Slavery* (Chicago: University of Chicago Press, 1945).

Asking Questions of the Documents

1. How did the coming of the Civil War make it easier for slaves to escape from bondage? Why do you think the actions of the contrabands made it harder for President Abraham Lincoln to ignore the question of emancipation as a war issue?

2. According to Frederick Douglass, why was it important for black men to enlist in the Union army? What did the war mean to African-American soldiers? What difficulties did they face in the conflict as a result of their race?

3. What roles did African-American women play during the war?

4. Why do you think the contrabands were so interested in obtaining an education? Why would northern free blacks believe that it was important to go South and teach them?

5. How did slaves react to the news of emancipation?

For Further Reading

Berlin, Ira, Barbara J. Fields, Steven F. Miller, Joseph P. Reidy, and Leslie S. Rowland, *Slaves No More: Three Essays on Emancipation and the Civil War*. New York: Cambridge University Press, 1992.

Cornish, Dudley T. *The Sable Arm: Black Troops in the Union Army, 1861–1865*. Lawrence, Ks.: University Press of Kansas, 1987.

Franklin, John Hope. *The Emancipation Proclamation*. New York: Doubleday, 1963.

Gerteis, Louis S. *From Contraband to Freedman: Federal Policy toward Southern Blacks, 1861-1865*. Westport, Conn.: Greenwood Press, 1973.

Litwack, Leon F. *Been in the Storm So Long: The Aftermath of Slavery*. New York: Alfred A. Knopf, 1979.

Quarles, Benjamin. *The Negro in the Civil War*. Boston: Little, Brown and Company, 1953.

Rose, Willie Lee. *Rehearsal for Reconstruction: The Port Royal Experiment*. Indianapolis: Bobbs-Merrill, 1964.

8

Dreams Deferred: The Promise and Failure of Reconstruction

The Civil War reunited the nation and ended slavery, but it left other important questions unanswered. What would happen to the states of the recently defeated Confederacy? What would freedom mean for the four million former slaves (now called freedmen) in the region? During the period from 1865 to 1877, usually known as Reconstruction, the federal government sought to answer these questions. This process was controlled after 1867 by so-called Radical Republicans in the U.S. Congress, who sought to punish ex-Confederates, grant basic rights to African Americans, and establish a strong Republican presence in the South. By 1870 all of the former Confederate states had been readmitted to the Union under Republican governments, and African Americans had been guaranteed important political and civil rights through a series of amendments to the U.S. Constitution.

Acting on definitions of freedom shaped during their years in bondage, the former slaves developed their own agenda for Reconstruction. They sought what had been denied them in slavery—a stable family life, education, their own institutions, and basic civil protections. But two rights seemed paramount. Freedmen insisted on the right to vote and run for office on the same basis as whites. Political power, they believed, would help them gain and protect other rights. They also sought economic autonomy, which they usually defined as owning and farming their own land. This would free them, they were persuaded, from continuing social control and economic exploitation by their former masters.

With the help of the Radical Republicans, African Americans achieved major political and social gains during Reconstruction. The Fourteenth Amendment (1868) guaranteed them citizenship, due process, and equal protection of the laws. The Fifteenth Amendment (1870) brought political empowerment, giving them the vote on the same basis as whites—universal male suffrage. Black men flocked to the polls in overwhelming numbers to support the Radical Republicans, and often used their new political power to elect other blacks to office. Some six hundred served in southern state legislatures during the period. One, P. B. S. Pinchback, briefly acted as governor of Louisiana. Fourteen were elected to the U.S. House of Representatives, and two—Hiram Revels and Blanche K. Bruce of Mississippi—served in the U.S. Senate. They used these offices to push for other gains, including the Civil Rights Act of 1875, which outlawed racial discrimination in hotels, theaters, railroad cars, and other public places.

Economic gains were far less substantial. Although the freedmen fervently hoped that each family of former slaves would be given "forty acres and a mule," land confiscated from Confederate masters was not redistributed. This seemed too extreme for most Radical Republicans. With land still in the hands of their former masters, most of the freedmen had to become sharecroppers, giving white landowners half of their annual crop in exchange for tools, seed, a cabin to live in, and the right to work the land. Although that arrangement kept them in poverty, it did provide far more social autonomy than had been possible in the slave quarters.

Reconstruction proved to be short-lived. Northern white commitment to the process, always based more on anger at white southerners than on support for African-American rights, faded as political scandals, economic depression, and other issues diverted attention away from the South. Southern white violence against both black and white Republicans, carried out by the Ku Klux Klan, White League, and similar groups, eventually restored Democratic opponents of Reconstruction to political control in the South. In 1877 northern Republicans finally capitulated and abandoned the Reconstruction experiment. African Americans saw many of their hard-won gains quickly evaporate. The black agenda for Reconstruction would have to wait nearly another century before again becoming a national issue.

The Freedmen's Agenda for Reconstruction

Once slavery ended, the former slaves moved boldly to give meaning to their incipient freedom. Throughout the South, they gathered in community meetings to press for their civil and political rights. One early example is the following list of resolutions approved by Norfolk blacks in June 1865, less than two months after the surrender of Confederate forces at Appomattox Court House had effectively ended the Civil War in Virginia. Apprehensive that local whites might try to limit their freedom, they assembled and outlined their requirements for a meaningful Reconstruction. The resolutions were drafted by a committee of eight local black leaders, most of whom had been free before the war.[*]

1st. *Resolved*, That the rights and interests of the colored citizens of Virginia are more directly, immediately and deeply affected in the restoration of the State to the Federal Union than any other class of citizens; and hence, that we have peculiar claims

---

[*] *Equal Suffrage: Address from the Colored Citizens of Norfolk, Va., to the People of the United States* (New Bedford, Mass., 1865).

to be heard in regard to the question of its reconstruction, and that we cannot keep silence without dereliction of duty to ourselves, to our country, and to our God.

2d. *Resolved*, That personal servitude having been abolished in Virginia, it behooves us, and is demanded of us, by every consideration of right and duty, to speak and act as freemen, and as such to claim and insist upon equality before the law, and equal rights of suffrage at the "ballot box."

3d. *Resolved*, That it is a wretched policy and most unwise statesmanship that would withhold from the laboring population of the country any of the rights of citizenship essential to their well-being and to their advancement and improvement as citizens.

4th. *Resolved*, That invidious political or legal distinctions, on account of color merely, if acquiesced in, or voluntarily submitted to, is inconsistent with our own self-respect, or to the respect of others, placing us at great disadvantages, and seriously retards our advancement or progress in improvement, and that the removal of such disabilities and distinctions are alike demanded by sound political economy, by patriotism, humanity and religion.

5th. *Resolved*, That we will prove ourselves worthy of the elective franchise, by insisting upon it as a right, by not tamely submitting to its deprivation, by never abusing it by voting the state out of the Union, and never using it for purposes of rebellion, treason, or oppression.

6th. *Resolved*, That the safety of all loyal men, black or white, in the midst of the recently slaveholding States, requires that all loyal men, black or white, should have equal political and civil rights, and that this is a necessity as a protection against the votes of secessionists and disloyal men.

7th. *Resolved*, That traitors shall not dictate or prescribe to us the terms or conditions of our citizenship, so help us God.

8th. *Resolved*, That as far as in us lies, we will not patronize or hold business relations with those who deny to us our equal rights.

Richard Harvey Cain, A Black Congressman Demands Equal Rights

Most of the hundreds of African-American legislators and officials elected during Reconstruction served with distinction. On many occasions, they used their positions to advance the rights and interests of their race. A good example is Richard Harvey Cain (1825–1887), who represented South Carolina in the U.S. House of Representatives during the 1870s. An African Methodist Episcopal clergyman from the North, he came to Charleston as a missionary at the end of the Civil War. He quickly became involved in local Republican politics and eventually served in the state legislature and in Congress. While in Washington, he fought for land for the freedmen and civil rights legislation. The following document is excerpted from his speech on the floor of the House in support of the Civil Rights Act of 1875.[*]

All we ask is that you, the legislators of this nation, shall pass a law so strong and so powerful that no one shall be able to elude it and destroy our rights under the Constitution and laws of our country. That is all we ask. . . .

We do not want any discriminations to be made. If discriminations are made in regard to schools, then there will be accomplished just what we are fighting against. If you say that the schools in the State of Georgia, for instance, shall be allowed to discriminate against colored people, then you will have discriminations made against us. We do not want any discriminations. I do not ask any legislation for the colored people of this country that is not applied to the white people. All that we ask is equal laws, equal legislation, and equal rights throughout the length and the breadth of this land.

[Another congressman] says that the colored men should not come here begging at the doors of Congress for their rights. I agree with him. I want to say that we do not come here begging for our rights. We come here clothed in the garb of American citizenship. We come demanding our rights in the name of justice. We come, with no arrogance on our part, asking that this great nation, which laid the foundations of civilization and progress more deeply and more securely than any other nation on the face of the earth, guarantee us protection from outrage. We come here, five millions of people—more than composed this entire nation when it had its great tea-party in Boston Harbor, and demanded its rights at the point of a bayonet—asking that unjust discriminations against us be forbidden. We come here in the name of justice, equity, and law, in the name of our children, in the name of our country, petitioning for our rights.

Harriet Hernandez, Political Terrorism by the Ku Klux Klan

Beginning in the late 1860s, white supremacist organizations such as the Ku Klux Klan began using political terrorism to diminish African-American political power in the South. They hoped to frighten Republicans—especially black ones—away from the polls. The following account by Harriet Hernandez (ca. 1837–?), a former slave of Spartanburg, South Carolina, describes how the Klan used threats and violence to intimidate black Republican voters in the region. It is excerpted from her testimony in December 1871 before a congressional committee appointed to investigate Klan activities. Such tactics eventually allowed Democrats to defeat Radical Republicans at the ballot box and to bring black political power—and with it, Reconstruction—to an end.*

Q: Did the Ku-Klux ever come to your house at any time?
A: Yes, sir; twice.
Q: Go on to the second time. . . .
A: They came in; I was lying in bed. Says he, "Come out here, sir; Come out here, sir!" They took me out of bed; they would not let me get out, but they took me up in their arms and toted me out—me and my daughter Lucy. He struck me on the forehead with a pistol, and here is the scar above my eye now. Says he, "Damn you, fall!" I fell. Says he, "Damn you, get up!" I got up. Says he, "Damn you, get over this fence!" And he kicked me over when I went to get over; and then he went to a brush pile, and they laid us right down there, both together. They laid us down twenty yards apart, I reckon. They had dragged and beat us along. They struck me right on the top of my head, and I thought they had killed me; and I said, "Lord o' mercy, don't, don't kill my child!" He gave me a lick on the head, and it liked to have killed me; I saw stars. He threw my arm over my head so I could not do anything with it for three weeks, and there are great knots on my wrist now.
Q: What did they say this was for?
A: They said, "You can tell your husband that when we see him we are going to kill him."
Q: Did they say why they wanted to kill him?
A: They said, "He voted the radical ticket, didn't he?" I said, "Yes, that very way."
Q: When did your husband get back after this whipping? He was not at home, was he?
A: He was lying out; he couldn't stay at home, bless your soul! . . .
Q: Has he been afraid for any length of time?
A: He has been afraid ever since last October. He has been lying out. He has not laid in the house ten nights since October.
Q: Is that the situation of the colored people down there to any extent?
A: That is the way they all have to do—men and women both.
Q: What are they afraid of?
A: Of being killed or whipped to death.
Q: What has made them afraid?
A: Because men that voted radical tickets they took the spite out on the women when they could get at them.
Q: How many colored people have been whipped in that neighborhood?
A: It is all of them, mighty near.

---

* *Report of the Joint Select Committee to Inquire into the Condition of Affairs in the Late Insurrectionary States* (Washington, 1872), vol. 5, South Carolina.

Bayley Wyatt, A Right to the Land

For many former slaves, freedom meant owning and working their own farms. Throughout the South, they squatted on vacant plots or waited for the federal government to redistribute plantation acreage confiscated from Confederate masters during the Civil War. They argued that their loyalty during the war and their years of unpaid labor as slaves gave them a right to the land. Bayley Wyatt, a Virginia freedman, articulates this view in the following document. After fleeing from slavery in central Virginia during the war, he was one of eight thousand contrabands who settled on land near Yorktown in 1863–1864. When Union army officials ordered them in 1866 to vacate their farms, he rose and offered this impromptu protest at a public meeting called to discuss the removal.[*]

We made bricks without straw under old Pharaoh. . . . We now, as a people desires to be elevated, and we desires to do all we can to be educated, and we hope our friends will aid us all they can. . . .

I may state to all our friends, and to all our enemies, that we has a right to the land where we are located. For why? I tell you. Our wives, our children, our husbands, has been sold over and over again to purchase the lands we now locate upon; for that reason we have a divine right to the land. . . .

And then didn't we clear the land and raise the crops of corn, of cotton, of tobacco, of rice, of sugar, of everything? And then didn't them large cities in the North grow up on the cotton and the sugars and the rice that we made? Yes! I appeal to the South and the North if I hasn't spoken the words of truth.

I say they have grown rich, and my people is poor.

Henry Blake, Working on Shares

With minor exceptions, confiscated plantations were never divided and redistributed among the freedmen. As a result, most former slaves had to become sharecroppers on land owned by whites, often by their former masters. Although this system allowed greater social autonomy than life in the slave quarters, it condemned most freedmen to permanent poverty and bound them to the land. Henry Blake, an

---

[*] Corrected version of speech reprinted in Bayley Wyatt, *A Freedman's Speech* (Philadelphia, 1867).

Arkansas freedman, explains the dangers of sharecropping in the following remarks to a Works Progress Administration interviewer in the 1930s. He was about eighty years old at the time.[*]

After freedom, we worked on shares a while. Then we rented. When we worked on shares, we couldn't make nothing—just overalls, and something to eat. Half went to the white man, and you would destroy your half, if you weren't careful. A man that didn't know how to count would always lose. He might lose anyhow. The white folks didn't give no itemized statements. No, you just had to owe so much. No matter how good account you kept, you had to go by their account, and—now, brother, I'm telling you the truth about this—it's been that way for a long time. You had to take the white man's words and notes on everything. Anything you wanted you could get, if you were a good hand. If you didn't make no money, that's all right; they would advance you more. But you better not try to leave and get caught. They'd keep you in debt. They were sharp. Christmas come, you could take up twenty dollars in somethin'-to-eat and as much as you wanted in whiskey. You could buy a gallon of whiskey—anything that kept you a slave. Because he was always right and you were always wrong, if there was a difference. If there was an argument, he would get mad and there would be a shooting take place.

The Changing Plantation Landscape

The rise of sharecropping brought dramatic changes to the landscape of most plantations in the South. The following maps of the Barrow plantation, a representative plantation in central Georgia, make this clear. The first map shows the plantation in 1860, the year before the Civil War began. The second shows the plantation in 1881, after the shift to sharecropping was complete.[†]

---

[*] George P. Rawick, ed., *The American Slave: A Composite Autobiography* (Westport, Conn., 1972), Ark. Narr., vol. 8.

[†] "A Georgia Plantation," *Scribner's Monthly* 21 (April 1881).

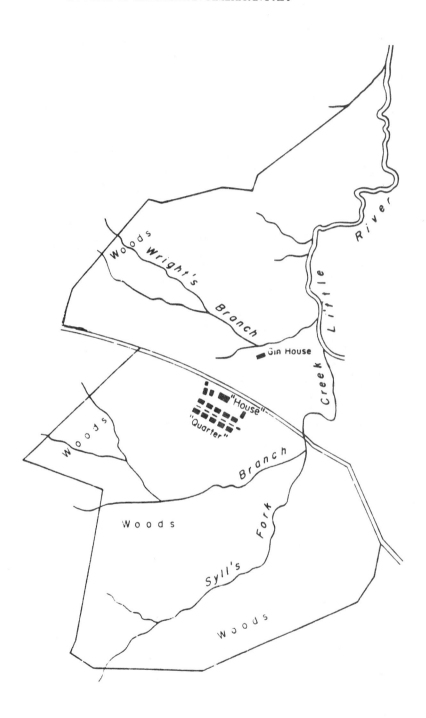

A Georgia plantation as it was in 1860

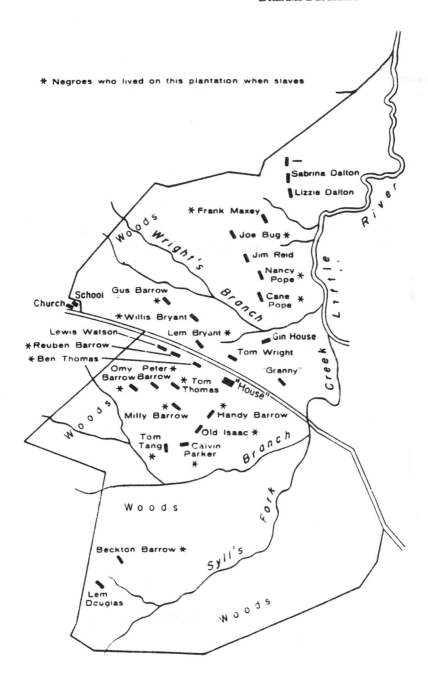

A Georgia plantation as it was in 1881.

Henry Adams, Leaving the South

After Reconstruction ended in 1877, some of the freedmen abandoned the South for a more hospitable place. Thousands of former slaves, known as Exodusters, left the poverty and violence of the region for Kansas or elsewhere in the West in 1879–1880. One of the leaders of this mass movement was Henry Adams (1843–?), a Louisiana freedman, who had served in the Union army in the West after the Civil War, then became active in Republican politics in Louisiana. The following testimony, given in 1879 before a U.S. Senate committee appointed to investigate the exodus, outlines its history and causes as Adams understood them.[*]

Q: Now tell us, Mr. Adams, what if anything, you know about the exodus of the colored people from the Southern to the Northern and Western States? . . .

A: Well, in 1870, I believe it was, . . . a parcel of us got together and said that we would organize ourselves into a committee and look into the true condition of our race, to see whether it was possible we could stay under a people who had held us under bondage or not. Then we did so and organized a committee. . . . We worked some of us, worked our way from place to place and went from State to State and worked—some of them did—amongst our people in the fields, everywhere, to see what sort of living our people lived; whether we could remain in the South amongst the people who had held us as slaves or not. We continued that on till 1874. . . .

Q: What did you do in 1874?

A: Well, along in August sometime in 1874, after the White League sprung up, they organized and said this is a white man's government, and the colored men should not hold any offices; they were no good but to work in the fields and take what they would give them and vote the Democratic ticket. That's what they would make public speeches and say to us, and we would hear them. We then organized an organization called the Colonization Council.

Q: What was the difference between that organization and your committee, as to its objects?

A: Well, the committee was to investigate the condition of our race. . . .

Q: Now, what was the purpose of this Colonization Council?

A: Well, it was to better our condition.

Q: In what way did you propose to do it?

---

[*] Senate Report 693, 46th Cong., 2nd Sess., pt. 2.

A: We first organized and adopted a plan to appeal to the President of the United States and to Congress to help us out of our distress, or to protect us in our rights and privileges.

Q: Well, what other plan had you?

A: And if that failed our idea was then to ask them to set apart a territory in the United States for us, somewhere where we could go and live with our families.

Q: You preferred to go off somewhere by yourselves?

A: Yes.

Q: Well, what then?

A: If that failed, our other object was to ask for an appropriation of money to ship us all to Liberia, in Africa; somewhere we could live in peace and quiet.

Q: Well, and what after that?

A: When that failed then our idea was to appeal to other governments outside of the United States to help us get away from the United States and go there and live under their flag.

Q: Well, what did your council do now under these various modes of relief which they had marked out for themselves?

A: Well, we appealed, as we promised. . . . We had much rather stayed there [in the South] if we could have had our rights. . . . In 1877 we lost all hopes . . . we found ourselves in such condition that we looked around and seed that there was no way on earth, it seemed, that we could better our condition there. . . . We said that the whole South—every State in the South—had got into the hands of the very men that held us slaves—from one thing to another and we thought that the men that held us slaves was holding the reins of government over our heads in every respect almost, even the constable up to the governor. We felt that we had almost as well be slaves under these men. In regard to the whole matter that was discussed, it came up in every council. Then we said that there was no hope for us and we had better go. . . .

Q: Now, Mr. Adams, you know, probably, more about the causes of the exodus from that country than any other man, from your connection with it; tell us in a few words what you believe to be the causes of these people going away?

A: Well, the cause is, in my judgment, and from what information I have received, and what I have seen with my own eyes—it is because the largest majority of the people, of the white people, that held us as slaves treats our people so bad in many respects that it is impossible for them to stand it. Now, in a great many parts of that country there our people most as well be slaves as to be free. ·

Asking Questions of the Documents

1.   What rights did the freedmen seek to give meaning to their incipient freedom? Which were the most important? Why?

2.   According to Richard Harvey Cain, why was additional civil rights legislation needed by the freedmen during the latter years of Reconstruction? What did he want such legislation to accomplish?

3. What degree of political power was achieved by African Americans in the South during Reconstruction? How did southern whites try to diminish this political power?

4. Why did most former slaves want land? Why did they believe they had a right to the land confiscated from Confederate masters during the Civil War?

5. Most freedmen were forced to become sharecroppers during Reconstruction. What were the benefits of this system? What were the drawbacks? How did the rise of this system change social and cultural life on most plantations?

6. Why did some African Americans leave the South after Reconstruction ended? What options did they explore? What did they hope to accomplish by emigrating?

For Further Reading

Foner, Eric. *Reconstruction: America's Unfinished Revolution, 1863-1877.* New York: Harper and Row, Publishers, 1988.

Magdol, Edward. *A Right to the Land: Essays on the Freedmen's Community.* Westport, Conn.: Greenwood Press, 1977.

Painter, Nell Irvin. *Exodusters: Black Migration to Kansas after Reconstruction.* Lawrence, Ks.: University Press of Kansas, 1976.

Rabinowitz, Howard N., ed. *Southern Black Leaders of the Reconstruction Era.* Urbana, Ill.: University of Illinois Press, 1982.

Ransom, Roger L., and Richard Sutch. *One Kind of Freedom: The Economic Consequences of Emancipation.* New York: Cambridge University Press, 1977.

Trelease, Allen W. *White Terror: The Ku Klux Klan Conspiracy and Southern Reconstruction.* New York: Harper and Row, Publishers, 1979.

9

The Color Line in the Era of Segregation

When Reconstruction ended, the vast majority of African Americans remained in the South, where they were subjected to increasingly harsh treatment. After 1890 southern state and local governments, now firmly in the hands of white Democrats, systematically overturned the political and social gains that blacks had made following the Civil War. A variety of ingenious disfranchisement devices—poll taxes, literacy tests, and white primary elections—circumvented the Fifteenth Amendment and effectively stripped southern blacks of their political rights. In Louisiana, for example, the number of black voters declined from 130,000 to 5,000 between 1896 and 1898 after such laws went into effect.

Segregation laws established a strict color line between the races in virtually all areas of southern life. Blacks and whites could not attend the same schools, drink from the same public water fountains, play in the same parks, ride in the same streetcars or railroad cars, be treated in the same hospitals, or even be buried in the same sections of cemeteries. This system became known as Jim Crow, named after an antebellum minstrel caricature of African Americans. Legal segregation was upheld by the U.S. Supreme Court in the case of *Plessy v. Ferguson* (1896), in which the court reasoned that mandating separate facilities for the races, as long as they were equal, did not violate the Fourteenth Amendment. In fact, Jim Crow facilities were rarely equal.

In addition to the legal restrictions of Jim Crow, African Americans were also expected to conform to a rigid code of racial etiquette that defined personal encounters with whites. Black men were to behave deferently around whites, bowing, removing their hats, and greeting them as "Mister" or "Miz." Actions that suggested equality between the races, such as shaking hands or eating together, were expressly forbidden. Blacks were required to enter the houses of whites and most public buildings by the side or rear door. Whenever the races worked together, blacks were confined to menial or subordinate tasks.

African Americans who failed to conform to this system of race relations were often lynched—executed by hanging, burning, or other methods, by a mob operating outside the law. Between 1882 and 1930 at least 3,295 blacks were lynched in the United States. Although murder or rape were frequently given as the justification for lynching, many occurred for other reasons, such as when blacks attempted to vote, talked back to a white person, or achieved economic success. Most lynchings took place in the rural South, but mob attacks on black communities were prevalent in the urban South and in the North. As the twentieth century dawned, most African Americans found themselves consigned to poverty, stripped of political power, and bound by a system of race relations that degraded and threatened them at every turn.

Richard Wright, Living Jim Crow

Living as an African American in the segregated South required careful attention to the color line. This meant following the Jim Crow laws that separated the races in various public arenas—schools, streetcars, railroad cars, parks, theaters, water fountains, restrooms, and the like. It also meant adhering to the unwritten code of racial etiquette that defined personal encounters between blacks and whites. Learning the latter involved a lengthy education in the southern system of race relations. In the following essay, African-American writer Richard Wright (1908–1960) describes his own childhood lessons in living Jim Crow. Wright, who is best known for his novel *Native Son* (1940) and the autobiographical *Black Boy* (1945), left the South in 1927 for Chicago, hoping to escape racism. But after flirting with the Communist Party in the 1930s and early 1940s, he abandoned the United States for self-imposed exile in Paris, France. This document remains one of the better accounts of the requirements of racial etiquette in the South during the era of segregation.

My first lesson in how to live as a Negro came when I was quite small. We were living in Arkansas. Our house stood behind the railroad tracks. Its skimpy yard was paved with black cinders. Nothing green ever grew in that yard.

The only touch of green we could see was far away, beyond the tracks, over where the white folks lived. But cinders were good enough for me and I never missed the green growing things. And anyhow cinders were fine weapons. You could always have a nice hot war with huge black cinders. All you had to do was crouch behind the brick pillars of a house with your hands full of gritty ammunition. And the first woolly black head you saw pop out from behind another row of pillars was your target. You tried your very best to knock it off. It was great fun.

I never fully realized the appalling disadvantages of a cinder environment till one day the gang to which I belonged found itself engaged in a war with the white boys who

Richard Wright, "The Ethics of Living Jim Crow," in *Uncle Tom's Children* (New York: Harper and Row, Publishers, 1938).

lived beyond the tracks. As usual we laid down our cinder barrage, thinking that this would wipe the white boys out. But they replied with a steady bombardment of broken bottles. We doubled our cinder barrage, but they hid behind trees, hedges, and the sloping embankments of their lawns. Having no such fortifications, we retreated to the brick pillars of our homes. During the retreat a broken milk bottle caught me behind the ear, opening a deep gash which bled profusely. The sight of blood pouring over my face completely demoralized our ranks. My fellow combatants left me standing paralyzed in the center of the yard, and scurried for their homes. A kind neighbor saw me and rushed me to a doctor, who took three stitches in my neck.

I sat brooding on my front steps, nursing my wound and waiting for my mother to come from work. I felt that a grave injustice had been done me. It was all right to throw cinders. The greatest harm a cinder could do was leave a bruise. But broken bottles were dangerous; they left you cut, bleeding, and helpless.

When night fell, my mother came from the white folks' kitchen. I raced down the street to meet her. I could just feel in my bones that she would understand. I knew she would tell me exactly what to do next time. I grabbed her hand and babbled out the whole story. She examined my wound, then slapped me.

"How come yuh didn't hide?" she asked me. "How come yuh awways fightin'?"

I was outraged and bawled. Between sobs I told her that I didn't have any trees or hedges to hide behind. There wasn't a thing I could have used as a trench. And you couldn't throw very far when you were hiding behind the brick pillars of a house. She grabbed a barrel stave, dragged me home, stripped me naked, and beat me till I had a fever of one hundred and two. She would smack my rump with the stave, and while the skin was still smarting, impart to me gems of Jim Crow wisdom. I was never to throw cinders any more. I was never to fight any more wars. I was never, never, under any conditions, to fight *white* folks again. And they were absolutely right in clouting me with the broken milk bottle. Didn't I know she was working hard every day in the hot kitchens of the white folks to make money to take care of me? When was I ever going to learn to be a good boy? She couldn't be bothered with my fights. She finished by telling me that I ought to be thankful to God as long as I lived that they didn't kill me.

All that night I was delirious and could not sleep.

Each time I closed my eyes I saw monstrous white faces suspended from the ceiling, leering at me.

From that time on, the charm of my cinder yard was gone. The green trees, the trimmed hedges, the cropped lawns grew very meaningful, became a symbol. Even today when I think of white folks, the hard, sharp outlines of white houses surrounded by trees, lawns, and hedges are present somewhere in the background of my mind. Through the years they grew into an overreaching symbol of fear.

It was a long time before I came in close contact with white folks again. We moved from Arkansas to Mississippi. Here we had the good fortune not to live behind the railroad tracks, or close to white neighborhoods. We lived in the very heart of the local Black Belt. There were black churches and black preachers; there were black schools and black teachers; black groceries and black clerks. In fact, everything was so solidly black that for a long time I did not even think of white folks, save in remote and vague terms. But this could not last forever. As one grows older one eats more. One's clothing costs more. When I finished grammar school I had to go to work. My mother could no longer feed and clothe me on her cooking job.

There is but one place where a black boy who knows no trade can get a job, and that's where the houses and faces are white, where the trees, lawns, and hedges are green. My first job was with an optical company in Jackson, Mississippi. The morning I applied I stood straight and neat before the boss, answering all his questions with sharp yessirs and nosirs. I was very careful to pronounce my *sirs* distinctly, in order that he might know that I was polite, that I knew where I was, and that I knew he was a *white* man.

I wanted that job badly.

He looked me over as though he were examining a prize poodle. He questioned me closely about my schooling, being particularly insistent about how much mathematics I had had. He seemed very pleased when I told him I had had two years of algebra.

"Boy, how would you like to learn something around here?" he asked me.

"I'd like it fine, sir," I said, happy. I had visions of "working my way up." Even Negroes have those visions.

"All right," he said. "Come on."

I followed him to the small factory.

"Pease," he said to a white man of about thirty-five, "this is Richard. He's going to work for us."

Pease looked at me and nodded. I was then taken to a white boy of about seventeen.

"Morrie, this is Richard, who's going to work for us." "Whut yuh sayin' there boy!" Morrie boomed at me. "Fine!" I answered.

The boss instructed these two to help me, teach me, give me jobs to do, and let me learn what I could in my spare time.

My wages were five dollars a week.

I worked hard, trying to please. For the first month I got along O.K. Both Pease and Morrie seemed to like me. But one thing was missing. And I kept thinking about it. I was not learning anything and nobody was volunteering to help me. Thinking they had forgotten that I was to learn something about the mechanics of grinding lenses, I asked Morrie one day to tell me about the work. He grew red.

"Whut yuh tryin' t'do, nigger, get smart?" he asked. "Naw; I ain't tryin' t' git smart," I said.

"Well, don't, if yuh know whut's good for yuh!"

I was puzzled. Maybe he just doesn't want to help me, I thought. I went to Pease.

"Say, are yuh crazy, you black bastard?" Pease asked me, his gray eyes growing hard.

I spoke out, reminding him that the boss had said I was to be given a chance to learn something.

"Nigger, you think you're *white*, don't you?"

"Naw, sir!"

"Well, you're acting mighty like it!"

"But, Mr. Pease, the boss said ..." Pease shook his fist in my face.

"This is a white man's work around here, and you better watch yourself!"

From then on they changed toward me. They said good-morning no more. When I was a bit slow performing some duty, I was called a lazy black son of a bitch.

Once I thought of reporting all this to the boss. But the mere idea of what would happen to me if Pease and Morrie should learn that I had "snitched" stopped me. And after all the boss was a white man, too. What was the use?

The climax came at noon one summer day. Pease called me to his work-bench. To get to him I had to go between two narrow benches and stand with my back against a wall.

"Yes, sir," I said.

"Richard, I want to ask you something," Pease began pleasantly, not looking up from his work.

"Yes, sir," I said again.

Morrie came over, blocking the narrow passage between the benches. He folded his arms, staring at me solemnly.

I looked from one to the other, sensing that something was coming.

"Yes, sir," I said for the third time.

Pease looked up and spoke very slowly.

"Richard, Mr. Morrie here tells me you called me *Pease.*"

I stiffened. A void seemed to open up in me. I knew this was the show-down.

He meant that I had failed to call him Mr. Pease. I looked at Morrie. He was gripping a steel bar in his hands.

I opened my mouth to speak, to protest, to assure Pease that I had never called him simply *Pease*, and that I had never had any intentions of doing so, when Morrie grabbed me by the collar, ramming my head against the wall.

"Now, be careful, nigger!" snarled Morrie, baring his teeth. "*I* heard yuh call 'im *Pease!* 'N' if you say yuh didn't, yuh're callin me a *lie*, see?" He waved the steel bar threateningly.

If I had said: No, sir, Mr. Pease, I never called you *Pease*, I would have been automatically calling Morrie a liar. And if I had said: Yes sir, Mr. Pease, I called you *Pease*, I would have been pleading guilty to having uttered the worst insult that a Negro can utter to a southern white man. I stood hesitating, trying to frame a neutral reply.

"Richard, I asked you a question!" said Pease. Anger was creeping into his voice.

"I don't remember calling you *Pease*, Mr. Pease," I said cautiously. "And if I did, I sure didn't mean..."

"You black son of a bitch! You called me *Pease*, then!" he spat, slapping me till I bent sideways over a bench. Morrie was on top of me demanding:

"Didn't yuh call 'im *Pease*? If yuh say yuh didn't I'll rip yo' gut string loose with this bar, yuh black granny dodger! Yuh can't call a white man a lie 'n' git erway with it, you black son of a bitch!"

I wilted. I begged them not to bother me. I knew what they wanted. They wanted me to leave.

"I'll leave," I promised. "I'll leave right *now.*"

They gave me a minute to get out of the factory. I was warned not to show up again, or tell the boss.

I went.

When I told the folks at home what had happened, they called me a fool. They told me that I must never again attempt to exceed my boundaries. When you are working for white folks, they said, you got to "stay in your place" if you want to keep working.

My Jim Crow education continued on my next job, which was portering in a clothing store. One morning, while polishing brass out front, the boss and his twenty-year-old son got out of their car and half dragged and half kicked a Negro woman into the store. A policeman standing at the corner looked on, twirling his night-stick. I watched out of the corner of my eye, never slackening the strokes of my chamois upon the brass. After a few minutes, I heard shrill screams coming from the rear of the store. Later the woman stumbled out, bleeding, crying, and holding her stomach. When she reached the end of the block, the policeman grabbed her and accused her of being drunk. Silently, I watched him throw her into a patrol wagon.

When I went to the rear of the store, the boss and his son were washing their hands in the sink. They were chuckling. The floor was bloody and strewn with wisps of hair and clothing. No doubt I must have appeared pretty shocked, for the boss slapped me reassuringly on the back.

"Boy, that's what we do to niggers when they don't want to pay their bills," he said, laughing.

His son looked at me and grinned.

"Here, hava cigarette," he said.

Not knowing what to do, I took it. He lit his and held the match for me. This was a gesture of kindness, indicating that even if they had beaten the poor old woman, they would not beat me if I knew enough to keep my mouth shut.

"Yes, sir," I said, and asked no questions.

After they had gone, I sat on the edge of a packing box and stared at the bloody floor till the cigarette went out.

That day at noon, while eating in a hamburger joint, I told my fellow Negro porters what had happened. No one seemed surprised. One fellow, after swallowing a huge bite, turned to me and asked:

"Huh! Is tha' all they did t' her?"

"Yeah. Wasn't tha' enough?" I asked.

"Shucks! Man, she's a lucky bitch!" he said, burying his lips deep into a juicy hamburger. "Hell, it's a wonder they didn't lay her when they got through."

I was learning fast, but not quite fast enough. One day, while I was delivering packages in the suburbs, my bicycle tire was punctured. I walked along the hot, dusty road, sweating and leading my bicycle by the handle-bars.

A car slowed at my side.

"What's the matter, boy?" a white man called.

I told him my bicycle was broken and I was walking back to town.

"That's too bad," he said. "Hop on the running board." He stopped the car. I clutched hard at my bicycle with one hand and clung to the side of the car with the other. "All set?"

"Yes, sir," I answered. The car started.

It was full of young white men. They were drinking. I watched the flask pass from mouth to mouth.

"Wanna drink, boy?" one asked.

I laughed as the wind whipped my face. Instinctively obeying the freshly planted precepts of my mother, I said:

"Oh, no!"

The words were hardly out of my mouth before I felt something hard and cold smash me between the eyes. It was an empty whisky bottle. I saw stars, and fell backwards from the speeding car into the dust of the road, my feet becoming entangled in the steel spokes of my bicycle. The white men piled out and stood over me.

"Nigger, ain' yuh learned no better sense'n tha' yet?" asked the man who hit me. "Ain' yuh learned t' say *sir* t' a white man yet?"

Dazed, I pulled to my feet. My elbows and legs were bleeding. Fists doubled, the white man advanced, kicking my bicycle out of the way.

"Aw, leave the bastard alone. He's got enough," said one.

They stood looking at me. I rubbed my shins, trying to stop the flow of blood. No doubt they felt a sort of contemptuous pity, for one asked:

"Yuh wanna ride t' town now, nigger? Yuh reckon yuh know enough t' ride now?"

"I wanna walk," I said, simply.

Maybe it sounded funny. They laughed.

"Well, walk, yuh black son of a bitch!" When they left they comforted me with: "Nigger, yuh sho better be damn glad it wuz us yuh talked t' tha' way. Yuh're a lucky bastard, 'cause if yuh'd said that't' somebody else, yuh might've been a dead nigger now."

Negroes who have lived South know the dread of being caught alone upon the streets in white neighborhoods after the sun has set. In such a simple situation as this the plight of the Negro in America is graphically symbolized. While white strangers may be in these neighborhoods trying to get home, they can pass unmolested. But the color of a Negro's skin makes him easily recognizable, makes him suspect, converts him into a defenseless target.

Late one Saturday night I made some deliveries in a white neighborhood. I was pedaling my bicycle back to the store as fast as I could, when a police car, swerving toward me, jammed me into the curbing.

"Get down and put up your hands!" the policemen ordered.

I did. They climbed out of the car, guns drawn, faces set, and advanced slowly.

"Keep still!" they ordered.

I reached my hands higher. They searched my pockets and packages. They seemed dissatisfied when they could find nothing incriminating. Finally, one of them said: "Boy, tell your boss not to send you out in white neighborhoods after sundown."

As usual, I said: "Yes, sir."

My next job was a hall-boy in a hotel. Here my Jim Crow education broadened and deepened. When the bell-boys were busy, I was often called to assist them. As many of the rooms in the hotel were occupied by prostitutes, I was constantly called to carry them liquor and cigarettes. These women were nude most of the time. They did not bother about clothing, even for bell-boys. When you went into their rooms, you were supposed to take their nakedness for granted, as though it startled you no more than a blue vase or a red rug. Your presence awoke in them no sense of shame, for you were not regarded as human. If they were alone, you could steal side-long glimpses at them. But if they were receiving men, not a flicker of your eyelids could show. I remember one incident vividly. A new woman, a huge, snowy-skinned blonde, took a room on my floor. I was sent to wait upon her. She was in bed with a thick-set man; both were nude and uncovered. She said she wanted some liquor and slid out of bed and waddled across the floor to get her money from a dresser drawer. I watched her.

"Nigger, what in hell are you looking at?" the white man asked me, raising himself upon his elbows. "Nothing," I answered, looking miles deep into the black wall of the room.

"Keep your eyes where they belong, if you want to be healthy!" he said.

"Yes, sir."

One of the bell-boys I knew in this hotel was keeping steady company with one of the Negro maids. Out of a clear sky the police descended upon his home and arrested him, accusing him of bastardy. The poor boy swore he had had no intimate relations with the girl. Nevertheless, they forced him to marry her. When the child arrived, it was found to be much lighter in complexion than either of the two supposedly legal parents. The white men around the hotel made a great joke of it. They spread the rumor that some white cow must have scared the poor girl while she was carrying the baby. If you were in their presence when this explanation was offered, you were supposed to laugh.

One of the bell-boys was caught in bed with a white prostitute. He was castrated and run out of town. Immediately after this all the bell-boys and hall-boys were called together and warned. We were given to understand that the boy who had been castrated was a "mighty, mighty lucky bastard." We were impressed with the fact that next time the management of the hotel would not be responsible for the lives of "trouble-making niggers." We were silent.

One night just as I was about to go home, I met one of the Negro maids. She lived in my direction, and we fell in to walk part of the way home together. As we passed the white night-watchman, he slapped the maid on her buttock. I turned around, amazed. The watchman looked at me with a long, hard, fixed-under stare. Suddenly he pulled his gun and asked:

"Nigger, don't yuh like it?"

I hesitated.

"I asked yuh don't yuh like it?" he asked again, stepping forward.

"Yes, sir," I mumbled.

"Talk like it, then!"

"Oh, yes, sir!" I said with as much heartiness as I could muster.

Outside, I walked ahead of the girl, ashamed to face her. She caught up with me and said: "Don't be a fool! Yuh couldn't help it!"

This watchman boasted of having killed two Negroes in self-defense.

Yet, in spite of all this, the life of the hotel ran with an amazing smoothness. It would have been impossible for a stranger to detect anything. The maids, the hall-boys, and the bell-boys were all smiles. They had to be.

I had learned my Jim Crow lessons so thoroughly that I kept the hotel job till I left Jackson for Memphis. It so happened that while in Memphis I applied for a job at a branch of the optical company. I was hired. And for some reason, as long as I worked there, they never brought my past against me.

Here my Jim Crow education assumed quite a different form. It was no longer brutally cruel, but subtly cruel. Here I learned to lie, steal, to dissemble. I learned to play that dual role which every Negro must play if he wants to eat and live.

For example, it was almost impossible to get a book to read. It was assumed that after a Negro had imbibed what scanty schooling the state furnished he had no further need for books. I was always borrowing books from men on the job. One day I mustered enough courage to ask one of the men to let me get books from the library in his name. Surprisingly, he consented. I cannot help but think that he consented because he was a Roman Catholic and felt a vague sympathy for Negroes, being himself an object of hatred. Armed with a library card, I obtained books in the following manner: I would write a note to the librarian, saying:

"Please let this nigger boy have the following books." I would then sign it with the white man's name.

When I went to the library, I would stand at the desk, hat in hand, looking as unbookish as possible. When I received the books desired I would take them home. If the books listed in the note happened to be out, I would sneak into the lobby and forge a new one. I never took any chances guessing with the white librarian about what the fictitious white man would want to read. No doubt if any of the white patrons had suspected that some of the volumes they enjoyed had been in the home of a Negro, they would not have tolerated it for an instant.

The factory force of the optical company in Memphis was much larger than that in Jackson, and more urbanized. At least they liked to talk, and would engage the Negro help in conversation whenever possible. By this means I found that many subjects were taboo from the white man's point of view. Among the topics they did not like to discuss with Negroes were the following: American white women; the Ku Klux Klan; France, and how Negro soldiers fared while there; French women; Jack Johnson; the entire northern part of the United States; the Civil War; Abraham Lincoln; U. S. Grant; General Sherman; Catholics; the Pope; Jews; the Republican Party; slavery; social equality; Communism; Socialism; the 13th and 14th Amendments to the Constitution; or any topic calling for positive knowledge or manly self-assertion on the part of the Negro. The most accepted topics were sex and religion.

There were many times when I had to exercise a great deal of ingenuity to keep out of trouble. It is a southern custom that all men must take off their hats when they enter an elevator. And especially did this apply to us blacks with rigid force. One day I stepped into an elevator with my arms full of packages. I was forced to ride with my hat on. Two white men stared at me coldly. Then one of them very kindly lifted my hat and placed it upon my armful of packages. Now the most accepted response for a Negro to make under such circumstances is to look at the white man out of the corner of his eye and grin. To have said: "Thank you!" would have made the white man *think* that you *thought* you were receiving from him a personal service. For such an act I have seen Negroes take a blow in the mouth. Finding the first alternative distasteful, and the second dangerous, I hit upon an acceptable course of action which fell safely between these two poles. I immediately—no sooner than my hat was lifted—pretended that my packages were about to spill, and appeared deeply distressed with keeping them in my arms. In this fashion I evaded having to acknowledge his service, and, in spite of adverse circumstances, salvaged a slender shred of personal pride.

How do Negroes feel about the way they have to live? How do they discuss it when alone among themselves? I think this question can be answered in a single sentence. A friend of mine who ran an elevator once told me:

"Lawd, man! Ef it wuzn't fer them polices 'n' them ol' lynching mobs, there wouldn't be nothin' but uproar down here!"

A Lynching in Mississippi

Conformity to the color line in the segregated South was often enforced through intimidation and violence. African Americans who violated community standards, especially the requirements of racial etiquette and the Jim Crow laws, were sometimes lynched as a warning to the rest of the local black community. Such lynchings were public rituals conducted by mobs and took place outside the scope of the legal process. One of the most famous was the lynching of Samuel Petty on 24 February 1914 in the river town of Leland, Mississippi. Petty, a local black, was accused of having killed Charles W. Kirkland, a deputy sheriff. When news of Kirkland's death reached the town, a mob quickly formed and advanced on Petty's cabin, then marched its victim to the town square and exacted its revenge. Lynchings of this kind were so common in the lower South that the local press made only brief mention of the event. But it became well known as a result of the following account by an anonymous correspondent to the *Crisis*, the monthly magazine of the National Association for the Advancement of Colored People (NAACP), the nation's leading civil rights organization during the first half of the twentieth century.[*]

The news spread like wildfire and in twenty minutes the entire white population was armed and headed for the cabin which was situated about a half mile from the depot, which is in the center of the town. I looked in every direction and could see men and mere boys, some not over 12 years old, carrying rifles, shotguns, pistols and, in fact, every imaginable thing that would shoot. They were acting as though there was an entire army of Negroes to be taken. The man who had killed the officer submitted to arrest by the mob, which by this time numbered about 400. Placing a rope around his neck he was led to the center of the town and in the presence of women and children they proceeded

---

[*] *Crisis* 8 (May 1914).

to hold a conference as to the kind of death that should be meted out to him. Some yelled to hang him; some to burn him alive. It was decided in a few minutes. Willing hands brought a large dry goods box, place it in the center of the street; in it was straw on which on which was poured a tub of oil; then the man was lifted with a rope around his neck and placed in this box head down, and then another tub of oil was poured over him. A man from the crowd deliberately lit a match and set fire to the living man. While in this position the flames shot up at great height. The crowd began to yell as the flames shot upward. In an instant the poor creature managed to lift himself out of the box, a mass of flames. He was fighting the flames with his hands in an effort to shield his face and eyes, and in this condition attempted to run. The crowd allowed him to run to the length of the rope, which was held by willing hands, until he reached a distance of about twenty feet; then a yell went up from the crowd to shoot. In an instant there were several hundred shots and the creature fell in his tracks. The crowd deliberately walked up to the prostrate form and shot the remainder of their guns into his lifeless body. With the flames still leaping into the air, he was pulled back into the fire that was now roaring with boxes and oil brought out of the different stores by men and boys. Every time they would throw on more oil and boxes the crowd would yell as though they were at a bull fight. Standing about fifty or seventy-five feet from the scene I could actually smell the flesh of the poor man as it was being burned. Not a voice was raised in the defense of the man. No one attempted to hide their identity. I looked into the faces of men whom I knew to be officers of the town lending a willing hand in the burning of this man. No wonder the coroner who held the inquest returned a verdict that the Negro came to his death "at the hands of an enraged mob unknown to the jury," because to get a jury in that town they had to get some who participated in the burning. I can never feel toward the white man as I have felt after seeing what I have attempted to describe. After burning the body into ashes the burned bones and ashes were buried in the edge of the street in front of a colored barber shop. May God forbid that any other living man will ever see a sight as I witnessed; this is the third Negro who has been killed in this vicinity in the last three weeks. The man burned was named Sam Pettie [sic], known by everybody to be quiet and inoffensive. I write this hoping you may get enough out of what I have tried to describe to tell your great number of readers what we are up against. To mention my name in connection with this would be equivalent to committing suicide.

Mary Church Terrell, The Causes of Lynching

In the 1890s African Americans began to confront the growing wave of lynchings, which took one black life nearly every two days during the decade. Black women were among the most vocal and effective critics of the practice. Ida B. Wells-Barnett (1862–1939) of Memphis editorialized against lynchings in her weekly newspaper, the *Free Speech and Headlight*, until threats of violence forced her to flee the South. She continued her crusade in a series of lectures in the North and in Europe, and finally published *The Red Record* (1895), a major exposé of the phenomenon. Another prominent critic was Mary Church Terrell (1863–1954) of Washington, D.C., the first president of the National Association of Colored Women and a leading figure in the woman suffrage movement. In the following essay, she explores the causes of lynching and demonstrates the fallacy of the argument that it was necessary to protect white womanhood.[*]

Hanging, shooting and burning black men, women and children in the United States have become so common that such occurrences create but little sensation and evoke but slight comment now. . . . In the discussion of this subject, four mistakes are commonly made.

In the first place, it is a great mistake to suppose that rape is the real cause of lynching in the South.

Beginning with the Ku Klux Klan, the negro has been constantly subjected to some form of organized violence ever since he became free. It is easy to prove that rape is simply the pretext and not the cause of lynching. Statistics show that, out of every 100 negroes who are lynched, from 75–85 are not even accused of this crime, and many who are accused of it are innocent. . . .

In the second place, it is a mistake to suppose that the negro's desire for social equality sustains any relation whatsoever to the crime of rape. . . . It is safe to assert that, among the negroes who have been guilty of ravishing white women, not one had been taught that he was the equal of white people or had ever heard of social equality. . . . Negroes who have been educated in Northern institutions of learning with white men and women, and who for that reason might have learned the meaning of social equality and have acquired a taste for the same, neither assault white women nor commit other crimes, as a rule. . . . Strange as it may appear, illiterate negroes, who are the only ones contributing largely to the criminal class, are coddled and caressed by the South. To the

[*] Mary Church Terrell, "Lynching from a Negro's Point of View," *North American Review* 178 (June 1904).

educated, cultivated members of the race, they are held up as a bright and shining examples of what a really good negro should be. The dictionary is searched in vain by Southern gentlemen and gentlewomen for words sufficiently ornate and strong to express their admiration for a dear old "mammy" or a faithful old "uncle," who can neither read nor write, and who assure their white friends they would not if they could. On the other hand, no language is sufficiently caustic, bitter and severe, to express the disgust, hatred and scorn which Southern gentlemen feel for what is called the "New Issue," which, being interpreted, means negroes who aspire to knowledge and culture, and who have acquired a taste for the highest and best things in life. At the door of this "New Issue," the sins and shortcomings of the whole race are laid. This "New Issue" is beyond hope of redemption, we are told, because somebody, nobody knows who, has taught it to believe in social equality, something, nobody knows what. The alledged fear of social equality has always been used by the South to explain its unchristian treatment of the negro and to excuse its many crimes. . . . In the North, which is the only section that accords the negro the scrap of social equality enjoyed by him in the United States, he is rarely accused of rape. The only form of social equality ever attempted between the two races, and practised to any considerable extent, is that which was originated by the white masters of slave women, and which has been perpetuated by them and their descendants even unto the present day. . . . There is no more connection between social equality and lynching today than there was between social equality and slavery before the war, or than there is between social equality and the convict-lease system, or any other form of oppression to which the negro has uniformly been subjected in the South.

The third error on the subject of lynching consists of the widely circulated statement that the moral sensibilities of the best negroes in the United States are so stunted and dull, and the standard of morality among even the leaders of the race is so low, that they do not appreciate the enormity and heinousness of rape. . . . Only those who are densely ignorant of the standards and sentiments of the best negroes, or who wish willfully to misrepresent and maliciously slander a race already resting under burdens greater than it can bear, would accuse its thousands of reputable men and women of sympathizing with rapists, either black or white, or of condoning their crime. . . .

What, then is the cause of lynching? At the last analysis, it will be discovered that there are just two causes of lynching. In the first place, it is due to race hatred, the hatred of a stronger people toward a weaker who were once held as slaves. In the second place, it is due to the lawlessness so prevalent in the section where nine-tenths of the lynchings occur. . . .

Lynching is the aftermath of slavery. The white men who shoot negroes to death and flay them alive, and the white women who apply flaming torches to their oil-soaked bodies today, are the sons and daughters of women who had but little, if any, compassion on the race when it was enslaved. The men who lynch negroes today are, as a rule, the children of women who sat by their firesides happy and proud in the possession and affection of their own children, while they looked with unpitying eye and adamantine heart upon the anguish of slave mothers whose children had been sold away, when not overtaken by a sadder fate. . . . It is impossible to comprehend the cause of the ferocity and barbarity which attend the average lynching-bee, without taking into account the brutalizing effect of slavery upon the people of the section where most of the lynchings occur. . . . It is too much to expect, perhaps, that the children of women who for generations looked upon the hardships and the degradation of their sisters of a darker hue with few if any protests, should have mercy and compassion upon the children of that oppressed race now. But what a tremendous influence for law and order, and what a mighty foe to mob violence Southern white women might be, if they would arise in the purity and power of their womanhood to implore their fathers, husbands and sons no longer to stain their hands with the black man's blood! . . . Whenever Southern white people discuss lynching, they are prone to slander the whole negro race. Not long ago, a Southern writer of great repute declared without qualification or reservation that "the crime of rape is well-nigh wholly confined to the negro race," and insisted that "negroes furnish most of the ravishers." These assertions are as unjust to the negro as they are unfounded in fact. According to statistics recently published, only one colored male in 100,000 over five years of age was accused of assault upon a white woman in the South in 1902, whereas one male out of every 20,000 over five years of age was charged with rape in Chicago during the same year. If these figures prove anything at all, they show that the men and boys in Chicago are many times more addicted to rape than are the negroes in the South. . . .

But even if the negro's morals were as loose and as lax as some claim them to be, and if his belief in the virtue of women were as slight as we are told, the South has nobody to blame but itself. . . . Men do not gather grapes of thorns nor figs of thistles. Throughout their entire period of bondage, colored women were debauched by their masters. From the day they were liberated to the present time, prepossessing young colored girls have been considered the rightful prey of white gentlemen in the South, and they have been protected neither by public sentiment nor by law. In the South, the negro's home is not considered sacred by the superior race. White men are neither punished for invading it, nor lynched for violating colored women and girls. . . .

How can lynching be extirpated in the United States? . . . Lynching can never be suppressed in the South, until the masses of ignorant white people in that section are educated and lifted to a higher moral plane. . . . Lynching cannot be suppressed in the South, until all classes of white people who dwell there . . . respect the rights of other human beings, no matter what may be the color of their skin. . . and learn a holy reverence for the law. . . .

Until there is a renaissance of popular belief in the principles of liberty and equality upon which this government was founded, lynching, the Convict-Lease System, the Disfranchisement Acts, the Jim Crow Car Laws, unjust discriminations in the professions and trades and similar atrocities will continue to dishearten and degrade the negro, and stain the fair name of the United States. For there can be no doubt that the greatest obstacle in the way of extirpating lynching is the general attitude of the public mind toward this unspeakable crime. The whole country seems tired of hearing about the black man's woes. The wrongs of the Irish, of the Armenians, of the Romanian and Russian Jews, of the exiles of Russia and of every other oppressed people upon the face of the globe, can arouse the sympathy and fire the indignation of the American public, while they seem to be all but indifferent to the murderous assaults upon the negroes in the South.

Asking Questions of the Documents

1. Describe the color line that separated the races in the South during the era of segregation. What racial etiquette were blacks expected to conform to in their personal encounters with whites? What happened to blacks who failed to conform? In what area of southern life were such encounters most likely to take place? Why? Describe the sexual double standard that existed along the color line.

2. What lessons of race and class did Richard Wright learn as part of his Jim Crow education? How did he learn them? Why did his mother punish him for getting into a cinder fight with white boys? Was she right to punish him? Why? What techniques did he eventually learn for deceiving whites?

3. What was lynching? Why was it done as a public ritual? Why was lynching especially effective in enforcing black conformity to the code of racial etiquette and the laws of segregation?

4. What, according to many whites, caused lynching? How does Mary Church Terrell demonstrate the fallacy of that argument? What does she suggest were the real causes of lynching?

For Further Reading

Brundage, W. Fitzhugh. *Lynching in the New South: Georgia and Virginia, 1880-1930.* Urbana, Ill.: University of Illinois Press, 1993.

Doyle, Bertram W. *The Etiquette of Race Relations in the South: A Study in Social Control.* Chicago: University of Chicago Press, 1937.

Harris, J. William. "Etiquette, Lynching, and Racial Boundaries in Southern History: A Mississippi Example." *American Historical Review* 100 (April 1995): 387-410.

McMillen, Neil R. *Dark Journey: Black Mississippians in the Age of Jim Crow.* Urbana, Ill.: University of Illinois Press, 1989.

Rabinowitz, Howard N. *Race Relations in the Urban South, 1865-1890.* New York: Oxford University Press, 1978.

Williamson, Joel. *The Crucible of Race: Black-White Relations in the American South since Emancipation.* New York: Oxford University Press, 1984.

Woodward C. Vann. *The Strange Career of Jim Crow.* 3d ed. New York: Oxford University Press, 1974.

10

Racial Alternatives
in the Progressive Era

The years between 1890 and 1915, usually known as the Progressive era, were a hopeful time for most Americans. A wave of social and economic reforms and technological inventions eased and improved their lives. But prospects looked bleak for African Americans in the South. Caught in a web of disfranchisement, Jim Crow laws, poverty, and lynching, they faced conditions that prompted one historian to call this period the "nadir" of African-American life.

African Americans responded to their plight in a variety of ways. This chapter presents four alternatives offered by five black leaders for improving the situation of their race in the South. Ida B. Wells-Barnett urged black communities to band together and pursue an aggressive policy of self-help. Booker T. Washington counseled patience and asked African Americans to seek economic advancement within the existing system of race relations in the South. Henry McNeal Turner argued that blacks could only improve their circumstances by returning to the African continent. As the twentieth century dawned, John Hope, W. E. B. Du Bois, and a host of younger activists advocated militant protest. After 1915, millions of ordinary blacks chose the additional alternative of migrating to the urban North—the subject of chapter eleven.

Ida B. Wells-Barnett, Self-Help

The fight against lynching helped energize the struggle for racial equality in the 1890s. Organizations such as the Afro-American League (1890) and the National Association of Colored Women (1895) emerged during the decade to develop a tradition of self-help among African Americans. One of the leading advocates of self-help was antilynching crusader Ida B. Wells-Barnett, the author of the following 1892 essay.*

In the creation of this healthier public sentiment, the Afro-American can do for himself what no one else can do for him. The world looks on with wonder that we have conceded so much and remain law-abiding under such great outrage and provocation.

To Northern capital and Afro-American labor the South owes its rehabilitation. If labor is withdrawn capital will not remain. The Afro-American is thus the backbone of the South. A thorough knowledge and judicious exercise of this power in lynching localities could many times effect a bloodless revolution. The white man's dollar is his god, and to stop this will be to stop outrages in many localities.

The Afro-Americans of Memphis denounced the lynching of three of their best citizens, and urged and waited for the authorities to act in the matter and bring the lynchers to justice. No attempt was made to do so, and the black men left the city by thousands, bringing about great stagnation in every branch of business. Those who remained so injured the business of the street car company by staying off the cars, that the superintendent, manager and treasurer called personally on the editor of the "Free Speech," asked them to urge our people to give them their patronage again. Other business men became alarmed over the situation, and the "Free Speech" was run away that the colored people might be more easily controlled. A meeting of white citizens in June, three months after the lynching, passed resolutions for the first time, condemning it. *But they did not punish the lynchers.* Every one of them was known by name, because they had been elected to do the dirty work, by some of the very citizens who passed these resolutions. Memphis is fast losing her black population, who proclaim as they go that there is no protection for the life and property of any Afro-American citizen in Memphis who is not a slave.

The Afro-American citizens of Kentucky, whose intellectual and financial improvement has been phenomenal, have never had a separate car law until now. Delegations and petitions poured into the Legislature against it, yet the bill passed and the Jim Crow Car of Kentucky is a legalized institution. Will the great mass of Negroes continue to patronize the railroad? A special from Covington, Ky., says: Covington, June 13th. The railroads of the State are beginning to feel very markedly, the effects of the separate coach bill recently passed by the Legislature. No class of people in the State has so many and so largely attended excursions as the blacks. All these have been abandoned, and regular travel is reduced to a minimum. A competent authority says the loss to the various roads will reach $1,000,000 this year.

A call to a State Conference in Lexington, Ky., last June had delegates from every county in the State. Those delegates, the ministers, teachers, heads of secret and other orders, and the head of every family should pass the word around for every member of the race in Kentucky to stay off railroads unless obliged to ride. If they did so, and their advice was followed persistently, the convention would not need to petition the Legislature to repeal the law or raise money to file a suit. The railroad corporations

---

* Ida B. Wells-Barnett, *Southern Horrors: Lynch Law in All Its Phases* (New York, 1892).

would be so effected they would in self-defense lobby to have the separate car law repealed. On the other hand, as long as the railroads can get Afro-American excursions they will always have plenty of money to fight all the suits brought against them. They will be aided in so doing by the same partisan public sentiment which passed the law. White men passed the law, and white judges and juries would pass upon the suits against the law, and render judgment in line with their prejudices and in deference to the greater financial power.

The appeal to the white man's pocket has ever been more effectual than all the appeals ever made to his conscience. Nothing, absolutely nothing, is to be gained by a further sacrifice of manhood and self-respect. By the right exercise of power as the industrial factor of the South, the Afro-American can demand and secure his rights, the punishment of lynchers, and a fair trial for accused rapists.

Of the many inhuman outrages of this present year, the only case where the proposed lynching did *not* occur, was where the men armed themselves in Jacksonville, Fla., and Paducah, Ky., and prevented it. The only times an Afro-American who was assaulted got away has been when he had a gun and used it in self-defense.

The lesson this teaches and which every Afro-American should ponder well, is that a Winchester rifle should have a place of honor in every black home, and it should be used for that protection which the law refuses to give. When the white man who is always the aggressor knows he runs as great risk of biting the dust every time his Afro-American victim does, he will have greater respect for Afro-American life. The more the Afro-American yields and cringes and begs, the more he has to do so, the more he is insulted, outraged and lynched.

Booker T. Washington, The "Atlanta Compromise"

Unlike Ida B. Wells-Barnett, Booker T. Washington urged African Americans to help themselves by temporarily accepting the racial status quo in the South and focusing on economic advancement— working hard, developing occupational skills, saving money, building businesses, and acquiring land. Washington (1856–1915), who had been born a slave in Virginia, was educated at Hampton Institute, which trained blacks in the practical skills needed to make a living in the Jim Crow South. Chosen in 1881 to create a similar facility in Alabama, he established Tuskegee Institute and used it to disseminate his views. Washington achieved national renown in 1895 as a result of this speech given at the Cotton States Exposition in Atlanta. Critics of the speech, which outlined his accommodationist approach, soon termed it the "Atlanta Compromise." But prominent whites and ordinary blacks endorsed Washington's views.*

Mr. President and Gentlemen of the Board of Directors and Citizens:

One-third of the population of the South is of the Negro race. No enterprise seeking the material, civil, or moral welfare of this section can disregard this element of our population and reach the highest success. I but convey to you, Mr. President and Directors, the sentiment of the masses of my race when I say that in no way have the value and manhood of the American Negro been more fittingly and generously recognized than by the managers of this magnificent Exposition at every stage of its progress. It is a recognition that will do more to cement the friendship of the two races than any occurrence since the dawn of our freedom.

Not only this, but the opportunity here afforded will awaken among us a new era of industrial progress. Ignorant and inexperienced, it is not strange that in the first years of our new life we began at the top instead of at the bottom; that a seat in Congress or the state legislature was more sought than real estate or industrial skill; that the political convention or stump speaking had more attractions than starting a dairy farm or truck garden.

A ship lost at sea for many days suddenly sighted a friendly vessel. From the mast of the unfortunate vessel was seen a signal, "Water, water; we die of thirst!" The answer from the friendly vessel at once came back, "Cast down your bucket where you are." A second time the signal, "Water, water; send us water!" ran up from the distressed vessel, and was answered, "Cast down your bucket where you are." And a third and fourth signal for water was answered, "Cast down your bucket where you are." The captain of the distressed vessel, at last heeding the injunction, cast down his bucket, and it came up full of fresh, sparkling water from the mouth of the Amazon River. To those of my race who depend on bettering their condition in a foreign land or who underestimate the importance of cultivating friendly relations with the Southern white man, who is their next-door neighbor, I would say: "Cast down your bucket where you are"—cast it down in making friends in every manly way of the people of all races by whom we are surrounded.

Cast it down in agriculture, mechanics, in commerce, in domestic service, and in the professions. And in this connection, it is well to bear in mind that whatever other sins the South may be called to bear, when it comes to business, pure and simple, it is in the South that the Negro is given a man's chance in the commercial world, and in nothing is this Exposition more eloquent than in emphasizing this chance. Our greatest danger is that in the great leap from slavery to freedom we may overlook the fact that the masses of us are to live by the productions of our hands, and fail to keep in mind that we shall prosper in proportion as we learn to dignify and glorify common labour, and put brains and skill into the common occupations of life; shall prosper in proportion as we learn to draw the line between the superficial and the substantial, the ornamental

---

* Booker T. Washington, *Up from Slavery* (Boston, 1901).

gewgaws of life and the useful. No race can prosper till it learns that there is as much dignity in tilling a field as in writing a poem. It is at the bottom of life we must begin, and not at the top. Nor should we permit our grievances to overshadow our opportunities.

To those of the white race who look to the incoming of those of foreign birth and strange tongue and habits for the prosperity of the South, were I permitted I would repeat what I say to my own race, "Cast down your bucket where you are." Cast it down among the eight millions of Negroes whose habits you know, whose fidelity and love you have tested in days when to have proved treacherous meant the ruin of your firesides. Cast down your bucket among these people who have, without strikes and labour wars, tilled your fields, cleared your forests, builded your railroads and cities, and brought forth treasures from the bowels of the earth, and helped make possible this magnificent representation of the progress of the South. Casting down your bucket among my people, helping and encouraging them as you are doing on these grounds, and to education of head, hand, and heart, you will find that they will buy your surplus land, make blossom the waste places in your fields, and run your factories. While doing this, you can be sure in the future, as in the past, that you and your families will be surrounded by the most patient, faithful, law-abiding, and unresentful people that the world has seen. As we have proved our loyalty to you in the past, in nursing your children, watching by the sick-bed of your mothers and fathers, and often following them with tear-dimmed eyes to their graves, so in the future, in our humble way, we shall stand by you with a devotion that no foreigner can approach, ready to lay down our lives, if need be, in defense of yours, interlacing our industrial, commercial, civil, and religious life with yours in a way that shall make the interests of both races one. In all things that are purely social we can be as separate as the fingers, yet one as the hand in all things essential to mutual progress.

There is no defense or security for any of us except in the highest intelligence and development of all. If anywhere there are efforts tending to curtail the fullest growth of the Negro, let these efforts be turned into stimulating, encouraging, and making him the most useful and intelligent citizen. Effort or means so invested will pay a thousand per cent interest. These efforts will be twice blessed—"blessing him that gives and him that takes."

There is no escape through law of man or God from the inevitable:

"The laws of changeless justice bind

Oppressor with oppressed;

And close as sin and suffering joined

We march to fate abreast."

Nearly sixteen millions of hands will aid you in pulling the load upward, or they will pull against you the load downward. We shall constitute one-third and more of the ignorance and crime of the South, or one-third [of] its intelligence and progress; we shall contribute one-third to the business and industrial prosperity of the South, or we shall prove a veritable body of death, stagnating, depressing, retarding every effort to advance the body politic.

Gentlemen of the Exposition, as we present to you our humble effort at an exhibition of our progress, you must not expect overmuch. Starting thirty years ago with ownership here and there in a few quilts and pumpkins and chickens (gathered from miscellaneous sources), remember the path that has led from these to the inventions and production of agricultural implements, buggies, steam-engines, newspapers, books, statuary, carving, paintings, the management of drug stores and banks, has not been trodden without contact with thorns and thistles. While we take pride in what we exhibit as a result of our independent efforts, we do not for a moment forget that our part in this exhibition would fall far short of your expectations but for the constant help that has come to our educational life, not only from the Southern states, but especially from Northern philanthropists, who have made their gifts a constant stream of blessing and encouragement.

The wisest among my race understand that the agitation of questions of social equality is the extremest folly, and that progress in the enjoyment of all privileges that will come to us must be the result of severe and constant struggle rather than of artificial forcing. No race that has anything to contribute to the markets of the world is long in any degree ostracized. It is important and right that all privileges of the law be ours, but it is vastly more important that we be prepared for the exercise of these privileges. The opportunity to earn a dollar in a factory just now is worth infinitely more than the opportunity to spend a dollar in an opera-house.

In conclusion, may I repeat that nothing in thirty years has given us more hope and encouragement, and drawn us so near to you of the white race, as this opportunity offered by the Exposition; and here bending, as it were, over the altar that represents the results of the struggles of your race and mine, both starting practically empty-handed three decades ago, I pledge that in your effort to work out the great and intricate problem which God has laid at the doors of the South, you shall have at all times the patient, sympathetic help of my race; only let this be constantly in mind, that, while from representations in these buildings of the product of field, of forest, of mine, of factory, letters, and art, much good will come, yet far above and beyond material benefits will be that higher good, that, let us pray God, will come, in a blotting out of sectional differences and racial animosities and suspicions in a determination to administer absolute justice, in a willing obedience among all classes to the mandates of law. This, coupled with our material prosperity, will bring into our beloved South a new heaven and a new earth.

Henry McNeal Turner, Back to Africa

Critics of Booker T. Washington's accommodationist approach offered a wide range of alternatives. Several continued to urge African Americans to leave the South for the West, the North, or even the African continent. The leading black emigrationist of the Progressive era was Henry McNeal Turner (1834–1915) of Georgia, a bishop in the African Methodist Episcopal church. Although he had actively pursued racial equality through Republican politics during Reconstruction, he later became disillusioned and—like Martin R. Delany in an earlier time—urged African Americans to go to Africa and build an independent black nation. In the following speech, given in December 1895 before a conference on African missions in Atlanta, Turner outlines his reasons for promoting an African "return." Although he visited Africa three times, and organized a society to recruit and assist potential migrants, very few blacks chose this alternative.*

There is no manhood future in the United States for the Negro. He may make out an existence for generations to come, but he can never be a *man*—full, symmetrical and undwarfed. Upon this point I know thousands who make pretensions to scholarship, white and colored, will differ and may charge me with folly, while I in turn pity their ignorance of history and political and civil sociology. We beg here to itemize and give a cursory glance at a few facts calculated to convince any man who is not biased or lamentably ignorant. Let us note a few of them.

1. There is a great chasm between the white and black, not only in this country, but in the West India Islands, South America, and as much as has been said to the contrary, I have seen inklings of it in Ireland, in England, in France, in Germany, and even away down in southern Spain in sight of Morocco in Africa. We will not, however, deal with foreign nations, but let us note a few facts connected with the United States.

I repeat that a great chasm exists between the two race varieties in this country. The white people, neither North or South, will have social contact as a mass between themselves and any portion of the Negroid race. Although they may be as white in appearance as themselves, yet a drop of African blood imparts a taint, and the talk about two races remaining in the same country with mutual interest and responsibility in its institutions and progress, with no social contact, is the jargon of folly, and no man who has read the history of nations and the development of countries, and the agencies which have culminated in the homogeneity of racial variations, will proclaim such a doctrine. Senator Morgan, of Alabama, tells the truth when he says that the Negro has nothing to expect without social equality with the whites, and that the whites will never grant it.

This question must be examined and opinions reached in the light of history and sociological philosophy, and not by a mere think-so on the part of men devoid of learning. When I use the term learning, I do not refer to men who have graduated from some college and have a smattering knowledge of Greek, Latin, mathematics and a few school books, and have done nothing since but read the trashy articles of newspapers. That is not scholarship. Scholarship consists in wading through dusty volumes for forty and fifty years. That class of men would not dare to predict symmetrical manhood for the Negroid race in this or any other country, without social equality. The colored man who will stand up and in one breath say that the Negroid race does not want social equality and in the next predict a great future in the face of all the proscription of which the colored man is the victim, is either an ignoramus, or is an advocate of the perpetual

* Henry McNeal Turner, "The American Negro and His Fatherland," in *Africa and the American Negro*, ed. John W. E. Bowen (Atlanta, 1896).

servility and degradation of his race variety. I know, as Senator Morgan says, and as every white man in the land will say, that the whites will not grant social equality to the Negroid race, nor am I certain that God wants them to do it. And as such, I believe that two or three millions of us should return to the land of our ancestors, and establish our own nation, civilization, laws, customs, style of manufacture, and not only give the world, like other race varieties, the benefit of our individuality but build up social conditions peculiarly our own, and cease to be grumblers, chronic complainers and a menace to the white man's country, or the country he claims and is bound to dominate.

The civil status of the Negro is simply what the white man grants of his own free will and accord. The black man can demand nothing. He is deposed from the jury and tried, convicted and sentenced by men who do not claim to be his peers. On the railroads, where the colored race is found in the largest numbers, he is the victim of proscription, and he must ride in the Jim Crow car or walk. The Supreme Court of the United States decided, October 15th, 1883, that the colored man had no civil rights under the general government, and the several States, from then until now, have been enacting laws which limit, curtail and deprive him of his civil rights, immunities and privileges, until he is now being disfranchised, and where it will end no one can divine.

They told me in the Geographical Institute in Paris, France, that according to their calculation there are not less than 400,000,000 of Africans and their descendants on the globe, so that we are not lacking in numbers to form a nationality of our own.

2. The environments of the Negroid race variety in this country tend to the inferiority of them, even if the argument can be established that we are equals with the white man in the aggregate, notwithstanding the same opportunities may be enjoyed in the schools. Let us note a few facts.

The discriminating laws, all will concede, are degrading to those against who they operate, and the degrader will be degraded also. "For all acts are reactionary, and will return in curses upon those who curse," said Stephen A. Douglass, the great competitor of President Lincoln. Neither does it require a philosopher to inform you that degradation begets degradation. Any people oppressed, proscribed, belied, slandered, burned, flayed and lynched will not only become cowardly and servile, but will transmit that same servility to their posterity, and continue to do so ad infinitum, and as such will never make a bold and courageous people. The condition of the Negro in the United States is so repugnant to the instincts of respected manhood that thousands, yea hundreds of thousands, of miscegenated will pass for white, and snub the people with whom they are identified at every opportunity, thus destroying themselves, or at least unracing themselves. They do not want to be black because of its ignoble condition, and they cannot be white, thus they become monstrosities. Thousands of young men who are even educated by white teachers never have any respect for people of their own color and spend their days as devotees of white gods. Hundreds, if not thousands, of the terms employed by the white race in the English language are also degrading to the black man. Everything that is satanic, corrupt, base and infamous is denominated black, and all that constitutes virtue, purity, innocence, religion, and that which is divine and heavenly, is represented as white. Our Sabbath-school children, by the time they reach proper consciousness, are taught to sing to the laudation of white and to the contempt of black. Can anyone with an ounce of common sense expect that these children, when they reach maturity, will ever have any respect for their black or colored faces, or the faces of their associates? But, without multiplying words, the terms used in our religious experience, and the hymns we sing in many instances, are degrading, and will be as long as the black man is surrounded by the idea that *white* represents God and *black* represents the devil. The Negro should, therefore, build up a nation of his own, and create a language in keeping with his color, as the whites have done. Nor will he ever respect himself until he does it.

3. In this country the colored man, with a few honorable exceptions, folds his arms and waits for the white man to propose, project, erect, invent, discover, combine, plan and execute everything connected with civilization, including machinery, finance, and indeed everything. This, in the nature of things, dwarfs the colored man and allows his great faculties to slumber from the cradle to the grave. Yet he possesses mechanical and inventive genius, I believe, equal to any race on earth. Much has been said about the natural inability of the colored race to engage in the profession of skilled labor. Yet before the war, right here in this Southland he erected and completed all of the fine edifices in which the lords of the land luxuriated. It is idle talk to speak of a colored man not being a success in skilled labor or the fine arts. What the black man needs is a country and surroundings in harmony with his color and with respect for his manhood. Upon this point I would delight to dwell longer if I had time. Thousands of white people in this country are ever and anon advising the colored people to keep out of politics, but they do not advise themselves. If the Negro is a man in keeping with other men, why should he be less concerned about politics than anyone else? Strange, too, that a number of would-be colored leaders are ignorant and debased enough to proclaim the same foolish jargon. For the Negro to stay out of politics is to level himself with a horse or a cow, which is no politician, and the Negro who does it proclaims his inability to take part in political affairs. If the Negro is to be a man, full and complete, he must take part in everything that belongs to manhood. If he omits a single duty, responsibility or privilege, to that extent he is limited and incomplete. . . .

I conclude by saying the argument that it would be impossible to transport the colored people of the United States back to Africa is an advertisement of folly. Two hundred millions of dollars would rid this country of the last member of the Negroid race, if such a thing was desirable, and two hundred and fifty millions would give every man, woman and child excellent fare, and the general government could furnish that amount and never miss it, and that would only be the pitiful sum of a million dollars a year for the time we labored for nothing, and for which somebody or some power is responsible. The emigrant agents at New York, Boston, Philadelphia, St. John, N.B., and Halifax, N.S., with whom I have talked, establish beyond contradiction, that over a million, and from that to twelve hundred thousand persons, come to this country every year, and yet there is no public stir about it. But in the case of African emigration, two or three millions only of self-reliant men and women would be necessary to establish the conditions we are advocating for in Africa.

John Hope, "Rise, Brothers!"

Many younger activists rejected Booker T. Washington's accommodationist approach in favor of militant protest. Among the first to do so was John Hope (1868–1936), a young instructor at Roger Williams University in Nashville. After returning home from the Cotton States Exposition, he openly criticized Washington's speech in a report to his students and colleagues. In the following address, delivered in February 1896 before the Colored Debating Society of Nashville, he offers a clear statement of the views of more protest-oriented blacks. Hope later served as president of Morehouse College and Atlanta University.[*]

If we are not striving for equality, in heaven's name for what are we living? I regard it as cowardly and dishonest for any of our colored men to tell white people or colored people that we are not struggling for equality. If money, education, and honesty will not bring to me as much privilege, as much equality as they bring to any American citizen, then they are to me a curse, and not a blessing. God forbid that we should get the implements with which to fashion our freedom, and then be too lazy or pusillanimous to fashion it. Let us not fool ourselves nor be fooled by others. If we cannot do what other freemen do, then we are not free. Yes, my friends, I want equality. Nothing less. I want all that my God-given powers will enable me to get, then why not equality? Now, catch your breath, for I am going to use an adjective: I am going to say we demand *social* equality. In this republic we shall be less than freemen, if we have a whit less than that which thrift, education, and honor afford other freemen. If equality, political, economic, and social, is the boon of other men in this great country of *ours*, then equality, political, economic, and social, is what we demand. Why build a wall to keep me out? I am no wild beast, nor am I an unclean thing.

Rise, Brothers! Come let us possess this land. Never say: "Let well enough alone." Cease to console yourselves with adages that numb the moral sense. Be discontented. Be dissatisfied. "Sweat and grunt" under present conditions. Be as restless as the tempestuous billows on the boundless sea. Let your discontent break mountain-high against the wall of prejudice, and swamp it to the very foundation. Then we shall not have to plead for justice nor on bended knee crave mercy; for we shall be men. Then and not until then will liberty in its highest sense be the boast of our Republic.

---

[*] Ridgely Torrence, *The Story of John Hope* (New York: Macmillan, 1948).

W.E.B. Du Bois, Organizing for Protest

Opponents of Booker T. Washington's accommodationist approach organized for protest during the first decade of the twentieth century. The clarion call was sounded by W. E. B. Du Bois's essay, "Of Mr. Booker T. Washington and Others," in *The Souls of Black Folk* (1903). Du Bois (1868–1963), an Atlanta University professor born and reared in Massachusetts, was exceptionally well educated and had studied with some of the greatest social thinkers of his time. In 1905 he and several younger black activists gathered at Niagara Falls, Canada, and developed a platform for aggressive action in pursuit of African-American rights. One year later, members of this Niagara Movement met at Harpers Ferry, West Virginia, the site of John Brown's famous 1859 raid, and drew up the following document (largely written by Du Bois); it outlined their demands and the means by which they intended to pursue them. In 1909 they joined like-minded blacks, several white progressives, and a few former abolitionists to create the NAACP, the nation's leading civil rights organization during the first half of the century.*

The men of the Niagara Movement coming from the toil of the year's hard work and pausing a moment from the earning of their daily bread turn toward the nation and again ask in the name of ten million the privilege of a hearing. In the past year the work of the Negro hater has flourished in the land. Step by step the defenders of the rights of American citizens have retreated. The work of stealing the black man's ballot has progressed and the fifty and more representatives of stolen votes still sit in the nation's capital. Discrimination in travel and public accommodation has so spread that some of our weaker brethren are actually afraid to thunder against color discrimination as such and are simply whispering for ordinary decencies.

Against this the Niagara Movement eternally protests. We will not be satisfied to take one jot or tittle less than our full manhood rights. W[ith] nastiness the new American creed says: Fear to let black men even try to claim for ourselves every single right that belongs to a freeborn American, political, civil, and social; and until we get these rights we will never cease to protest and assail the ears of America. The battle we wage is not for ourselves alone but for all true Americans. It is a fight for ideals, lest this, our common fatherland, false to its founding, become in truth the land of the thief and the home of the Slave—a by-word and a hissing among the nations for its sounding pretensions and pitiful accomplishments.

---

* W. E. B. Du Bois, "Niagara Address of 1906," W. E. B. Du Bois Manuscripts, University of Massachusetts, Amherst, Massachusetts.

Never before in the modern age has a great and civilized folk threatened to adopt so cowardly a creed in the treatment of its fellow-citizens born and bred on its soil. Stripped of verbiage and subterfuge and in its naked [form] rise lest they become the equals of the white. And this is the land that professes to follow Jesus Christ. The blasphemy of such a course is only matched by its cowardice.

In detail our demands are clear and unequivocal. First. We would vote; with the right to vote goes everything: Freedom, manhood, the honor of your wives, the chastity of your daughters, the right to work, and the chance to rise, and let no man listen to those who deny this.

We want full manhood suffrage, and we want it now, henceforth and forever.

Second. We want discrimination in public accommodation to cease. Separation in railway and street cars, based simply on race and color, is un-American, undemocratic, and silly. We protest against all such discrimination.

Third. We claim the right of freemen to walk, talk, and be with them that wish to be with us. No man has a right to choose another man's friends, and to attempt to do so is an impudent interference with the most fundamental human privilege.

Fourth. We want the laws enforced against rich as well as poor; against Capitalist as well as Laborer; against white as well as black. We are not more lawless than the white race; we are more often arrested, convicted and mobbed. We want justice even for criminals and outlaws. We want the Constitution of the country enforced. We want Congress to take charge of Congressional elections. We want the Fourteenth Amendment carried out to the letter and every State disfranchised in Congress which attempts to disenfranchise its rightful voters. We want the Fifteenth Amendment enforced and no State allowed to base its franchise simply on color.

The failure of the Republican Party in Congress at the session just closed to redeem its pledge of 1904 with reference to suffrage conditions [in] the South seems a plain, deliberate, and premeditated breach of promise, and stamps that party as guilty of obtaining votes under false pretense.

Fifth. We want our children educated. The school system in the country districts of the South is a disgrace and in few towns and cities are the Negro schools what they ought to be. We want the national government to step in and wipe out illiteracy in the South. Either the United States will destroy ignorance or ignorance will destroy the United States.

And when we call for education we mean real education. We believe in work. We ourselves are workers, but work is not necessarily education. Education is the development of power and ideal. We want our children trained as intelligent human beings should be, and we will fight for all time against any proposal to educate black boys and girls simply as servants and underlings, or simply for the use of other people. They have a right to know, to think, to aspire.

These are some of the chief things which we want. How shall we get them? By voting where we may vote, by persistent, unceasing agitation, by hammering at the truth, by sacrifice and work.

We do not believe in violence, neither in the despised violence of the raid nor the lauded violence of the soldier, nor the barbarous violence of the mob, but we do believe in John Brown, in that incarnate spirit of justice, that hatred of a lie, that willingness to sacrifice money, reputation, and life itself on the altar of right. And here on the scene of John Brown's martyrdom we reconsecrate ourselves, our honor, our property to the final emancipation of the race which John Brown died to make free.

Our enemies, triumphant for the present, are fighting the stars in their courses. Justice and humanity must prevail. We live to tell these dark brothers of ours—scattered in counsel, wavering and weak—that no bribe of money or notoriety, no promise of wealth or fame, is worth the surrender of a people's manhood or the loss of a man's self-respect. We refuse to surrender the leadership of this race to cowards and trucklers. We are men; we will be treated as men. On this rock we have planted our banners. We will never give up, though the trump of doom find us still fighting.

And we shall win. The past promised it, the present foretells it. Thank God for John Brown! Thank God for . . . all the hallowed dead who died for freedom! Thank God for all those today, few though their voices be, who have not forgotten the divine brotherhood of all men, white and black, rich and poor, fortunate and unfortunate.

We appeal to the young men and women of this nation, to those whose nostrils are not yet befouled by greed and snobbery and racial narrowness: Stand up for the right, prove yourselves worthy of your heritage and whether born north or south dare to treat men as men. Cannot the nation that has absorbed ten million foreigners into its political life without catastrophe absorb ten million Negro Americans into that same political life at less cost than their unjust and illegal exclusion will involve?

Courage, brothers! The battle for humanity is not lost or losing. All across the skies sit signs of promise. The Slav is rising in his might, the yellow millions are tasting liberty, the black Africans are writhing toward the light, and everywhere the laborer, with ballot in his hand, is voting open the gates of Opportunity and Peace. The morning breaks over blood-stained hills. We must not falter, we may not shrink. Above are the everlasting stars.

Asking Questions of the Documents

1. What did Ida B. Wells-Barnett mean by self-help? How did she think that blacks could best fight for racial equality in the South?

2. How did Booker T. Washington think that blacks could best improve their circumstances in the South? What did he ask them to give up—at least temporarily? Why would prominent whites approve of his approach?

3. Why did Henry McNeal Turner think that blacks should migrate to the African continent? Why did he believe it was impossible for blacks ever to gain equality in the United States?

4. What subtle (and not so subtle) criticisms did John Hope, W. E. B. Du Bois, and the members of the Niagara Movement make of Washington's approach? What strategy did they suggest? What specific goals did they seek? Why did they believe that they would achieve these goals? Why did the Niagara Movement meet in 1906 at Harpers Ferry?

5.   Compare and contrast the racial alternatives presented in this chapter. Which would have been the best one for blacks in the South during the Progressive era? Which would be best for African Americans today? Why?

For Further Reading

Harlan, Louis R. *Booker T. Washington: The Making of a Black Leader, 1856–1901.* New York: Oxford University Press, 1972.

Harlan, Louis R. *Booker T. Washington: The Wizard of Tuskegee, 1901–1915.* New York: Oxford University Press, 1983.

Holt, Thomas C. "The Lonely Warrior: Ida B. Wells-Barnett and the Struggle for Black Leadership." In *Black Leaders of the Twentieth Century,* ed. John Hope Franklin and August Meier, 39–61. Urbana, Ill.: University of Illinois Press, 1982.

Lewis, David Levering. *W. E. B. Du Bois: Biography of a Race, 1868–1919.* New York: Henry Holt and Company, 1993.

Meier, August. *Negro Thought in America, 1880–1915: Racial Ideologies in the Age of Booker T. Washington.* Ann Arbor, Mich.: University of Michigan Press, 1963.

Redkey, Edwin S. *Black Exodus: Black Nationalist and Back-to-Africa Movements, 1890–1910.* New Haven: Yale University Press, 1969.

11

The Great War
and the Great Migration

The outbreak of World War I (known as the Great War) in Europe brought the beginnings of a major transformation in African-American life. The war slowed the flow of immigrants from Europe to a trickle, cutting off a major source of labor for American industry. As the United States prepared to enter the war in 1917, another four million workers enlisted or were drafted into the armed services. Desperate for laborers to meet the needs of wartime production, American industry looked for the first time to African Americans in the South. Soon black newspapers like the *Chicago Defender*, labor agents, and letters home from family and friends heralded the advantages of migrating to one of the industrial cities of the North.

Thousands of blacks left plantations, villages, and southern cities in a movement that became known as the Great Migration. Some 500,000 blacks went North between 1915 and 1920, and another million migrated during the following decade. Hoping for a better life than they had left behind in the South, they crowded into urban ghettoes such as Harlem, Chicago's South Side, and Philadelphia's Seventh Ward. Here they rebuilt their lives in a new and often strange setting, establishing new institutions, such as storefront churches, to meet their spiritual and social needs. These ghettoes became vibrant centers of African-American culture; many housed black newspapers, jazz and blues clubs, and literary salons.

With the migration came a new militancy, a new outlook, and, according to Alain Locke, the creation of "a New Negro." A number of movements arose that gave expression to this new mood. The Harlem Renaissance, a literary and artistic movement, helped the literate elite of the ghettoes develop their cultural identity. For the first time, black artists and writers openly embraced their folk culture and their African past. Garveyism, the first nationalist mass movement among African Americans, raised black political consciousness and increased black cultural pride. As Locke explained: "In the very process of being transplanted, the Negro is being transformed."

Causes of the Migration

A number of factors caused the Great Migration. Many blacks were attracted by the opportunity for good jobs and a freer life in the North; others sought to flee the poverty, lynching, disfranchisement, and segregation of the Jim Crow South. Most probably came North for a combination of reasons, some of which are poignantly explained in the following two letters from potential migrants to the *Chicago Defender.*[*]

NEWBERN, ALA.

4/7/1917

Dear Sir:

I am in receipt of a letter from __ of __, __, in regards to placing two young women of our community in positions in the North or West; as he was unable to give the above assistance he enclosed your address. We desire to know if you are in a position to put us in touch with any reliable firm or private family that desire to employ two young women; one is a teacher in the public school of this county, and has been for the past six years; having duties of a mother and sister to care for she is forced to seek employment else where as labor is very cheap here. The other is a high school pupil, is capable of doing the work of a private family with much credit.

Doubtless you have learned of the great exodus of our people to the north and west from this and other southern states. I wish to say that we are forced to go when one thinks of a grown man wages is only fifty to seventy five cents per day for all grades of work. He is compelled to go where there is better wages and sociable conditions, believe me. When I say that many places here in this state the only thing that the black man gets is a peck of meal and from three to four lbs. of bacon per week, and he is treated as a slave. As leaders we are powerless for we dare not resent such or to show even the slightest disapproval. Only a few days ago more than 1,000 people left here for the North and West. They cannot stay here. The white man is saying that you must not go, but they are not doing anything by way of assisting the black man to stay. As a minister of the Methodist Episcopal Church (north) I am on the verge of starvation simply because of the above conditions. I shall be glad to know if there is any possible way by which I could be of real service to you as director of your society. Thanking you in advance for an early reply, and for any suggestions that you may be able to offer.

With best wishes for your success, I remain, very sincerely yours.

---

[*] Emmett J. Scott, "Letters of Negro Migrants of 1916-1918," *Journal of Negro History* 4 (July and November 1919).

PALESTINE, TEX.

1/2/17

Dear Sir:

I hereby enclose you a few lines to find out some few things if you will be so kind to word them to me. I am a southerner lad and has never ben in the north no further than Texas and I has heard so much talk about the north and how much better the colard people are treated up there than they are down here and I has ben striveing so hard in my coming up and now I see that I cannot get up there without the ade of some one and I wants to ask you Dear Sir to please direct me in your best manner the step that I shall take to get there and if there are any way that you can help me to get there I am kindly asking you for your ade. And if you will ade me please notify me by return mail because I am sure ancious to make it in the north because these southern white people ar so mean and they seems to be getting worse and I wants to get away and they wont pay enough for work for a man to save up enough to get away and live to. If you will not ade me in getting up there please give me some information how I can get there I would like to get there in the early spring, if I can get there if possible. Our Southern white people are so cruel we collard people are almost afraid to walke the streets after night. So please let me hear from you by return mail. I will not say very much in this letter I will tell you more about it when I hear from you please ans. soon to

Yours truly.

W.E.B. Du Bois, Returning Soldiers

Some 370,000 African Americans served in the U.S. armed forces during World War I. More than a quarter fought in Europe, especially in France. The French treated black soldiers as equals and welcomed them into their restaurants, clubs, hotels, and houses. But when they returned home, they faced racial violence and continued discrimination. In the following editorial written for the *Crisis*, the magazine of the NAACP, W. E. B. Du Bois sounded a call for black veterans to fight as valiantly for their rights at home as they had for democracy abroad. This was representative of the new militancy in the African-American community during the Great Migration.[*]

---

[*] W. E. B. Du Bois, "Returning Soldiers," *Crisis* 13 (May 1919).

We are returning from war. The *Crisis* and tens of thousands of black men were drafted into a great struggle. For bleeding France and what she means and has meant and will mean to us and humanity and against the threat of German race arrogance, we fought gladly and to the last drop of blood; for America and her highest ideals, we fought in far-off hope; for the dominant southern oligarchy entrenched in Washington, we fought in bitter resignation. For the America that represents and gloats in lynching, disfranchisement, caste, brutality and devilish insult—for this, in the hateful upturning and mixing of things, we were forced by vindictive fate to fight, also.

But to-day we return! We return from the slavery of uniform which the world's madness demanded us to don to the freedom of civil garb. We stand again to look America squarely in the face and call a spade a spade. We sing: This country of ours, despite all its better souls have done and dreamed, is yet a shameful land.

It *lynches*.

And lynching is barbarism of a degree of contemptible nastiness unparalleled in human history. Yet for fifty years we have lynched two Negroes a week, and we have kept this up right through the war.

It *disfranchises* its own citizens.

Disfranchisement is the deliberate theft and robbery of the only protection of poor against rich and black against white. The land that disfranchises its citizens and calls itself a democracy lies and knows it lies.

It encourages *ignorance*.

It has never really tried to educate the Negro. A dominant minority does not want Negroes educated. It wants servants, dogs, whores and monkeys. And when this land allows a reactionary group by its stolen political power to force as many black folk into these categories as it possible can, it cries in contemptible hypocrisy: "They threaten us with degeneracy; they cannot be educated."

It *steals* from us.

It organizes industry to cheat us. It cheats us out of our land; it cheats us out of our labor. It confiscates our savings. It reduces our wages. It raises our rent. It steals our profit. It taxes us without representation. It keeps us consistently and universally poor, and then feeds us on charity and derides our poverty.

It *insults* us.

It has organized a nation-wide and latterly a world-wide propaganda of deliberate and continuous insult and defamation of black blood wherever found. It decrees that it shall not be possible in travel nor residence, work nor play, education nor instruction for a black man to exist without tacit or open acknowledgment of his inferiority to the dirtiest white dog. And it looks upon any attempt to question or even discuss this dogma as arrogance, unwarranted assumption and treason.

This is the country to which we Soldiers of Democracy return. This is the fatherland for which we fought! But it is our fatherland. It was right for us to fight. The faults of *our* country are *our* faults. Under similar circumstances, we would fight again. But by the God of Heaven, we are cowards and jackasses if now that that war is over, we do not marshal every ounce of our brain and brawn to fight a sterner, longer, more unbending battle against the forces of hell in our own land.

We *return*.

We *return from fighting*.
We *return fighting*.
Make way for Democracy! We saved it in France, and by the Great Jehovah, we will save it in the United States of America, or know the reason why.

Alain Locke, The New Negro

Black veterans were not the only African Americans to display this new militant mood. Some observers witnessed it throughout the Great Migration. Alain Locke (1886–1954), a Harvard-educated philosopher and literary critic saw about him a "New Negro" with a "new psychology" and a "new outlook." In the following document, his most famous essay on the "New Negro," Locke looks at the causes, consequences, and evidences of this phenomenon. He believed that, from that time on, white Americans would have to reckon with an African-American population that was "fundamentally changed." Locke taught philosophy at Howard University from 1918 until the year before his death.[*]

In the last decade something beyond the watch and guard of statistics has happened in the life of the American Negro, and the three norns who have traditionally presided over the Negro problem have a changeling in their laps. The Sociologist, the Philanthropist, the Race leader are not unaware of the New Negro, but they are at a loss to account for him. He simply cannot be swathed in their formulae. For the younger generation is vibrant with a new psychology; the new spirit is awake in the masses, and under the very eyes of the professional observers is transforming what has been a perennial problem into the progressive phases of contemporary Negro life.

Could such a metamorphosis have taken place as suddenly as it has appeared to? The answer is no; not only because the New Negro is not here, but because the Old Negro had long become more of a myth than a man. The Old Negro, we must remember, was a creature of moral debate and historical controversy. His has been a stock figure perpetuated as an historical fiction partly in innocent sentimentalism, partly in deliberate reactionism. The Negro himself has contributed his share to this through a sort of protective social mimicry forced upon him by the adverse circumstances of dependence. So for generations in the mind of America, the Negro has been more of a formula than a human being—a something to be argued about, condemned or defended, to be "kept down," or "in his place," or "helped up," to be worried with or worried over, harassed or patronized, a social bogey or a social burden. The thinking Negro even has

[*] Alain Locke, ed., *The New Negro: An Interpretation* (New York: Macmillan, 1925).

been induced to share this same general attitude, to focus his attention on controversial issues, to see himself in the distorted perspective of a social problem. His shadow, so to speak, has been more real to him than his personality. Through having had to appeal from the unjust stereotypes of his oppressors and traducers to those of his liberators, friends and benefactors he has had to subscribe to the traditional positions from which his case has been viewed. Little true social or self understanding has or could come from such a situation.

But while the minds of most of us, black and white, have thus burrowed in the trenches of the Civil War and Reconstruction, the actual march of development has simply flanked these positions, necessitating a sudden reorientation of view. . . . The mind of the Negro seems suddenly to have slipped from under the tyranny of social intimidation and to be shaking off the psychology of imitation and implied inferiority. By shedding the old chrysalis of the Negro problem we are achieving something like a spiritual emancipation. Until recently, lacking self-understanding, we have been almost as much of a problem to ourselves as we still are to others. But the decade that found us with a problem has left us with only a task. The multitude perhaps feels as yet only a strange belief and a new vague urge, but the thinking few know that in the reaction the vital inner grip of prejudice has been broken.

With this renewed self-respect and self-dependence, the life of the Negro community is bound to enter a new dynamic phase, the buoyancy from within compensating for whatever pressure there may be of conditions from without. The migrant masses, shifting from countryside to city, hurdle several generations of experience at a leap, but more important, the same thing happens spiritually in the life-attitudes and self-expression of the Young Negro, in his poetry, his art, his education and his new outlook, with the additional advantage, of course, of the poise and greater certainty of knowing what it is all about. From this comes the promise and warrant of a new leadership. . . .

This is what, even more than any "most creditable record of fifty years of freedom," requires that the Negro of to-day be seen through other than the dusty spectacles of past controversy. The day of "aunties," "uncles" and "mammies" is equally gone. Uncle Tom and Sambo have passed on, and even the "Colonel" and "George" play barnstorm roles from which they escape with relief when the public spotlight is off. The popular melodrama has about played itself out, and it is time to scrap the fictions, garret the bogeys and settle down to a realistic facing of facts.

First we must observe some of the changes which since the traditional lines of opinion were drawn have rendered these quite obsolete. A main change has been, of course, that shifting of the Negro population which has made the Negro problem no longer exclusively or even predominantly Southern. Why should our minds remain sectionalized, when the problem itself no longer is? Then the trend of migration has not only been toward the North and the Central Midwest, but city-ward and to the great centers of industry—the problems of adjustment are new, practical, local and not peculiarly racial. Rather they are an integral part of the large industrial and social problems of our present-day democracy. And finally, with the Negro rapidly in process of class differentiation, if it ever was warrantable to regard and treat the Negro *en masse* it is becoming with every day less possible, more unjust and more ridiculous.

In the very process of being transplanted, the Negro is being transformed.

The tide of Negro migration, northward and city-ward, is not to be fully explained as a blind flood started by the demands of war industry coupled with the shutting off of foreign migration, or by the pressure of poor crops coupled with increased social terrorism in certain sections of the South and Southwest. Neither labor demand, the boll-weevil nor the Ku Klux Klan is a basic factor, however contributory any or all of them may have been. The wash and rush of this human tide on the beach line of the northern city centers is to be explained primarily in terms of a new vision of opportunity, of social and economic freedom, of a spirit to seize, even in the face of an extortionate and heavy toll, a chance for the improvement of conditions. With each successive wave of it, the movement of the Negro becomes more and more a mass movement toward the larger and the more democratic chance—in the Negro's case a deliberate flight not only from countryside to city, but from medieval America to modern.

Take Harlem as an instance of this. Here is Manhattan is not merely the largest Negro community in the world, but the first concentration in history of so many diverse elements of Negro life. It has attracted the African, the West Indian, the Negro American; has brought together the Negro of the North and the Negro of the South; the man from the city and the man from the town and village; the peasant, the student, the business man, the professional man, artist poet, musician, adventurer and worker, preacher and criminal, exploiter and social outcast. Each group has come with its own separate motives and for its own special ends, but their greatest experience has been the finding of one another. Proscription and prejudice have thrown these dissimiliar elements into a common area of contact and interaction. Within this area, race sympathy and unity have deterimined a further fusing of sentiment and experience. So what began in terms of segregation becomes more and more, as its elements mix and react, the laboratory of a great race-welding. Hitherto, it must be admitted that American Negroes have been a race more in name than in fact, or to be exact, more in sentiment than in experience. The chief bond between them has been that of a common condition rather than a common consciousness; a problem in common rather than a life in common. In Harlem, Negro life is seizing upon its first chances for group expression and self-determination. It is—or promises at least to be—a race capital. That is why our comparison is taken with those nascent centers of folk-expression and self-determination which are playing a creative part in the world to-day. Without pretense to their political significance, Harlem has the same role to play for the New Negro as Dublin has had for the New Ireland or Prague for the New Czechoslovakia.

Harlem, I grant you, isn't typical—but it is significant, it is prophetic. No sane observer, however sympathetic to the new trend, would contend that the great masses are articulate as yet, but they stir, they move, they are more than physically restless. The challenge of the new intellectuals among them is clear enough—the "race radicals" and realists who have broken with the old epoch of philanthropic guidance, sentimental appeal and protest. But are we after all only reading into the stirrings of a sleeping giant the dreams of an agitator? The answer is in the migrating peasant. It is the "man farthest down" who is most active in getting up. One of the most characteristic symptoms of this is the professional man, himself migrating to recapture his constituency after a vain effort to maintain in some Southern corner what for years back seemed an established living and clientele. The clergyman following his errant flock, the physician or lawyer trailing his clients, supply the true clues. In a real sense it is the rank and file who are leading, the leaders who are following. A transformed and transforming psychology permeates the masses.

When the racial leaders of twenty years ago spoke of developing race-pride and stimulating race-consciousness, and of the desirability of race-solidarity, they could not in any accurate degree have anticipated the abrupt feeling that has surged up and now pervades the awakened centers. Some of the recognized Negro leaders and a powerful section of white opinion identified with "race work" of the older order have indeed attempted to discount this feeling as a "passing phase," an attack of "race nerves" so to speak, an "aftermath of the war," and the like. It has not abated, however, if we are to gauge by the present tone and temper of the Negro press, or by the shift in popular support from the officially recognized and orthodox spokesmen to those of the independent, popular, and often radical type who are unmistakable symptoms of a new order. It is a social disservice to blunt the fact that the Negro of the Northern centers has reached a stage where tutelage, even of the most interested and well-intentioned sort, must give place to new relationships, where positive self-direction must be reckoned with in ever increasing measure. The American mind must reckon with a fundamentally changed Negro.

Harlem Renaissance Poetry

One of the best evidences of the "new Negro" was the Harlem Renaissance, a literary, artistic, and intellectual movement that flowered in Harlem—soon to be known as the cultural capital of black America—from World War I to the early 1930s. The movement explored previously untapped themes, such as black folk culture and the African past, and kindled a new and more strident black cultural identity. The nucleus of the movement included poets Claude McKay (1890–1948), a migrant from Jamaica; Langston Hughes (1902–1967), from Kansas; and Countee Cullen (1903–1946), a native New Yorker. The following poems by these three men represent the range of themes explored by writers and artists of the Harlem Renaissance.[*]

---

[*] Claude McKay, "If We Must Die," in *Liberator* 2 (July 1919); Langston Hughes, "The Negro Speaks of Rivers," in *The Weary Blues* (New York: Alfred A. Knopf, Inc., 1926); Countee Cullen, "Yet Do I Marvel," in *Color* (New York: Harper and Brothers, Publishers, 1925).

If We Must Die

If we must die—let it not be like hogs
Hunted and penned in an inglorious spot,
While round us bark the mad and hungry dogs,
Making their mock at our accursed lot.
If we must die—oh, let us nobly die,
So that our precious blood may not be shed
In vain; then even the monsters we defy
Shall be constrained to honor us though dead!
Oh Kinsmen! We must meet the common foe;
Though far outnumbered, let us show us brave,
And for their thousand blows deal one deathblow!
What though before us lies the open grave?
Like men we'll face the murderous, cowardly pack,
Pressed to the wall, dying, but fighting back!

Claude McKay

The Negro Speaks of Rivers

I've known rivers:
I've known rivers ancient as the world and older than the flow of human
	blood in human veins.
My soul has grown deep like the rivers.
I bathed in the Euphrates when dawns were young.
I built my hut near the Congo and it lulled me to sleep.
I looked upon the Nile and raised the pyramids above it.
I heard the singing of the Mississippi when Abe Lincoln went down to New
	Orleans, and I've seen its muddy bosom turn all golden in the sunset.
I've known rivers:
Ancient, dusky rivers.
My soul has grown deep like the rivers.

Langston Hughes

Yet Do I Marvel

I doubt not God is good, well-meaning, kind,
And did He stoop to quibble could tell why
The little buried mole continues blind,
Why flesh that mirrors Him must someday die,

Make plain the reason tortured Tantalus
Is baited by the fickle fruit, declare
If merely brute caprice dooms Sisyphus
To struggle up a never ending stair.

Inscrutable His ways are, and immune
To catechism by a mind too strewn
With petty cares to slightly understand
What awful brain compels His awful hand.
 Yet do I marvel at this curious thing:
To make a poet black, and bid him sing!

Countee Cullen

Marcus Garvey, "African Fundamentalism"

Another manifestation of the "New Negro" was the Garvey movement. Marcus Garvey (1887–1940), a black Jamaican, brought his Universal Negro Improvement Association (UNIA) to Harlem in 1916 and forged it into the largest African-American secular organization to that time. It claimed more than a million members, mostly in the black communities of the urban North. A strident black nationalist, Garvey sought to raise the political consciousness, race pride, and economic power of people of African descent throughout the world. In the following editorial, which appeared in 1925 in the *Negro World*, a UNIA publication, he outlined the goals and beliefs of his movement. After the failure of one UNIA business, the Black Star Line, in 1922, Garvey was convicted of mail fraud, imprisoned, and eventually deported. Without his charismatic presence, the movement soon declined. But Garvey's ideas later influenced the development of the Nation of Islam and the Black Power Movement of the 1960s.[*]

Fellow Men of the Negro Race, Greeting:

The time has come for the Negro to forget and cast behind him his hero worship and adoration of other races, and to start out immediately, to create and emulate heroes of his own.

We must canonize our own saints, create our own martyrs, and elevate to positions of fame and honor black men and women who have made their distinct contributions to our racial history. Sojourner Truth is worthy of the place of sainthood alongside of Joan of Arc; Crispus Attucks and George William Gordon are entitled to the halo of martyrdom with no less glory than that of the martyrs of any other race. Toussaint L'Ouverture's brilliancy as a soldier and statesman outshone that of a Cromwell,

---

[*] Marcus Garvey, "African Fundamentalism," *Negro World* (New York), 6 June 1925.

Napoleon and Washington; hence, he is entitled to the highest place as a hero among men. Africa has produced countless numbers of men and women, in war and in peace, whose lustre and bravery outshine that of any other people. Then why not see good and perfection in ourselves?

We must inspire a literature and promulgate a doctrine of our own without any apologies to the powers that be. The right is ours and God's. Let contrary sentiment and cross opinions go to the winds. Opposition to race independence is the weapon of the enemy to defeat the hopes of an unfortunate people. We are entitled to our own opinions and not obligated to or bound by the opinions of others.

If others laugh at you, return the laughter to them; if they mimic you, return the compliment with equal force. They have no more right to dishonor, disrespect and disregard your feeling and manhood than you have in dealing with them. Honor them when they honor you; disrespect and disregard them when they vilely treat you. T heir arrogance is but skin deep and an assumption that has no foundation in morals or in law. They have sprung from the same family tree of obscurity as we have; their history is as rude in its primitiveness as ours; their ancestors ran wild and naked, lived in caves and in the branches of trees, like monkeys, as ours; they made human sacrifices, ate the flesh of their own dead and the raw meat of the wild beast for centuries even as they accuse us of doing; their cannibalism was more prolonged than ours; when we were embracing the arts and sciences on the banks of the Nile their ancestors were still drinking human blood and eating out of the skulls of their conquered dead; when our civilization had reached the noonday of progress they were still running naked and sleeping in holes and caves with rats, bats and other insects and animals. After we had already unfathomed the mysteries of the stars and reduced the heavenly constellations to minute and regular calculus they were still backwoodsmen, living in ignorance and blatant darkness.

The world today is indebted to us for the benefits of civilization. They stole our arts and sciences from Africa. Then why should we be ashamed of ourselves? Their MODERN IMPROVEMENTS are but DUPLICATES of a grander civilization that we reflected thousands of years ago, without the advantage of what is buried and still hidden, to be resurrected and reintroduced by the intelligence of our generation and our prosperity. Why should we be discouraged because somebody laughs at us today? Who [is] to tell what tomorrow will bring forth? Did they not laugh at Moses, Christ and Mohammed? Was there not a Carthage, Greece and Rome? We see and have changes every day, so pray, work, be steadfast and be not dismayed.

As the Jew is held together by his RELIGION, the white races by the assumption and the unwritten law of SUPERIORITY, and the Mongolian by the precious tie of BLOOD, so likewise the Negro must be united in one GRAND RACIAL HIERARCHY. Our UNION MUST KNOW NO CLIME, BOUNDARY, or NATIONALITY. Like the great Church of Rome, Negroes the world over MUST PRACTICE ONE FAITH, that of Confidence in themselves, with One God! One Aim! One Destiny! Let no religious scruples, no political machination divide us, but let us hold together under all climes and in every country, making among ourselves a Racial Empire upon which "the sun shall never set."

Let no voice but your own speak to you from the depths. Let no influence but your own raise you in time of peace and time of war. Hear all, but attend only that which concerns you.

Your first allegiance shall be to your God, then to your family, race and country. Remember always that the Jew in his political and economic urge is always first a Jew; the white man is first a white man under all circumstances, and you can do no less than being first and always a Negro, and then else will take care of itself. Let no one inoculate you for their own conveniences. There is no humanity before that which starts with yourself. "Charity begins at home." First to thyself be true, and "thou canst not then be false to any man."

God and Nature first made us what we are, and then out of our own creative genius we make ourselves what we want to be. Follow always that great law.

Let the sky and God be our limit, and Eternity our measurement. There is no height to which we cannot climb by using the active intelligence of our minds. Mind creates, and as much as we desire in Nature we can have through the creation of our own minds. Being at present the scientifically weaker race, you shall treat others only as they treat you; but in your homes and everywhere possible you must teach the higher development of science to your children; and be sure to develop a race of scientists par excellence, for in science and religion lies our only hope to withstand the evil designs of modern materialism. Never forget your God. Remember, we live, work and pray for the establishing of a great and binding RACIAL HIERARCHY, the founding of a RACIAL EMPIRE whose only natural, spiritual and political limits shall be God and "Africa, at home and abroad."

Asking Questions of the Documents

1. What were the causes of the Great Migration? Which of these seems to have been the most important?

2. What contradictions were raised by the participation and treatment of black soldiers in World War I?

3. What was the "New Negro"? What did Alain Locke see as the cause of this phenomenon? as the consequences? How was the emergence of the "New Negro" linked to the Great Migration?

4. What were the major themes in the poetry of the Harlem Renaissance?

5. What were the goals and beliefs of the Garvey movement?

6. How did the Harlem Renaissance and the Garvey movement reflect the new militancy of African Americans during the Great Migration?

For Further Reading

Barbeau, Arthur E. and Florette Henri. *Unknown Soldiers: Black American Troops in World War I.* Philadelphia: Temple University Press, 1974.

Cronon, E. David. *Black Moses: The Story of Marcus Garvey and the Universal Negro Improvement Association.* Madison, Wisc.: University of Wisconsin Press, 1955.

Grossman, James R. *Land of Hope: Chicago, Black Southerners, and the Great Migration.* Chicago: University of Chicago Press, 1989.

Huggins, Nathan I. *Harlem Renaissance.* New York: Oxford University Press, 1971.

Lewis, David Levering. *When Harlem Was in Vogue.* New York: Oxford University Press, 1979.

Marks, Carole. *Farewell—We're Good and Gone: The Great Black Migration.* Bloomington, In.: Indiana University Press, 1989.

Stein, Judith. *The World of Marcus Garvey: Race and Class in Modern Society.* Baton Rouge, La.: Louisiana State University Press, 1986.

12

A New Deal for African Americans?

The coming of the Great Depression slowed the migration of blacks to America's cities. After the stock market crash of 1929, the nation slipped into an economic decline that brought massive unemployment and suffering. African Americans, who had remained at the bottom of the economic ladder during the 1920s, were hit especially hard. In the cities, black unemployment reached well over 50 percent, more than twice the national average. In the countryside, cotton prices dropped precipitously, forcing thousands of sharecroppers off the land and forcing many more into even greater poverty.

As the depression worsened between 1929 and 1932, the administration of President Herbert Hoover responded slowly and cautiously, employing a "trickle-down" approach that benefited few working Americans—black or white. In the face of unrelieved suffering, many blacks explored new political and organizational solutions to their social and economic ills. Some became Communists or Socialists; others embraced the fledgling Congress of Industrial Organizations, which finally welcomed blacks into the labor union movement. In at least twenty-five cities, blacks organized "Don't Buy Where You Can't Work" campaigns to force more equitable hiring by employers. But after 1932, with the election of Franklin D. Roosevelt, a growing number looked to the federal government. The New Deal—a collection of federal programs created by FDR to bring relief, recovery, and reform to the economy and the nation—helped ordinary blacks and raised their hopes. As a result, a majority of African Americans switched their political allegiance from Republican (the party of Lincoln) to Democrat (the party of FDR).

Despite the enthusiasm of average blacks, the New Deal achieved a mixed record on matters of race. New Deal programs assisted many blacks. FDR listened attentively to black advisers and dramatically increased the number of black employees in the federal government. Federal restrooms, cafeterias, and secretarial pools began to be desegregated. Both FDR and first lady Eleanor Roosevelt invited prominent blacks to the White House and visited and spoke to African-American organizations. But black critics found much to condemn in New Deal programs. Fearful of alienating white voters in the South, a traditional Democratic base, FDR refused to mount direct attacks on Jim Crow. Segregation and discrimination were widespread in the local administration of New Deal agencies, especially in the South. Nonetheless, the 1930s brought a new relationship between African Americans and the federal government, stimulating their hopes for racial change.

Joseph D. Bibb, Flirting with Radicalism

The failure of the Hoover administration to aggressively combat the depression prompted many African Americans to explore radical political and economic alternatives. The Communist Party, which promised an America free of race and class distinctions, actively recruited black members in northern industrial centers and the sharecropping districts of the lower South. Growing black enthusiasm for Communism is the subject of the following editorial by Joseph D. Bibb, a young graduate of Yale Law School and the editor of the Chicago *Whip*. This militant black newspaper, which sometimes openly challenged capitalist values, was a leading advocate of labor unionism among African Americans.*

Contrary to the conciliatory policies of . . . our conservative leaders and erstwhile voicers of black public opinion, the overtures of the Communists and other radical political and economic groups to Negroes are not falling on deaf ears. In most of these cases, the prophecies are begotten of the wish, but the evidence to the contrary is too apparent everywhere about us to be contradicted on such slim rebuttal and words. When thousands of colored men and women gather every night of the week at the open air forums held by these radical groups in the parks and on the street corners of nearly all of our large cities to listen with rapt attention and enthusiasm to doctrines of a radical reorganization of our political and economic organization, the evidence to the contrary of the declaration that "Negroes will never take to Communis[m]" is too strong to be ignored. When Negro miners in the coal and iron districts join in strikes and face starvation to cast their lot with the brother workers, no mere mouthing of platitudes will suffice to hoodwink the thinking masses of our people. When the enslaved and peon-ized sharecroppers of the South dare bravely a certain threat of rope and faggot to follow radical leadership with organized demands for a newer and squarer deal, it fairly shouts from the house tops that the working Negro is part and parcel of the seething discontent which has swept across the entire world.

The rottenness, the injustice, the grim brutality and cold unconcern of our present system has become too irksome to the man farthest down to be longer endured in silence and pacifism. It is high time that those who would stem a revolution busied themselves in sweeping and lasting cures to the cancerous sores which fester upon our body politic and fiercely competitive society. The Communists have framed a program of social remedies which cannot fail to appeal to the hungry and jobless millions, who live in barren want, while everywhere about them is evidence of restricted plenty in the greedy hands of the few. Safety and security, peace and plenty are the things most dear to the hearts of the inarticulate lowly, and these are the things which the radicals hold out as bait to the

---

* *Whip* (Chicago), 1 August 1931.

masses, white as well as black. To argue that they cannot give them but begs the question, for the obvious answer is that our present systems HAVE not given them, and offer no promise of them.

If our two major parties would stem this rising tide of Communism, let them take steps to provide for such immediate needs as are virtually hurling the masses into the ranks of radicalism. Food, shelter and clothing, adequate employment are the only answer to the challenge of Communism, not mere word of mouth denials. The demand among both black and white alike is insisting for improvement—or change.

Virgil Johnson, Switching Party Allegiance

The New Deal reawakened black hopes for American democratic capitalism. For the first time since Reconstruction, many African Americans believed that the federal government cared for their interests. As New Deal relief and recovery programs began to benefit millions of poor and unemployed Americans, blacks, who were disproportionately represented among those two groups, started to switch their allegiance from the Republican Party to FDR and the Democrats. Robert L. Vann, the editor of the Pittsburgh *Courier*, had urged fellow blacks in 1932 to "turn Lincoln's picture to the wall" and vote for FDR. But most of them, moved by decades of tradition, still marked their ballots for Hoover. In 1936, however, blacks voted in record numbers and most of them supported FDR. The following document, excerpted from an interview with Virgil Johnson (1871–?), an aging North Carolina sharecropper, typifies the enthusiasm for FDR and rejection of the Republicans among ordinary blacks.[*]

If I was to vote today, I'd vote for Roosevelt. I don't care if he is a Democrat, he helps the poor man and the farmer. They say that Hoover told 'em over the radio that the jobs should be given to the whites and the colored people could go rabbit-hunting. People can't live on rabbits. Hoover don't care for the workin' man and he has said they's no better than dogs. Roosevelt has held cotton up to nine cents and if they gives up the allotments, it will drop to four cents.

Ever since the war, the colored folks has looked upon the elephant as the animal that helps 'em. But I'm coming to believe that the elephant may be all right in Africa but the American niggers had better stay close to the American mule. I honors Lincoln for freein' us. But the Republican Party has changed. The G.O.P. stands for the rich man.

---

[*] Virgil Johnson Interview, 22 November 1938, Federal Writers Project #3709, Southern Historical Collection, University of North Carolina, Chapel Hill, North Carolina.

They just counted on the colored man voting right and didn't do nothing for us. Roosevelt is for all the poor folks, white and black. You know, as well as I do that they ain't one rich nigger in a thousand. If the Democrats keep bein' friendly to the poor, there soon won't be one Republican in a thousand colored people. Some of the colored people tries to hide it that they's votin' for Roosevelt. . . . But I talks for him and I don't care if I do get scolded for it. The best friend a colored man has is a white Democrat. Just as sure as most of my race gets to votin' Democratic the South is goin' to give 'em back the vote. Northern Republicans don't like us colored people except at a distance. When they moves down here they don't know how to treat us. The only white people that is interested enough to get along with us is the ones that has lived here all their lives. I tells my colored neighbors that the sooner they forget the Republicans the better off they'll be.

Mary McLeod Bethune, A Black Adviser to FDR

African Americans demonstrated renewed political importance in the 1930s. Although a majority were still disfranchised in the South, the Great Migration had made them a potent political force in the urban North. One evidence of this significance was their growing presence in the federal government. FDR tripled the number of black federal employees from 50,000 in 1933 to 150,000 in 1941. And he appointed more than one hundred to administrative posts, including a close circle of advisers known as the "Black Cabinet." One of the most influential was Mary McLeod Bethune (1875–1955), the founder and president of Bethune-Cookman College and a leading activist in the black women's club movement. From 1936 to 1943, she served as director of Minority Affairs in the National Youth Administration, a New Deal agency that provided part-time work to more than two million youths. In this post, she frequently advised FDR on minority concerns. She recounts her relationship with and assessment of FDR in the following document, a magazine article written four years after his death.[*]

I knew Franklin D. Roosevelt as a friend and as a political leader. I talked with him personally on scores of occasions. . . . I discussed with him the problems of my people in many an off-the-record private talk held in the President's study in the White House. I loved that voice and was thrilled by it on innumerable occasions. To me it represented the voice of sanity and progress and humanism. . . .

There are those who criticize FDR's slowness to move against basic evils in our midst and his obvious dislike of extreme methods of achieving his objectives. But it is

---

[*] Mary McLeod Bethune, "My Secret Talks with FDR," *Ebony* 4 (April 1949).

important to understand that his methods were those of a man of great experience and insight. He was a man of great depth of mind and seldom made rash moves. I had many opportunities to study the man at work and in the midst of a crisis, and I was struck by the calm, exact, almost mathematical way in which he thought and moved.

I often expressed to him my impatience with the slowness of the democratic process. I remember going to see him one evening. . . . I was feeling particularly distressed that day over reports I had received on flagrant bias shown against Negroes seeking to enter the National Youth Administration in certain parts of the South. I called him direct that afternoon, and must have sounded awfully agitated.

"Anything wrong?" he asked in that fine strong voice.

"Yes," I answered, "quite a lot."

"Come over after dinner, Mrs. Bethune," he said, "I'll be glad to see you."

I entered the White House in a grim mood, and was escorted upstairs by an attendant who took me up in the President's private elevator.

"He's waiting for you now," the attendant said with a smile. I walked down the hallway to the President's private study and found him waiting for me with a pleasant smile on his face. Sitting in his chair near the door, he waved a greeting with his hand which held his famous cigarette holder.

"Come in, Mrs. Bethune," he called out. "I'm always glad to see you. And do you know why?" I said I didn't.

"Because you always come for others and never for yourself," he said.

His face relaxed and his eyes, though still bright, were searching my features. "How are you," he asked gently. "What can I do for you?"

I told him about the situation in NYA in the South, about the lack of training facilities for Negroes in certain Southern states and of the refusal of state governments to allocate funds for Negro NYA activities. Negroes could not enter the technical training schools established under NYA.

I was visibly disturbed and made the President aware of how I felt. I caught his arm and clung to him. "The Negro people need all of the strength that you can give, Mr. President, in opening up opportunities for them," I told him.

He looked at me seriously for a few seconds, and then said, "Mrs. Bethune, I shall not fail you. I'll see [that] everything that can be done to open up these sections of the South to NYA training for Negroes will be done. Your people and all minorities shall have their chance."

Altogether, I suppose, we talked for 40 minutes, touching on such subjects as anti-Negro discrimination. . . . As I left, I shook his hand warmly and told him: "Mr. President, the common people feel they have someone in the White House who cares." The President smiled gratefully and waved a goodbye.

That was not the last time that I felt impelled to speak out strongly to the President on conditions confronting Negroes in the South. More than once I proposed pretty drastic steps to end the hideous discriminations and second-class citizenship which make the South a blot upon our democracy. But FDR usually demurred, pointing out that a New Reconstruction would have to keep pace with democratic progress on a national scale. He strove to bring the whole country into a unified understanding of freedom. He tried to hold the whole country together so that the whole might be one.

But President Roosevelt did not complete his work. Had he lived I am convinced that he would have launched new, bold offensives against bigotry and Jim Crow everywhere. But it would have been according to *his* plan.

Frequently I would ask him with some impatience why this couldn't be done at once or that done immediately. He would think awhile, and then say very carefully and patiently, "Mrs. Bethune, if we do that now, we'll hurt our program over there. We must do this thing stride by stride, but leaving no stone unturned."

FDR taught me much about practical politics and how important it is that we understand their meaning if we are to make progress in the political arena. My contact with him was one of the great experiences of my life.

He would say things that would remain with you for the rest of your life. Thus, one day, I think it was at a reception in 1940, he beckoned to me and opened up a conversation I shall always remember. "You know, Mrs. Bethune," he said, looking out of the window and yet speaking directly to me, "people like you and me are fighting, and must continue to fight, for the day when a man will be regarded as a man regardless of his race or faith or country. That day will come, but we must pass through perilous times before we realize it, and that's why it's so difficult today because that new idea is being born and many of us flinch from the thought of it. Justice must and will prevail."

That is why I believed so deeply in Franklin D. Roosevelt.

Roy Wilkins, A Black Assessment of the New Deal

The New Deal achieved a mixed record on matters of race. One black critic, John P. Davis, openly castigated FDR's programs as a "raw deal" for African Americans. But most blacks recognized that they had benefited to some extent from New Deal programs. In the following document, written in 1940, NAACP official Roy Wilkins (1901–1981) offers a balanced assessment of the New Deal, describing both successes and failures. He noted evidence of segregation and discrimination in agencies such as the Tennessee Valley Authority (TVA), Federal Housing Authority (FHA), and Civilian Conservation Corps (CCC). He reminded readers that FDR had consistently failed to support a bill to make lynching a federal crime. But he also noted that African Americans had been well served by the Works Progress Administration (WPA), Farm Security Administration (FSA), federal relief programs, the National Labor Relations Act (which established a right to collective bargaining), and the Fair Labor Standards Act (which set a minimum wage and maximum workweek of forty hours). Wilkins later served as executive director of the NAACP during the 1950s and 1960s.[*]

On the subject of the Negro, the Roosevelt record is spotty, as might be expected in an administration where so much power is in the hands of the southern wing of the Democratic Party. And yet Mr. Roosevelt, hobbled as he has been by the Dixie die-hards, has managed to include Negro citizens in practically every phase of the administration program. In this respect, no matter how far behind the ideal he may be, he is far ahead of any other Democratic president, and of recent Republican ones.

The best proof that Mr. Roosevelt has not catered always to the South and has insisted on carrying the Negro along with his program is to be found in the smearing, race-hating propaganda used against him in the 1936 campaign by southern white groups. Both he and Mrs. Roosevelt were targets of filthy mud-slinging simply because they did not see eye-to-eye with the South on the Negro.

This does not mean that the Roosevelt administration has done all that it could have done for the race. Its policies in many instances have done Negroes great injustice and have helped to build more secure walls of segregation.

On the anti-lynching bill Mr. Roosevelt has said not a mumbling word. His failure to endorse this legislation, to bring pressure to break the filibuster, is a black mark against him. It does no good to say that the White House could not pass down some word on this bill. The White House spoke on many bills. Mr. Roosevelt might have pressed the anti-lynching bill to a vote, especially during January and February 1938, when there was tremendous public opinion supporting the bill. His failure to act, or even speak, on the anti-lynching bill was the more glaring because, while mobs in America were visiting inhumanities upon Negroes, Mr. Roosevelt periodically was rebuking some foreign government for inhumanity, and enunciating high sentiments of liberty, tolerance, justice, etc.

To declare that the Roosevelt administration has tried to include the Negro in nearly every phase of its program for the people of the nation is not to ignore the instances where government policies have harmed the race.

At Boulder dam, for example, the administration continued the shameful policy begun by Hoover of forbidding Negroes to live in Boulder City, the government-built town. And in its own pet project, the TVA, the administration forbade Negroes to live in Norris, another government-built town at Norris dam.

Full credit must go to the administration for its program of low-cost housing, so sorely needed by low-income families. No one pretends that the American housing program is more than a beginning, but Negroes have shared in it in the most equitable manner. However, there were, outside the slum-clearance program, some damaging practices. The FHA, which insures mortgages for home buyers, has enforced a regulation which puts the power and approval of the government on ghetto life. No Negro family which sought a home outside the so-called "Negro" neighborhood could get a FHA-insured loan.

---

[*] [Roy Wilkins], "The Roosevelt Record," *Crisis* 47 (November 1940).

The vast program for youth, the CCC and the NYA, has included our young people, but in the CCC a justifiable complaint has been that Negro instructors, advisers, and reserve army officers were not appointed in any but the tiniest proportion.

There is little need to mention relief and the WPA. Mr. Roosevelt's critics concede what his administration has done in these two branches of his program by concentrating their attack upon the relief that the New Deal has given Negroes. In relief the government set the tone. That tone was so much higher than the city, the county, and state standards for Negroes in certain areas that, even though differentials existed, the net result was more than it would have been without government supervision. Collective bargaining and the Wages and Hours Act have aided Negro workers in private industry.

The farm program has not been ideally administered, but colored people have shared in the benefits. More than 50,000 families have been assisted by the Farm Security Administration.

Mr. Roosevelt had the courage to appoint a Negro to a federal judgeship, the first in the history of the country. His nominee was confirmed by a Democratic Senate without a murmur. Complaint has been made that in naming about a score of colored administrative assistants and advisers, Mr. Roosevelt has kept Negroes out of any real posts in the government. If it be true that Mr. Roosevelt has created Negro appendages to various bureaus, it cannot be denied that colored people know more about their government and have penetrated nearer to policy-making desks than ever before.

Heavily on the debit side is Mr. Roosevelt's approval of the War Department's notorious Jim Crow in the armed services.

[The] most important contribution of the Roosevelt administration to the age-old color line problem in America has been its doctrine that Negroes are a part of the country and must be considered in any program for the country as a whole. The inevitable discriminations notwithstanding, this thought has been driven home in thousands of communities by a thousand specific acts. For the first time in their lives, government has taken on meaning and substance for the Negro masses.

Asking Questions of the Documents

1. What prompted African Americans to explore radical political and economic alternatives such as Communism during the Great Depression? What did Joseph D. Bibb suggest "would stem this rising tide of Communism" among blacks? Is this what the New Deal accomplished?

2. Why did blacks support FDR? Was this the only reason they began to switch party allegiance to the Democrats in the mid-1930s?

3. What did Mary McLeod Bethune mean by "practical politics"? Should a politician immediately confront racial wrongs in American society or employ "practical politics" to slowly bring about change? Do you agree with Bethune's assessment of FDR? Why?

4. What were the major failures of the New Deal on matters of race? What were its major successes? What did Roy Wilkins think was the major benefit of the New Deal

for African Americans? Do you agree that the federal government provided a "New Deal" for African Americans during the 1930s? Why?

For Further Reading

Grant, Nancy L. *TVA and Black Americans: Planning for the Status Quo.* Philadelphia: Temple University Press, 1990.

Kelley, Robin D. G. *Hammer and Hoe: Alabama Communists during the Great Depression.* Chapel Hill, N.C.: University of North Carolina Press, 1990.

Kirby, John B. *Black Americans in the Roosevelt Era: Liberalism and Race.* Knoxville, Tenn.: University of Tennessee Press, 1980.

Naison, Mark. *Communists in Harlem during the Depression.* Urbana, Ill: University of Illinois Press, 1983.

Sitkoff, Harvard. *A New Deal for Blacks: The Emergence of Civil Rights as a National Issue.* New York: Oxford University Press, 1978.

Weiss, Nancy. *Farewell to the Party of Lincoln: Black Politics in the Age of F.D.R.* Princeton, N.J.: Princeton University Press, 1983.

Wolters, Raymond. *Negroes and the Great Depression: The Problem of Economic Recovery.* Westport, Conn.: Greenwood Press, 1970.

13

World War II:
Fighting on Two Fronts

On the eve of World War II, African Americans stood ready to consolidate the gains they had made over the previous decade and to press ahead for full equality. As the United States mobilized for war, blacks were presented with opportunities and new strategies for attacking racial injustice. The federal government's need for social harmony in the face of international conflict meant that Washington was more likely than ever to acquiesce to black demands for change. The March-on-Washington Movement (MOWM) in 1941 demonstrated the effectiveness of a new tactic—nonviolent direct action—and opened jobs in the nation's defense industries to blacks for the first time. When America finally entered the war, most African Americans agreed with Robert Vann of the *Pittsburgh Courier* that they should mount a "Double V" campaign—fighting fascism abroad while continuing to struggle against Jim Crow at home.

Having gained new opportunities to work in defense industries, hundreds of thousands of African Americans migrated during the war to port and industrial cities from Norfolk to Detroit to Oakland. But southern whites streamed into the same cities, bringing their racial attitudes with them. This led to frequent racial disturbances over jobs and housing in many urban centers during the war. In 1943 these tensions erupted into a full-scale race riot in Detroit. Smaller riots occurred in other cities.

Black soldiers fared no better. The armed forces remained segregated during the war. In addition, most black soldiers were trained at camps in the rural South, increasing the likelihood of racial tensions and discriminatory treatment, both on and off base.

The war spawned optimism and rising militancy among blacks. In addition to the success of the MOWM, the NAACP continued to challenge the color line, winning a judicial victory in 1944 against white primary elections in the U.S. Supreme Court. NAACP membership soared during the war, growing from 50,000 in 1940 to over 450,000 in 1946. Many of these new members were black soldiers. A new civil rights organization, the Congress of Racial Equality (CORE), was created in 1942. An interracial group, it pioneered sit-ins, picketing and other innovative tactics, and desegregated restaurants, movie theaters, and other public accommodations in a few northern cities. When the war ended in 1945, African Americans were ready for a full-scale assault on the walls of Jim Crow, confident that they would finally succeed.

A. Philip Randolph, The March-on-Washington Movement

The March-on-Washington Movement, the brainchild of black labor leader A. Philip Randolph (1889–1979), offered African Americans an opportunity to challenge their exclusion from defense industries and segregation within the military. Randolph, the founder of the Brotherhood of Sleeping Car Porters, was a well-respected activist for black rights. In the following summons, published in the May 1941 issue of the *Black Worker*, he called for a mass march on Washington by blacks to protest inequalities in the nation's defense effort and to pressure FDR for change. Six days before the scheduled march, FDR issued Executive Order 8802, which barred racial discrimination in the defense industries and set up the Fair Employment Practices Committee as an enforcement device. Willing to accept the partial victory, Randolph cancelled the march. But black leaders had learned the value of this technique. They would employ it again in another famous march on Washington twenty-two years later.[*]

Greetings:

We call upon you to fight for jobs in National Defense. We call upon you to struggle for the integration of Negroes in the armed forces, such as the Air Corps, Navy, Army and Marine Corps of the Nation.

We call upon you to demonstrate for the abolition of Jim-Crowism in all Government departments and defense employment.

This is an hour of crisis. It is a crisis of democracy. It is a crisis of minority groups. It is a crisis of Negro Americans.

What is this crisis?

To American Negroes, it is the denial of jobs in Government defense projects. It is racial discrimination in Government departments. It is widespread Jim-Crowism in the armed forces of the Nation.

While billions of the taxpayers' money are being spent for war weapons, Negro workers are finally being turned away from the gates of factories, mines and mills—being flatly told, "NOTHING DOING." Some employers refuse to give Negroes jobs when they are without "union cards," and some unions refuse to Negro workers union cards when they are "without jobs."

What shall we do?

What a dilemma!

What a runaround!

What a disgrace!

---

[*] A. Philip Randolph, "Call to Negro America 'To March on Washington for Jobs and Equal Participation in National Defense,' July 1, 1941," *Black Worker* 14 (May 1941).

What a blow below the belt!

'Though dark, doubtful and discouraging, all is not lost, all is not hopeless. 'Though battered and bruised, we are not beaten, broken, or bewildered.

Verily, the Negroes' deepest disappointments and direst defeats, their tragic trials and outrageous oppressions in these dreadful days of destruction and disaster to democracy and freedom, and the rights of minority peoples, and the dignity and independence of the human spirit, is the Negroes' greatest opportunity to rise to the highest heights of struggle for freedom and justice in Government, in industry, in labor unions, education, social service, religion and culture.

With faith and confidence of the Negro people in their own power for self-liberation, Negroes can break down the barriers of discrimination against employment in National Defense. Negroes can kill the deadly serpent of race hatred in the Army, Navy, Air and Marine Corps, and smash through and blast the Government, business and labor-union red tape to win the right to equal opportunity in vocational training and re-training in defense employment.

Most important and vital of all, Negroes, by the mobilization and coordination of their mass power, can cause PRESIDENT ROOSEVELT TO ISSUE AN EXECUTIVE ORDER ABOLISHING DISCRIMINATIONS IN ALL GOVERNMENT DEPARTMENTS, ARMY, NAVY, AIR CORPS AND NATIONAL DEFENSE JOBS.

Of course, the task is not easy. In very truth, it is big, tremendous and difficult.

It will cost money.

It will require sacrifice.

It will tax the Negroes' courage, determination and will to struggle. But we can, must and will triumph.

The Negroes' stake in national defense is big. It consists of jobs, thousands of jobs. It may represent millions, yes, hundreds of millions of dollars in wages. It consists of new industrial opportunities and hope. This is worth fighting for.

But to win our stakes, it will require an "all-out," bold and total effort and demonstration of colossal proportions.

Negroes can build a mammoth machine of mass action with a terrific and tremendous driving and striking power that can shatter and crush the evil fortress of race prejudice and hate, if they will only resolve to do so and never stop, until victory comes.

Dear fellow Negro Americans, be not dismayed in these terrible times. You possess power, great power. Our problem is to harness and hitch it up for action on the broadest, daring and most gigantic scale.

In this period of power politics, nothing counts but pressure, more pressure, and still more pressure, through the tactic and strategy of broad, organized, aggressive mass action behind the vital and important issues of the Negro. To this end, we propose that ten thousand Negroes MARCH ON WASHINGTON FOR JOBS IN NATIONAL DEFENSE AND EQUAL INTEGRATION IN THE FIGHTING FORCES OF THE UNITED STATES.

An "all-out" thundering march on Washington, ending in a monster and huge demonstration at Lincoln's Monument will shake up white America.

It will shake up official Washington.

It will give encouragement to our white friends to fight all the harder by our side, with us, for our righteous cause.

It will gain respect for the Negro people.

It will create a new sense of self-respect among Negroes.

But what of national unity?

We believe in national unity which recognizes equal opportunity of black and white citizens to jobs in national defense and the armed forces, and in all other institutions and endeavors in America. We condemn all dictatorships, Fascist, Nazi and Communist. We are loyal, patriotic Americans all.

But if American democracy will not defend its defenders; if American democracy will not protect its protectors; if American democracy will not give jobs to its toilers because of race or color; if American democracy will not insure equality of opportunity, freedom and justice to its citizens, black and white, it is a hollow mockery and belies the principles for which it is supposed to stand.

To the hard, difficult and trying problem of securing equal participation in national defense, we summon all Negro Americans to march on Washington. We summon Negro Americans to form committees in various cities to recruit and register marchers and raise funds through the sale of buttons and other legitimate means for the expenses of marchers to Washington by buses, train, private automobiles, trucks, and on foot.

We summon Negro Americans to stage marches on their City Halls and Councils in their respective cities and urge them to memorialize the President to issue an executive order to abolish discrimination in the Government and national defense.

However, we sternly counsel against violence and ill-considered and intemperate action and the abuse of power. Mass power, like physical power, when misdirected is more harmful that helpful.

We summon you to mass action that is orderly and lawful, but aggressive and militant, for justice, equality and freedom.

Crispus Attucks marched and died as a martyr for American independence. Nat Turner, Denmark Vesey, Gabriel Prosser, Harriet Tubman and Frederick Douglass fought, bled and died for the emancipation of Negro slaves and the preservation of American democracy.

Today, we call upon President Roosevelt, a great humanitarian and idealist, to follow in the footsteps of his noble and illustrious predecessor and take the second decisive step in this world and national emergency and free American Negro citizens of the stigma, humiliation and insult of discrimination and Jim-Crowism in Government departments and national defense.

The Federal Government cannot with clear conscience call upon private industry and labor unions to abolish discrimination based on race and color as long as it practices discrimination itself against Negro Americans.

NEGROES' COMMITTEE TO MARCH ON WASHINGTON
FOR EQUAL PARTICIPATION IN NATIONAL DEFENSE.

Walter White, Race Relations in Wartime Detroit

Just as in World War I, the Second World War saw a flood of African Americans move to cities; but this time the migration was more broadly located throughout the nation. This so-called Second Migration would continue until 1970, carrying an additional one and a half million blacks into urban America each decade. The initial stimulus for this Second Migration was the opportunity to work in defense industries, coupled with the growing mechanization of cotton agriculture in the South, which lessened the need for black farmworkers. The influx of blacks into urban centers brought them into direct competition with older residents and newer white migrants (mostly from the South) for housing and employment. On 20 June 1943, black-white tensions erupted into a bloody race riot in Detroit, one of the leading destinations of migrants from the South. Only the intervention of federal troops restored order in the "Motor City." When the smoke cleared, thirty-four people lay dead and two million dollars in property had been destroyed. Walter White (1893–1955), the executive director of the NAACP from 1931 until his death, investigated the riot and wrote the following analysis of its causes, providing a window on race relations in wartime Detroit. By the end of the year, another 241 similar disturbances had broken out in cities throughout the nation.[*]

In 1916 there were 8,000 Negroes in Detroit's population of 536,650. In 1925 the number of Negroes in Detroit had been multiplied by ten to a total of 85,000. In 1940, the total had jumped to 149,119. In June 1943, between 190,000 and 200,000 lived in the Motor City.

According to the War Manpower Commission, approximately 500,000 in-migrants moved to Detroit between June 1940 and June 1943. Because of discrimination against employment of Negroes in industry, the overwhelming majority—between 40,000 and 50,000—of the approximately 50,000 Negroes who went to Detroit in this three-year period moved there during the fifteen months prior to the race riot of June 1943. According to Governor Harry S. Kelly, of Michigan, a total of 345,000 persons moved into Detroit during the same fifteen-month period. There was comparatively little out-migration as industry called for more and more workers in one of the tightest labor markets in the United States. The War Manpower Commission failed almost completely to enforce its edict that no in-migration be permitted into any industrial area until all available local labor was utilized. Thus a huge reservoir of Negro labor existed in

---

[*] Walter White, "What Caused the Detroit Riots?," in *What Caused the Detroit Riots?* (New York: NAACP, 1943).

Detroit, crowded into highly-congested slum areas. But they did have housing of a sort and this labor was already in Detroit.

[Housing]

The coming of white workers recruited chiefly in the South not only gravely complicated the housing, transportation, educational and recreational facilities of Detroit, but they brought with them traditional prejudices of Mississippi, Arkansas, Louisiana, and other Deep South states against the Negro. . . . The overwhelming majority retained and even increased their hostility to Negroes. This was particularly noticeable when Negroes were forced by sheer necessity to purchase homes outside the so-called Negro areas. For years preceding the riot, there had been mob attacks . . . upon the homes of Negroes. In some instances there had been police connivance in these attacks. In practically no case had there been arrests of whites who had stoned or bombed the houses of Negroes. During July 1941, there had been an epidemic of riots, allegedly by Polish youths, which had terrorized colored residents in Detroit. . . . Homes of Negroes on . . . streets close to but outside of the so-called Negro areas were attacked by mobs with no police interference.

Detroit's 200,000 Negroes are today largely packed into two segregated areas. . . . In addition to these two wholly Negro areas, there are scattered locations throughout Detroit of mixed occupancy in which, significantly, there was during the riot less friction than in any other area. The desperate scarcity of housing for whites, however, limited Negroes in finding places to live outside of the Negro areas.

The Detroit newspapers have contained for months many advertisements offering rewards for housing of any nature or quality for whites. Meantime, but little public housing was created to meet the tragic need for housing for both whites and Negroes in Detroit. Even this was characterized by shameless vacillation and weakness in Washington, which only added fuel to the flames of racial tension in Detroit. The notorious riots revolving about the question of who should occupy the Sojourner Truth Housing Project in February 1942 are an example of this. These riots resulted when fascist elements, emboldened by the vacillation of the National Housing Administration, which reversed itself several times on Negro occupancy, joined with real estate interests to bring to a head the mob violence which led to the smashing of the furniture and the beating of Negro tenants attempting to move into the project.

Previously, the Public Works Administration had built the Brewster Project of 701 units in 1938, to which the United States Housing Authority has added the Brewster addition of 240 units completed in 1940 and 1941. All these provided housing for only about 3,000 Negroes, however.

From all other public housing projects erected in Detroit, Negroes were totally excluded, although Negroes and whites had lived together in complete amity in some of the areas on which these public housing projects, erected through the taxation of Negro as well as white Americans, were built.

Equally contributory to the explosion which was to come has been the attitude of the Detroit Real Estate Association. Mention has already been made of the opposition of the real estate interests to public housing in Detroit. Their contention was that such housing as Detroit needed should be created by private interests. By the time private interests were ready to begin erections of homes for the greatly augmented population of wartime Detroit, priorities on building materials were put into effect. Meanwhile, every train, bus, or other public conveyance entering Detroit disgorged an ever increasing torrent of men, women, and children demanding places to live while they earned the war wages Detroit factories were paying. Overcrowding, lack of sanitation, a mounting disease rate resulting in absenteeism and a severe tax on the hospital and clinical facilities of Detroit were bad enough among whites. Among Negroes it resulted in a scandalous condition.

Jobs

The Ku Klux Klan . . . has had its numbers and agents industriously organizing anti-Negro sentiment among those with racial prejudice against the Negro in several of the Detroit plants. "Strikes" against the employment or promotion of Negroes can be traced to these agitators in the Dodge Truck Plant, the Hudson Arsenal, the Packard Plant, and other plants. The Klan has been active in Detroit as far back as the early 20's. Early in the 20's it almost succeeded in electing a Mayor of Detroit. It was shortly after this disaster was averted that a series of attacks upon the homes of Negroes took place, culminating in . . . 1925. Following this . . . , the Klan in Detroit dropped out of existence, along with its demise in other parts of the country. But agencies with similar methods and ideologies succeeded it.

Though short-lived, a vicious successor was the notorious Black Legion, which . . . began as an offshoot of the Ku Klux Klan. Originally conceived to secure and insure jobs for white Southerners, the organization soon expanded its fields of activity to include putting down by violence, if necessary, all movements the Black Legion decided were "alien" or "un-American." After the conviction of its leader, [a] former Klanman, for the murder of . . . a Detroit Catholic, the 4-year-old, crime-besmirched Black Legion virtually expired, but was followed quickly by others of similar purpose and method, among them the National Workers League (held chiefly responsible for the Sojourner Truth riot . . .), which is reputedly financed in part by Nazi Bund and Silver Shirt money.

Gerald L. K. Smith, former assistant and protege of the late Huey Long, has been long active in stirring up discord and dissension in the Detroit area. His activities in America First, anti-union, and other similar groups have been greatly increased in effectiveness by his also being a Southerner trained in the art of demagogy by Huey Long, and provided with a fertile field due to the predominantly Southern white psychology of Detroit. Active also have been the followers of Father [Charles] Coughlin, some Polish and Italian Catholic priests and laymen, and others who, wittingly or otherwise, have utilized anti-Negro sentiment for selfish and sometimes sinister objectives in much the same manner that the Nazis utilized anti-Semitism in Germany during the late 20's. Ingrained or stimulated prejudice against the Negro has been used as much against organized labor as it has been against the Negro. . . . It has been frequently charged . . . that some of the employers have financed or contributed heavily to some of the organizations which have organized and capitalized upon race prejudice as a means of checking the organization of workers in Detroit plants. . . .

Law Enforcement Agencies

Politically minded public officials have winked at the activities of agencies like the Klan, the Black Legion, the National Workers League, the followers of Father Coughlin and other similar groups. During the 30's especially when there was keen competition for jobs because of the depression, Southern whites sought and secured jobs on the police force of Detroit and in the courts. There was a period of years when cold-blooded killings of Negroes by policemen were a constant source of bitterness among Negroes. Eventually, protest by such organizations as the Detroit branch of the NAACP and other Negro and inter-racial groups led to a diminution and eventually a practical cessation of such killings. But a residue of distrust of the police remained. When the riot of June 1943 broke forth, this suspicion of police by Negroes was more than justified. . . .

The willful inefficiency of the Detroit police in its handling of the riot is one of the most disgraceful episodes in American history. When the riot broke out on Sunday night, June 20, following a dispute between a white and Negro motorist on the Belle Isle Bridge, an efficient police force armed with night sticks and fire hoses could have broken up the rioting . . . and broken the back of the insurrection, had the police been determined to do so. Instead, the police did little or nothing. . . .

The anti-Negro motivation of the Detroit police department is further illustrated by these facts and figures. It has already been pointed out that the Negro population of Detroit at the time of the riot was 200,000 or less, out of a total population of more than 2,000,000. The inevitable riot was the product of anti-Negro forces which had been allowed to operate without check or hindrance by the police over a period of many years. But 29 of the 35 persons who died during the riot were Negroes. An overwhelming majority of the more than 600 injured were Negroes. Of the 1,832 persons arrested for rioting, more than 85 percent were Negroes. And this in the face of the indisputable fact that the aggressors over a period of years were not Negroes but whites.

A Black Soldier in a Jim Crow Army

Some one million African-American men and women served in the U.S. armed forces during World War II. Nearly half of these saw action overseas in either the European or Pacific theaters. Although they continued to fight in segregated units, blacks made some significant advancements during the war, gaining admission to the Marine Corps and Air Corps and breaking through other military assignment ceilings. But most experienced incidents of racial mistreatment—both from civilians and fellow soldiers—that reminded them of the importance of the "Double V" campaign. This is made clear in the following letter from an anonymous black soldier to Truman K. Gibson, the civilian aide to the secretary of war. The author clearly intended that the letter would be published and reach a wider African-American audience.

November 5, 1943

Truman K. Gibson, Jr.
Civilian Aide to the Secretary of War
Washington, D.C.

Dear Mr. Gibson:

And I fight—for Democracy?

Upon reading the title of this article the average reader would assume that I am a member of the armed forces in the U.S.A. In your assumption, reader, you are definitely correct. I was selected by the President and citizens, to fight for a "non-existing Democracy." I am one soldier who waited to be drafted. I didn't volunteer out. I am learning to fight to protect whatever cause for which the Allies are fighting. I am forced to learn to be ready to kill or be killed—for "Democracy." When fighting time arrives I will fight for __?

I learned early in life that for the Negro there is no Democracy. Of course I know the principles set forth in the Amendments and the Bill of Rights. I learned that I knew nothing of the operation of a true democratic form of government. I found that a Negro in civilian life has [a] very tough time with segregation in public places and discrimination in industry. I knew this and I thought that white people would react differently toward a colored soldier.

I had heard and read of the cruel treatment given colored soldiers and somehow, even among existing conditions of civilian life, I couldn't understand how white people could be so down on one who wears the uniform of the fighting forces of their country. From civilian life I was drafted and now I prepare to fight for——The continuation of discriminatory practices against me and my people.

I have long known that the fighting forces are composed of two divisions. Namely, a white division composed of Germans, Jews, Italians, Dutch and all white people of the remaining countries (The question is: Are they loyal?). A Negro division composed of American Negroes and all dark skin people. The American Negro has fought in every war since the Revolutionary War. There can be no question as to his loyalty. He is put into a division composed of the members of his race not because of his educational qualities, his fighting abilities or his inability to live with others, but he's put into a separate division because of the color of his skin.

This is serious since the Negroes are trained to a large extent in Southern States whose white civilians are more drastic in showing their dislike than in Northern white people.

* "A Loyal Negro Soldier" to Truman K. Gibson, Jr., 5 November 1943, Civilian Aide to the Secretary of War Subject File, 1940-1947, Record Group 107, National Archives, Washington, D.C.

I prayed that I'd be sent to a camp in my home state or that I'd be sent to some camp in a Northern State. My prayers weren't answered and I find myself at this outpost of civilization. I never wanted to be within twenty hundred miles of Alexandria, Louisiana. I am here and I can do nothing to improve my condition. Nevertheless, I prepare to fight for a country where I am denied the rights of being a full-fledged citizen.

A few weeks after my arrival at this camp, I went to a post exchange on my regimental area. I knew that each area has an exchange but I thought that I could make my purchase at any of them. Upon entering I could feel the place grow cold. All conversation ceased. It was then that I noticed that all the soldiers and the saleswomen were white. Not to be outdone I approached the counter and was told (even before asking for the article) that, "Negroes are not served here. This post exchange is for white soldiers. You have one near your regiment. Buy what you want there."

My answer to these abrupt and rudely made statements was in the form of a question—"I thought that post exchanges are for soldiers regardless of color, am I right?"

I left this post exchange and returned to my regimental area. I know that these saleswomen knew not the way of a true democracy.

As long as I am a soldier I fight for a mock Democracy. I was called to report to the camp hospital for an eye examination last week. I was surprised to find the waiting room full of Negro and white soldiers who were sharing the same seats and reading the same newspapers. I was shocked. I didn't believe that the camp hospital could be so free from segregation while the camp itself was built on prejudice.

My second surprise came when registering. Each person filled out a blank and all blanks were placed in the same basket in order of the entrance regardless of the race of the entree. I was just beginning to feel proud of the hospital when a list of names were called off and my name was last on the list. I found myself in line of sixteen (16) men, seven of whom were white. The white men gradually fell out of line and the Negroes found themselves continually waiting . . . waiting for the white soldiers to finish their examinations.

It wouldn't have been noticed had not the sergeant in charge been contented to carry only those white soldiers in the line, but he proceeded to bring more from the waiting room. When I could stand this no longer I protested.

Result: We were immediately examined and allowed to return to our regimental area. I was asked a few days later, "Don't you want to fight for the U.S.A. and its policies?"

I am a soldier; I made no answer, but deep down inside I knew when I faced America's enemies I will fight for the protection of my loved ones at home.

Listen, Negro America, I am writing this article believing that it will act as a stimulant. You need awakening. Many of you have come to realize that your race is fighting on the battlefields of the world, but do you know why they fight? I can answer this question.

The right on the battlefield is for your existence, not for Democracy. It is upon you that each soldier depends. In my fight my thoughts will invariably return to you who can fight for Democracy. You must do this for the soldiers because Democracy will be, and Democracy must, must be won at home—not on battlefields but through your bringing pressure to bear on Congress.

A Loyal Negro Soldier

Asking Questions of the Documents

1. What were the specific goals of the March-on-Washington Movement? How did A. Philip Randolph hope that FDR would implement these goals? What tactical measure did Randolph recommend to achieve these goals? Why did he think they were achievable?

2. What were the causes of the Detroit riot of 1943? To what extent was the riot a product of wartime factors? To what extent was it a product of tensions building long before the war began? Who bears the greatest responsibility for the riot: white workers, racist organizations, industrialists, the police, public officials, the African-American community, or the federal government?

3. What conditions and treatment were faced by black soldiers in the Jim Crow army during World War II? How did the letter by "A Loyal Negro Soldier" illustrate a "Double V" campaign?

For Further Reading

Capeci, Dominic J., Jr. *Race Relations in Wartime Detroit: The Sojourner Truth Housing Controversy of 1942*. Philadelphia: Temple University Press, 1984.

_____and Martha Wilkerson. *Layered Violence: The Detroit Rioters of 1943*. Jackson, Miss.: University Press of Mississippi, 1991.

Dalfiume, Richard M. *Desegregation of the U.S. Armed Forces: Fighting on Two Fronts, 1939–1953*. Columbia, Mo.: University of Missouri Press, 1969.

_____, "The 'Forgotten Years' of the Negro Revolution." *Journal of American History* 55 (June 1968): 90–106.

Garfinkel, Herbert. *When Negroes March: The March on Washington Movement in the Organizational Politics of FEPC*. New York: Atheneum, 1959.

Jakeman, Robert J. *The Divided Skies: Establishing Segregated Flight Training at Tuskegee, Alabama, 1934–1942*. Tuscaloosa, Ala.: University of Alabama Press, 1992.

Wynn, Neal A. *The Afro–American and the Second World War*. New York: Holmes & Meier, 1975.

14

The School Segregation Cases

African Americans emerged from World War II ready to launch a full-scale assault on Jim Crow and convinced that conditions were ripe for change. Having helped to defeat fascism abroad, they were determined to end racial injustice at home. Many barriers began to fall. In 1948 President Harry S Truman ordered the desegregation of the U.S. armed forces. Between 1945 and 1950, blacks broke the color line in professional sports as the National Football League, major-league baseball, and the National Basketball Association all signed African-American athletes.

The major challenge of the postwar years was a legal campaign by the NAACP against segregated public education, which more than anything else symbolized the inequalities of Jim Crow. A series of suits before 1950 forced improvements in the condition of black schools. Then in 1950, the NAACP initiated a direct challenge to the constitutionality of segregated public education. In their decision in the case of *Brown v. The Board of Education of Topeka* (1954), the U.S. Supreme Court agreed that segregated education was "inherently unequal" and must be ended. But as the white South resisted implementation of the decision, many African Americans looked to other strategies in pursuit of their civil rights.

Charles Hamilton Houston, Launching the Campaign

The NAACP's campaign against segregated public education was part of a two-phase process begun before World War II. During the first phase, started in 1935, the NAACP pressed state and federal courts to end inequalities between black and white public schools in the South. The second phase, initiated in 1950, directly challenged the constitutionality of segregated public education. The architect of this plan was Charles Hamilton Houston (1895–1950), the NAACP's chief attorney and the former dean of Howard University Law School. Houston, who viewed the law as a tool for "social engineering," especially against Jim Crow, had used his law school to train a cadre of talented, well-trained, and highly dedicated black lawyers. One of these, Thurgood Marshall (1908–1993), became his protege and after 1938 was the chief attorney for the school campaign. In the following document, Houston launches the NAACP's campaign and explains its objectives. Marshall, of course, eventually convinced the U.S. Supreme Court to end school segregation and in 1967 became the first black named to the Court.[*]

The National Association for the Advancement of Colored People is launching an active campaign against race discrimination in public education. The campaign will reach all levels of public education from the nursery school through the university. The ultimate objective of the association is the abolition of all forms of segregation in public education, whether in the admission of students, the appointment or advancement of teachers, or administrative control. The association will resist any attempt to extend segregated schools. Where possible it will attack segregation in schools. Where segregation is so firmly entrenched by law that a frontal attack cannot be made, the association will throw its immediate force toward bringing Negro schools up to an absolute equality with white schools. If the white South insists upon its separate schools, it must not squeeze the Negro schools to pay for them.

It is not the purpose or the function of the national office of the N.A.A.C.P. to force a school fight upon any community. Its function is primarily to expose the rotten conditions of segregation to point out the evil consequences of discrimination and injustice to both Negroes and whites, and to map out ways and means by which these evils may be corrected. The decision for action rests with the local community itself. If the local community decides to act and asks the N.A.A.C.P. for aid, the N.A.A.C.P. stands ready with advice and assistance.

The N.A.A.C.P. proposes to use every legitimate means at its disposal to accomplish actual equality of educational opportunity for Negroes. A legislative program is being formulated. Court action has already begun in Maryland to compel the University of Maryland to admit a qualified Negro boy to the law school of the university. Court action is imminent in Virginia to compel the University of Virginia to admit a qualified Negro girl in the graduate department of that university. Activity in politics will be fostered due to the political set-up of and control over public school systems. The press and the public forum will be enlisted to explain to the public the issues involved and to make both whites and Negroes realize the blight which inferior education throws over them, their children and their communities.

---

[*] Charles Houston, "Educational Inequalities Must Go!," *Crisis* 42 (October 1935).

Septima Clark, Black Schools in the Jim Crow South

The NAACP campaign against segregated schools was motivated by the deplorable condition of public education for African Americans in the South. In the following document, Septima Clark (1898–1987) describes the horrible inequalities she witnessed while teaching in a black school on Johns Island, South Carolina, as a young woman. Fired in 1956 from a position in the nearby Charleston school system for being a member of the NAACP, she devoted the remainder of her life to the fight for civil rights.[*]

Here I was, a high-school graduate, eighteen years old, principal in a two-teacher school with 132 pupils ranging from beginners to eighth graders, with no teaching experience, a schoolhouse constructed of boards running up and down, with no slats in the cracks, and a fireplace at one end of the room that cooked the pupils immediately in front of it but allowed those in the rear to shiver and freeze on their uncomfortable, hard, back-breaking benches. . . .

I had the older children, roughly the fifth, sixth, seventh and eighth grades. The other teacher had those through the fourth. But my pupils in the seventh and eighth grades . . . were most erratic in their attendance, for they were old enough to work in the fields. They didn't come in until the cotton had been picked, and often it was Christmas and sometimes even January before all the cotton was gleaned. To add to this difficulty, most of the children had to stop school in early spring to begin preparing the fields for the new crop. Naturally, the attendance varied greatly from day to day.

We tried as best we could to classify these children. But it was difficult. Some subjects I was able to teach most of them at the same time, and so was the other teacher; we could make better time that way. But there were subjects that required almost individual teaching. Another problem was the lack of textbooks. There were so few, and what we had were not uniform. In the spelling classes, I remember, I often wrote out lists of words to be studied. . . .

In those days the state financed the schools, but sometimes the counties provided small supplements and Charleston County was one of them. Soon I was getting a supplement of five dollars, which made my salary $35 a month. But right across from me—it happened that the white school and Negro school in this community were not far apart—was the white teacher getting $85 a month and teaching three—yes, three—pupils.

It wasn't fair, of course; it was the rankest discrimination.

---

[*] Septima Clark, *Echo in My Soul* (New York: E. P. Dutton & Company, 1962).

The Argument in *Brown v. Board of Education*

After thoroughly documenting the condition of black public schools in the South, the NAACP challenged educational inequality in the region in a series of cases before the U.S. Supreme Court between 1935 and 1950. By the latter date, the Court held that separate schools for blacks and whites must be substantially equal. The NAACP then directly contested the constitutionality of segregated education. They pressed five cases challenging Jim Crow schools through the federal courts, eventually bringing the issue before the Supreme Court in *Brown v. The Board of Education of Topeka*. Arguing from constitutional principle, as well as social science evidence demonstrating the damaging effects of segregation on African-American children, Thurgood Marshall and a team of NAACP lawyers pressed the Court to end segregated public education. The following document is a summary of their constitutional argument in *Brown*. In a unanimous 1954 decision, the Court held that separate schools were "inherently unequal" and must be desegregated, overturning *Plessy v. Ferguson* and nearly six decades of constitutional support for the Jim Crow system.*

These cases consolidated for argument before this Court present in different factual contexts essentially the same ultimate legal questions.

The substantive question common to all is whether a state can, consistently with the Constitution, exclude children, solely on the ground that they are Negroes, from public schools which otherwise they would be qualified to attend. It is the thesis of this brief, submitted on behalf of the excluded children, that the answer to the question is in the negative: the Fourteenth Amendment prevents states from according differential treatment to American children on the basis of their color or race. Both the legal precedents and the judicial theories, . . . and the evidence concerning the intent of the framers of the Fourteenth Amendment and the understanding of Congress and the ratifying states, . . . support this proposition.

Denying this thesis, the school authorities, relying in part on language originating in this Court's opinion in *Plessy v. Ferguson*, . . . urge that exclusion of Negroes, *qua* Negroes, from designated public schools is permissible when the excluded children are afforded admittance to other schools especially reserved for Negroes, *qua* Negroes, if such schools are equal.

The procedural question common to all the cases is the role to be played, and the time-table to be followed, by this Court and the lower courts in directing an end to the

* NAACP Legal Defense and Education Fund, Inc., "Summary of Argument," in the Supreme Court of the United States, *Brown v. Board of Education of Topeka*, 347 US 483 (1954).

challenged exclusion, in the event that this Court determines, with the respect to the substantive question, that exclusion of Negroes, *qua* Negroes, from public schools contravenes the Constitution.

The importance to American democracy of the substantive question can hardly be overstated. The question is whether a nation founded on the proposition that "all men are created equal" is honoring its commitments to grant "due process of law" and "the equal protection of the laws" to all within its borders when it, or one of its constituent states, confers or denies benefits on the basis of color or race.

1. Distinctions drawn by state authorities on the basis of color or race violate the Fourteenth Amendment. . . . This has been held to be true even as to the conduct of educational institutions. . . . Whatever other purposes the Fourteenth Amendment may have had, it is indisputable that its primary purpose was to complete the emancipation provided by the Thirteenth Amendment by ensuring to the Negro equality before the law. . . .

2. Even if the Fourteenth Amendment did not *per se* invalidate racial distinctions as a matter of law, the racial segregation challenged in the instant cases would run afoul of the conventional test established for application of the equal protection clause because the racial classifications here have no reasonable relation to any legislative purpose. . . .

3. Appraisal of the facts requires rejection of the contention of the school authorities. The educational detriment involved in racially constricting a student's associations has already been recognized by this Court. . . .

4. The argument that the requirements of the Fourteenth Amendment are met by providing alternative schools rests, finally, on reiteration of the separate but equal doctrine enunciated in *Plessy v. Ferguson*. Were these ordinary cases, it might be enough to say that the *Plessy* case can be distinguished—that it involved only segregation in transportation. But these are not ordinary cases, and in deference to their importance it seems more fitting to meet the *Plessy* doctrine head-on and to declare that doctrine erroneous.

Candor requires recognition that the plain purpose and effect of segregated education is to perpetuate an inferior status for Negroes which is America's sorry heritage from slavery. But the primary purpose of the Fourteenth Amendment was to deprive the states of *all* power to perpetuate such a caste system.

5. The . . . questions propounded by this Court requested enlightenment as to whether the Congress which submitted, and the state legislatures and conventions which ratified, the Fourteenth Amendment contemplated or understood that it would prohibit segregation in public schools, either of its own force or through subsequent legislative or judicial action. The evidence, both in Congress and in the legislatures of the ratifying states, reflects the substantial intent of the Amendment's proponents and the substantial understanding of its opponents that the Fourteenth Amendment would, of its own force, proscribe all forms of state-imposed racial distinctions, thus necessarily including all racial segregation in public education.

The Fourteenth Amendment was actually the culmination of the determined efforts of the Radical Republican majority in Congress to incorporate into our fundamental law the well-defined equalitarian principle of complete equality for all without regard to race or color. The debates in the 39th Congress and succeeding Congresses clearly reveal the intention that the Fourteenth Amendment would work a revolutionary change in our state-federal relationship by denying to the states the power to distinguish on the basis of race.

The Civil Rights Bill of 1866, as originally proposed, possessed scope sufficiently broad in the opinion of many Congressmen to entirely destroy all state legislation based on race. A great majority of the Republican Radicals—who later formulated the Fourteenth Amendment—understood and intended that the Bill would prohibit segregated schools. Opponents of the measure shared this understanding. The scope of this legislation was narrowed because it was known that the Fourteenth Amendment was in process of preparation and would itself have scope exceeding that of the original draft of the Civil Rights Bill.

6. The evidence makes clear that it was the intent of the proponents of the Fourteenth Amendment, and the substantial understanding of its opponents, that it would, of its own force, prohibit all state action predicated upon race or color. The intention of the framers with respect to any specific example of caste state action—in the instant cases, segregated education—cannot be determined solely on the basis of a tabulation of contemporaneous statements mentioning the specific practice. The framers were formulating a constitutional provision setting broad standards for determining the relationship of the state to the individual. In the nature of things they could not list all the specific categories of existing and prospective state activity which were to come within the constitutional prohibitions. The broad general purpose of the Amendment—obliterations of race and color distinctions—is clearly established by the evidence. So far as there was consideration of the Amendment's impact upon the undeveloped educational systems then existing, both proponents and opponents of the Amendment understood that it would proscribe all racial segregation in public education.

7. While the Amendment conferred upon Congress the power to enforce its prohibitions, members of the 39th Congress and those of subsequent Congresses made it clear that the framers understood and intended that the Fourteenth Amendment was self-executing and particularly pointed out that the federal judiciary had authority to enforce its prohibitions without Congressional implementation.

8. The evidence as to the understanding of the states is equally convincing. Each of the eleven states that had seceded from the Union ratified the Amendment, and concurrently eliminated racial distinctions from its laws, and adopted a constitution free of requirement or specific authorization of segregated schools. Many rejected proposals for segregated schools, and none enacted a school segregation law until after readmission. The significance of these facts is manifest from the consideration that ten of these states, which were required, as a condition of readmission, to ratify the Amendment and to modify their constitutions and laws in conformity therewith, considered that the Amendment required them to remove all racial distinctions from their existing and prospective laws, including those pertaining to public education.

Twenty-two of the twenty-six Union states also ratified the Amendment. Although unfettered by Congressional surveillance, the overwhelming majority of the Union states acted with an understanding that it prohibited racially segregated schools and necessitated conformity of their school laws to secure consistency with that understanding.

9. In short, the historical evidence fully sustains this Court's conclusion in [a previous case] that the Fourteenth Amendment was designed to take from the states all power to enforce caste or class distinctions.

Elizabeth Eckford, The First Day of School in Little Rock

The U.S. Supreme Court ordered that the *Brown* decision be implemented "with all deliberate speed." The upper South began to draft and implement desegregation plans. But the lower South embarked on a campaign of "massive resistance" to preserve segregated schools. State legislatures passed hundreds of laws designed to circumvent the ruling—closing schools faced with desegregation orders, allowing white children to tranfer from integrated schools, providing state funding for all-white private schools, and targeting the NAACP as a subversive organization. In Little Rock, Arkansas, resistance to integration provoked a direct federal response. When local school officials moved to comply in 1957, Governor Orval Faubus blocked desegregation by deploying the Arkansas National Guard to keep out nine black students. One of those students, Elizabeth Eckford, recounts her experience on that first day of school in the following document. After she and her fellow students were denied entry to Central High School, President Dwight D. Eisenhower ordered in the 101st Airborne Division to preserve order and enforce the desegregation plan. Despite this localized success, integration of public education continued to move slowly throughout most of the lower South.[*]

I was about the first one up. While pressing my black-and-white dress—I had made it to wear on the first day of school—my little brother turned on the TV set. They started telling about a large crowd gathered at the school. The man on TV said he wondered if we were going to show up that morning. . . .

Before I left home Mother called us into the living room. She said we should have a word of prayer. Then I caught the bus and got off a block from the school. I saw a large crowd of people standing across the street from the soldiers guarding Central. As I walked on, the crowd suddenly got very quiet. Superintendent Blossom told us to enter by the front door. I looked at all the people and thought, "Maybe I will be safer if I walk down the block to the front entrance behind the guards."

---

[*] Elizabeth Eckford, "The First Day: Little Rock, 1957," in *Growing Up Southern: Southern Exposure Looks at Childhood, Then and Now*, ed. Chris Mayfield (New York: Random House, 1981).

At the corner I tried to pass through the long line of guards around the school so as to enter the grounds behind them. One of the guards pointed across the street. So I pointed in the same direction and asked whether he meant for me to cross the street and walk down. He nodded "yes." So, I walked across the street conscious of the crowd that stood there, but they moved away from me.

For a moment all I could hear was the shuffling of their feet. Then someone shouted, "Here she comes, get ready!" I moved away from the crowd on the sidewalk and into the street. If the mob came at me I could then cross back over so the guards could protect me.

The crowd moved in closer and then began to follow me, calling me names. I still wasn't afraid. Just a little bit nervous. Then my knees started to shake all of a sudden and I wondered if I could make it to the center entrance a block away. It was the longest block I ever walked in my whole life.

Even so, I still wasn't too scared because all the time I kept thinking that the guards would protect me.

When I got in front of the school, I went up to a guard again. But this time he just looked straight ahead and didn't move to let me pass him. I didn't know what to do. Then I looked and saw that the path leading to the front entrance was a little further ahead. So I walked until I was right in front of the path to the front door.

I stood looking at the school—it looked so big! Just then the guards let some white students through.

The crowd was quiet. I guess they were waiting to see what was going to happen. When I was able to steady my knees, I walked up to the guard who had let the white students in. He too didn't move. When I tried to squeeze past him, he raised his bayonet and then the other guards moved in and they raised their bayonets.

They glared at me with a mean look and I was very frightened and didn't know what to do. I turned around and the crowd came toward me.

They moved closer and closer. Somebody started yelling, "Lynch her! Lynch her!"

I tried to see a friendly face somewhere in the mob—someone who maybe would help. I looked into the face of an old woman and it seemed a kind face, but when I looked at her again she spat on me.

They came closer, shouting, "No nigger bitch is going to get in our school! Get out of here."

I turned back to the guards but their faces told me I wouldn't get any help from them. Then I looked down the block and saw a bench at the bus stop. "If I can only get there I will be safe." I don't know why the bench seemed a safe place to me, but I started walking toward it. I tried to close my mind to what they were shouting, and kept saying to myself, "If I can only make it to the bench I will be safe."

When I finally got there, I don't think I could have gone another step. I sat down and the mob crowded up and began shouting all over again. Someone hollered, "Drag her over to this tree! Let's take care of that nigger." Just then a white man sat down beside me, put his arm around me and patted my shoulder.

Asking Questions of the Documents

1. What were the objectives of the NAACP's campaign against racial discrimination in segregated public education? What strategies did they employ to achieve those objectives? How did the NAACP attempt to convince observers that they were not "outside agitators" stirring up fights over educational inequalities in local communities?

2. Describe the deplorable conditions in public education for African Americans in the Jim Crow South.

3. What constitutional question was involved in the *Brown* case? What formed the basis of the NAACP's argument? What formed the basis of their opponents' argument? How did the NAACP argue that segregated public education violated the Fourteenth Amendment?

4. How did southern whites react to attempts to implement the *Brown* decision? How do you think that Elizabeth Eckford (and her eight black fellow students) felt toward whites after her experience on the first day of school in 1957 at Central High School in Little Rock? Why?

For Further Reading

Bartley, Numan V. *The Rise of Massive Resistance: Race and Politics in the South during the 1950s.* Baton Rouge, La.: Louisiana State University Press, 1969.

Burk, Robert F. *The Eisenhower Administration and Black Civil Rights.* Knoxville, Tenn.: University of Tennessee Press, 1984.

Kluger, Richard. *Simple Justice: The History of Brown v. Board of Education and Black America's Struggle for Equality.* New York: Alfred A. Knopf, 1975.

McNeil, Genna Rae. *Groundwork: Charles Hamilton Houston and the Struggle for Civil Rights.* Philadelphia: University of Pennsylvania Press, 1983.

Tushnet, Mark V. *Making Civil Rights Law: Thurgood Marshall and the Supreme Court, 1936–1961.* New York: Oxford University Press, 1994.

Wolters, Raymond. *The Burden of Brown: Thirty Years of School Desegregation.* Knoxville, Tenn.: University of Tennessee Press, 1984.

15

The Civil Rights Movement

In 1955 a bus boycott in Montgomery, Alabama, initiated a new phase in the African-American struggle for racial justice. Civil rights activists now employed a new strategy—nonviolent direct action—which used marches, boycotts, and similar mass actions to create crises intended to force segregated southern communities to abandon their Jim Crow laws and practices. It called for nonviolence on the part of participants, in spite of racial taunts, arrest, or physical attack. The most visible and eloquent spokesman for this approach was a black Baptist preacher named Martin Luther King Jr. (1929–1968), who had studied the ideas and technique of India's Mohandas Gandhi and sought to apply a similar method in the struggle for black equality. As the leader of the Southern Christian Leadership Conference (SCLC), he set out to employ his nonviolent strategy in community after community throughout the South. King became an internationally known figure and in 1964 won the Nobel Peace Prize for his civil rights activities. Although assassinated in 1968, he remains the most potent symbol of the Civil Rights Movement.

As King and SCLC brought their strategy to communities throughout the South, new groups adopted the technique. In February 1960 four black college students sat down at a "whites only" lunch counter in Greensboro, North Carolina, and refused to leave unless they were served. Within weeks, the sit-in movement had spread to seventy southern cities and attracted thousands of black college students. Many of them came together in April to form the Student Nonviolent Coordinating Committee (SNCC). Their tactics were soon expanded to include kneel-ins at segregated churches and wade-ins at segregated public pools. In 1961 the Congress of Racial Equality (CORE) sent an interracial group of "freedom riders" across the South on buses to force compliance with a federal ban on segregation in interstate travel. After repeated physical assaults in Alabama forced them to go home, SNCC volunteers carried on the so-called Freedom Rides. In 1962 SNCC turned its attention to a voter registration campaign, with the assistance of SCLC, CORE, and the NAACP.

Before 1963 the Civil Rights Movement achieved many local successes. In that year, it started to pressure the federal government for sweeping change. This resulted in several landmark pieces of civil rights legislation. In August the March on Washington for Jobs and Freedom brought more than 200,000 Americans to the nation's capital to demonstrate on behalf of a pending civil rights bill. It was capped by King's stirring "I Have a Dream" speech envisioning an integrated America. Congress responded by passing the Civil Rights Act of 1964, the most comprehensive civil rights law it had ever enacted. This act prohibited discrimination or segregation in employment and public facilities, outlawed bias in federally assisted programs, and authorized the attorney general to institute lawsuits challenging discrimination in public schools and other facilities operated by state and local governments.

The movement then stepped up its campaign for voting rights. In 1964 the Twenty-fourth Amendment to the Constitution was ratified, ending use of the poll tax. After a Selma-to-Montgomery march in Alabama publicized continuing disfranchisement, Congress passed the Voting Rights Act of 1965, which outlawed literacy tests and similar devices and sent federal examiners to register voters in areas that had historically excluded blacks from the ballot. A century after emancipation, African Americans had finally gained legal equality.

Rosa Parks, The Montgomery Bus Boycott

The Montgomery bus boycott brought new leadership and a new strategy to the struggle for civil rights. It began on 1 December 1955, when Rosa Parks (1913–), a seamstress and former secretary of the local NAACP chapter, refused to give up her bus seat to a white passenger. Montgomery's Jim Crow laws required a complex form of segregation on the city's bus line. Whites were to begin seating from the front of each bus, blacks from the back. If the bus was crowded, blacks closest to the white section were required to give up their seats. On this occasion, Parks refused and was arrested. In the following document, she recounts the event in her own words. Her courageous act prompted a boycott of the buses by the city's African-American community. For one year, blacks walked, carpooled, and hired black-owned taxis in lieu of riding the buses, despite legal harrassment, intimidation, and violence. The boycott ended in December 1956, after the U.S. Supreme Court ruled Alabama's segregated bus systems to be unconstitutional. Along the way, it made a national figure of Martin Luther King Jr., the boycott's spokesman, and attracted attention to the strategy of nonviolent direct action. Many historians view this event as the beginning of a new Civil Rights Movement.[*]

---

[*] Rosa L. Parks, "Recollections," in *My Soul is Rested: Movement Days in the Deep South Remembered*, ed. ⁓ ⁓aines (New York: G. P. Putnam's Sons, 1977).

As I got up on the bus and walked to the seat, I saw that there was only one vacancy that was just back of where it was considered the white section. So this was the seat that I took, next to the aisle, and a man was sitting next to me. Across the aisle there were two women, and there were a few seats at this point in the very front of the bus that was called the white section. I went on to one stop, and I didn't particularly notice the other people getting on. And on the third stop there were some people getting on, and at this point all the front seats were taken. Now in the beginning, at the very first stop I had got on the bus, the back of the bus was filled up with people standing in the aisle, and I don't know why this one vacancy that I took was left, because there were quite a few people already standing toward the back of the bus. The third stop is when all the seats were taken, and this one man was standing, and when the driver looked around and saw he was standing, he asked the four of us, the man in the seat with me and the two women across the aisle, to let him have those front seats.

At his first request, didn't any of us move. Then he spoke again and said, "You'd better make it light on yourselves and let me have those seats." At this point, of course, the passenger who would have taken the seat hadn't said anything. In fact, he never did speak to my knowledge. When the three people, the man who was in the seat with me and the two women, stood up and moved into the aisle, I remained where I was. When the driver saw that I was still there, he asked if I was going to stand up. I told him, no, I wasn't. He said, "Well, if you don't stand up, I'm going to have you arrested." I told him to go on and have me arrested.

He got off the bus and came back shortly. A few minutes later, two policemen got on the bus, and they approached me and asked if the driver had asked me to stand up, and I said yes, and they wanted to know why I didn't. I told them I didn't think I should have to stand up. After I had paid my fare and occupied my seat, I didn't think I should have to give it up. They placed me under arrest then.

Martin Luther King Jr., The Strategy of Nonviolent Direct Action

---

The lessons of Montgomery convinced King and other civil rights activists to employ the strategy of nonviolent direct action against Jim Crow throughout the South. In 1957 they gathered in Atlanta and formed SCLC for that purpose. Under King's leadership, SCLC organized nonviolent direct action campaigns in dozens of cities over the next few years, most notably Birmingham, Albany, and St. Augustine. But the strategy was not without its critics, especially among whites. After being jailed in Birmingham in 1963 for leading a protest march, King received a letter from a group of white Alabama clergymen criticizing his timing and tactics and accusing him and other SCLC officials of being "outside agitators." In his famous "Letter from

Birmingham Jail," from which the following document is excerpted, he answered their charges and explained nonviolent direct action. Once again, SCLC's strategy worked. Before the year was out, the campaign in Birmingham had forced a negotiated end to the city's Jim Crow rules.*

My dear Fellow Clergymen,

While confined here in the Birmingham city jail, I came across your recent statement calling our present activities "unwise and untimely." Seldom, if ever, do I pause to answer criticism of my work and ideas. If I sought to answer all of the criticisms that cross my desk, my secretaries would be engaged in little else in the course of the day, and I would have no time for constructive work. But since I feel thay you are men of genuine good will and your criticisms are sincerely set forth, I would like to answer your statement in what I hope will be patient and reasonable terms.

I think I should give the reason for my being in Birmingham, since you have been influenced by the argument of "outsiders coming in." I have the honor of serving as president of the Southern Christian Leadership Conference, an organization operating in every southern state, with headquarters in Atlanta, Georgia. We have some eighty-five affiliate organizations all across the South, one being the Alabama Christian Movement for Human Rights. Whenever necessary and possible, we share staff, educational and financial resources with our affiliates. Several months ago our local affiliate here in Birmingham invited us to be on call to engage in a nonviolent direct-action program if such were deemed necessary. We readily consented, and when the hour came we lived up to our promises. So I am here, along with several members of my staff, because we were invited here. I am here because I have basic organizational ties here.

Beyond this, I am in Birmingham because injustice is here. Just as the eighth century prophets left their little villages and carried their "thus saith the Lord" far beyond the boundaries of their hometowns; and just as the Apostle Paul left his little village of Tarsus and carried the gospel of Jesus Christ to practically every hamlet and city of the Graeco-Roman world, I too am compelled to carry the gospel of freedom beyond my particular hometown. Like Paul, I must constantly respond to the Macedonian call for aid.

Moreover, I am cognizant of the interrelatedness of all communities and states. I cannot sit idly by in Atlanta and not be concerned about what happens in Birmingham. Injustice anywhere is a threat to justice everywhere. We are caught in an inescapable network of mutuality, tied in a single garment of destiny. Whatever affects one directly affects all indirectly. Never again can we afford to live with the narrow, provincial "outside agitator" idea. Anyone who lives in the United States can never be considered an outsider anywhere in this country.

You deplore the demonstrations that are presently taking place in Birmingham. But I am sorry that your statement did not express a similar concern for the conditions that

---

* Martin Luther King, Jr., "Letter from Birmingham Jail," in *Why We Can't Wait* (New York: Harper and Row Publishers, 1963).

brought the demonstrations into being. I am sure that each of you would want to go beyond the superficial social analyst who looks merely at effects, and does not grapple with underlying causes. I would not hesitate to say that it is unfortunate that so-called demonstrations are taking place in Birmingham at this time, but I would say in more emphatic terms that it is even more unfortunate that the white power structure of this city left the Negro community with no other alternative.

In any nonviolent campaign there are four basic steps: (1) collection of the facts to determine whether injustices are alive, (2) negotiation, (3) self-purification, and (4) direct action. We have gone through all of these steps in Birmingham. There can be no gainsaying of the fact that racial injustice engulfs this community.

Birmingham is probably the most thoroughly segregated city in the United States. Its ugly record of police brutality is known in every section of this country. Its unjust treatment of Negroes in the courts is a notorious reality. There have been more unsolved bombings of Negro homes and churches in Birmingham than any city in this nation. These are the hard, brutal and unbelievable facts. On the basis of these conditions Negro leaders sought to negotiate with the city fathers. But the political leaders consistently refused to engage in good faith negotiation.

Then came the opportunity last September to talk with some of the leaders of the economic community. In these negotiating sessions certain promises were made by the merchants—such as the promise to remove the humiliating racial signs from the stores. On the basis of these promises . . . the leaders of the Alabama Christian Movement for Human Rights agreed to call a moratorium on any type of demonstrations. As the weeks and months unfolded we realized that we were the victims of a broken promise. The signs remained. Like so many experiences of the past we were confronted with blasted hopes, and the dark shadow of a deep disappointment settled upon us. So we had no alternative except that of preparing for direct action, whereby we would present our very bodies as a means of laying our case before the conscience of the local and national community. We were not unmindful of the difficulties involved. So we decided to go through a process of self-purification. We started having workshops on nonviolence and repeatedly asked ourselves the questions, "Are you able to accept blows without retaliating?" "Are you able to endure the ordeals of jail?" We decided to set our direct-action program around the Easter season, realizing that with the exception of Christmas, this was the largest shopping period of the year. Knowing that a strong economic withdrawal program would be the by-product of direct action, we felt that this was the best time to bring pressure on the merchants for the needed changes. Then it occurred to us that the March election was ahead and so we speedily decided to postpone action until after election day. When we discovered that [racist police commissioner "Bull"] Connor was in the run-off, we decided again to postpone action so that the demonstrations could not be used to cloud the issues. At this time we agreed to begin our nonviolent witness the day after the run-off.

This reveals that we did not move irresponsibly into direct action. We too wanted to see Mr. Connor defeated; so we went through postponement after postponement to aid in this community need. After this we felt that direct action could be delayed no longer.

You may ask, "Why direct action? Why sit-ins, marches, etc.? Isn't negotiation a better path?" You are exactly right in your call for negotiation. Indeed, this is the purpose of direct action. Nonviolent direct action seeks to create such a crisis and establish such creative tension that a community that has constantly refused to negotiate is forced to confront the issue. It seeks so to dramatize the issue that it can no longer be ignored. I just referred to the creation of tension as a part of the work of the nonviolent resister. This may sound rather shocking. But I must confess that I am not afraid of the word tension. I have earnestly worked and preached against violent tension, but there is a type of constructive nonviolent tension that is necessary for growth. Just as Socrates felt that it was necessary to create a tension in the mind so that individuals could rise from the bondage of myths and half-truths to the unfettered realm of creative analysis and objective appraisal, we must see the need of having nonviolent gadflies to create the kind of tension in society that will help men to rise from the dark depths of prejudice and racism to the majestic heights of understanding and brotherhood. So the purpose of the direct action is to create a situation so crisis-packed that it will inevitably open the door to negotiation. We, therefore, concur with you in your call for negotiation. Too long has our beloved Southland been bogged down in the tragic attempt to live in monologue rather than dialogue.

One of the basic points in your statement is that our acts are untimely. Some have asked, "Why didn't you give the new administration time to act?" The only answer that I can give to this inquiry is that the new administration must be prodded about as much as the outgoing one before it acts. We will be sadly mistaken if we feel that the election of Mr. Boutwell will bring the millennium to Birmingham. While Mr. Boutwell is much more articulate and gentle than Mr. Connor, they are both segregationists, dedicated to the task of maintaining the status quo. The hope I see in Mr. Boutwell is that he will be reasonable enough to see the futility of massive resistance to desegregation. But he will not see this without pressure from the devotees of civil rights. My friends, I must say to you that we have not made a single gain in civil rights without determined legal and nonviolent pressure. History is the long and tragic story of the fact that privileged groups seldom give up their privileges voluntarily. Individuals may see the moral light and voluntarily give up their unjust posture; but as Reinhold Niebuhr has reminded us, groups are more immoral than individuals.

We know through painful experience that freedom is never voluntarily given by the oppressor; it must be demanded by the oppressed. Frankly, I have never yet engaged in a direct-action movement that was "well timed," according to the timetable of those who have not suffered unduly from the disease of segregation. For years now I have heard the word "Wait!" It rings in the ear of every Negro with a piercing familiarity. This "Wait!" has almost always meant "Never." It has been a tranquilizing thalidomide, relieving the emotional stress for a moment, only to give birth to an ill-formed infant of frustration. We must come to see with the distinguished jurist of yesterday that "justice too long delayed is justice denied."

We have waited for more than 340 years for our constitutional and God-given rights. The nations of Asia and Africa are moving with jetlike speed toward the goal of political independence, and we still creep at horse and buggy pace toward the gaining of a cup of coffee at a lunch counter. I guess it is easy for those who have never felt the stinging darts of segregation to say, "Wait." But when you have seen vicious mobs lynch your mothers and fathers at will and drown your sisters and brothers at whim; when you have seen hate-filled policemen curse, kick, brutalize and even kill your black brothers and sisters with impunity; when you see the vast majority of your twenty million Negro brothers smothering in an airtight cage of poverty in the midst of an affluent society; when you suddenly find your tongue twisted and your speech stammering as you seek to explain to your six-year-old daughter why she can't go to the public amusement park that has just been advertised on television, and see tears welling up in her little eyes when she is told that Funtown is closed to colored children, and see the depressing clouds of inferiority begin to form in her little mental sky, and see her begin to distort her little personality by unconsciously developing a bitterness toward white people; when you have to concoct an answer for a five-year-old son asking i n agonizing pathos: "Daddy, why do white people treat colored people so mean?"; when you take a cross-country drive and find it necessary to sleep night after night in the uncomfortable corners of your automobile because no motel will accept you; when you are humiliated day in and day out by nagging signs reading "white" and "colored"; when your first name becomes "nigger" and your middle name becomes "boy" (however old you are) and your last name becomes "John," and when your wife and mother are never given the respected title "Mrs."; when you are harried by day and haunted by night by the fact that you are a Negro, living constantly at tiptoe stance never quite knowning what to expect next, and plagued with inner fears and outer resentments; when you are forever fighting a degenerating sense of "nobodiness"; then you will understand why we find it difficult to wait. There comes a time when the cup of endurance runs over, and men are no longer willing to be plunged into an abyss of injustice where they experience the blackness of corroding despair. I hope, sirs, you can understand our legitimate and unavoidable impatience.

You express a great deal of anxiety over our willingness to break laws. This is certainly a legitimate concern. Since we so diligently urge people to obey the Supreme Court's decision of 1954 outlawing segregation in the public schools, it is rather strange and paradoxical to find us consciously breaking laws. One may well ask, "How can your advocate breaking some laws and obeying others?" The answer is found in the fact that there are two types of laws: there are *just* and there are *unjust* laws. I would agree with Saint Augustine that "An unjust law is no law at all."

Now what is the difference between the two? How does one determine when a law is just or unjust? A just law is a man-made code that squares with the moral law or the law of God. An unjust law is a code that is out of harmony with the moral law. To put it in the terms of Saint Thomas Aquinas, an unjust law is a human law that is not rooted in eternal and natural law. Any law that degrades human personality is unjust. All segregation statutes are unjust because segregation distorts the soul and damages the personality. It gives the segregator a false sense of superiority, and the segregaated a false sense of inferiority. . . . So I can urge men to disobey segregation ordinances because they are morally wrong. . . .

First, I must confess that over the last few years I have been gravely disappointed with the white moderate. I have almost reached the regrettable conclusion that the Negro's great stumbling block in the stride toward freedom is not the White Citizen's Counciler or the Ku Klux Klanner, but the white moderate who is more devoted to "order" than to justice; who prefers a negative peace which is the absence of tension to a positive peace which is the the presence of justice; who constantly says, "I agree with you in the goal you seek, but I can't agree with your methods of direct action"; who paternalistically feels that he can set the timetable for another man's freedom; who lives by the myth of time and who constantly advised the Negro to wait until a "more convenient season." Shallow understanding from people of good will is more frustrating than absolute misunderstanding from people of ill will. Lukewarm acceptance is much more bewildering that outright rejection.

I had hoped that the white moderate would understand that law and order exist for the purpose of establishing justice, and that when they do fail to do this they become dangerously structured dams that block the flow of social progress. I had hoped that the white moderate would understand that the present tenion of the South is merely a necessary phase of the transition from an obnoxious negative peace, where the Negro passively accepted his unjust plight, to a substance-filled positive peace, where all men will respect the dignity and worth of human personality. Actually, we who engage in nonviolent direct action are not the creators of tension. We merely bring to the surface the hidden tension that is already alive. We bring it out in the open where it can be seen and dealt with. Like a boil that can never be cured as long as it is covered up but must be opened with all its pus-flowing ugliness to the natural medicines of air and light, injustice must likewise be exposed, with all of the tension its exposing creates, to the light of human conscience and the air of national opinion before it can be cured.

In your statement you asserted that our actions, even though peaceful, must be condemned because they precipitate violence. But can this assertion be logically made? Isn't this like condemning the robbed man because his possession of money precipitated the evil act of robbery? Isn't this like condemning Socrates because his unswerving commitment to truth and his philosophical delvings precipitated the misguided popular mind to make him drink the hemlock? Isn't this like condemning Jesus because His unique God consciousness and never-ceasing devotion to his will precipitated the evil act of crucifixion? We must come to see, as federal courts have consistently affirmed, that it is immoral to urge an individual to withdraw his efforts to gain his basic constitutional rights because the quest precipitates violence. Society must protect the robbed and punish the robber.

I had also hoped that the white moderate would reject the myth of time. I received a letter this morning from a white brother in Texas which said: "All Christians know that the colored people will receive equal rights eventually, but it is possible that you are in too great of a religious hurry. It has taken Christianity almost two thousand years to accomplish what it has. The teachings of Christ take time to come to earth." All that is said here grows out of a tragic misconception of time. It is the strangely irrational notion that there is something in the very flow of time that will inevitably cure all ills. Actually time is neutral. It can be used either destructively or constructively. I am coming to feel that the people of ill will have used time much more effectively than the people of good will. We will have to repent in this generation not merely for the vitriolic words and actions of the bad people, but for the appalling silence of the good people. We must come to see that human progress never rolls in on wheels of inevitability. It comes through the tireless efforts and persistent work of men willing to be co-workers with God, and without this hard word time itself becomes an ally of the forces of social stagnation. We must use time creatively, and forever realize that the time is always ripe to do right. Now is the time to make real the promise of democracy, and transform our pending national elegy into a creative psalm of brotherhood. Now is the time to lift our national policy from the quicksand of racial injustice to the solid rock of human dignity.

You spoke of our activity in Birmingham as extreme. At first I was rather disappointed that fellow clergymen would see my nonviolent efforts as those of the extremist. . . . But as I continued to think about the matter I gradually gained a bit of satisfaction from being considered an extremist. Was not Jesus an extremist in love—"Love your enemies, bless them that curse you, pray for them that despitefully use you." Was not Amos an extremist for justice—"Let justice roll down like waters and righteousness like a mighty stream." Was not Paul and extremist for the gospel of Jesus Christ—"I bear in my body the marks of the Lord Jesus." Was not Martin Luther an extremist—"Here I stand; I can do none other so help me God." Was not John Bunyan an extremist—"I will stay in jail to the end of my days before I make a Butchery of my conscience." Was not Abraham Lincoln an extremist—"This nation cannot survive half slave and half free." Was not Thomas Jefferson an extremist—"We hold these truths to be self-evident, that all men are created equal." So the question is not whether we will be extremist but what kind of extremist will we be. Will we be extremists for hate or will we be extremists for love? Will we be extremists for the preservation of injustice—or will we be extremists for the cause of justice? In that dramatic scene on Calvary's hill, three men were crucified. We must not forget that all three were crucified for the same crime—the crime of extremism. Two were extremists for immorality, and thusly fell below their environment. The other, Jesus Christ, was an extremist for love, truth, and goodness, and thereby rose above his environment. So, after all, maybe the South, the nation and the world are in dire need of creative extremists.

I had hoped that the white moderate would see this. Maybe I was too optimistic. Maybe I expected too much. I guess I should have realized that few members of a race that has oppressed another race can understand or appreciate the deep groans and passionate yearnings of those that have been oppressed, and still fewer have the vision to see that injustice must be rooted out by strong, persistent and determined action. I am thankful, however, that some of our white brothers have grasped the meaning of this social revolution and committed themselves to it. . . .

Yours for the Cause of Peace and Brotherhood

Martin Luther King Jr.

Fannie Lou Hamer, Fighting for the Vote in Mississippi

While national attention focused on King and other prominent figures in the Civil Rights Movement, the success of the struggle depended upon mobilizing the African-American masses. Even though SCLC,

SNCC, and other civil rights organizations sent trained workers into southern communities to coordinate campaigns against Jim Crow laws and disfranchisement, those campaigns required the courage and determination of local people. In 1962 SNCC initiated a voter registration drive in Mississippi, where only 5 percent of the black residents were registered to vote. One of the first local blacks to respond was a sharecropper named Fannie Lou Hamer (1917–1977). But after attempting to register to vote, she was subjected to unceasing economic intimidation, arrest, and physical violence. In 1964 she joined the Mississippi Freedom Democratic Party (MFDP), which organized mock elections among blacks in the state and sought representation in that year's Democratic National Convention. The following testimony by Hamer before the convention's Credentials Committee exposed the hazards of trying to vote in Mississippi and called for the nation to live up to its democratic ideals. *

Mr. Chairman and the Credentials Committee, my name is Mrs. Fannie Lou Hamer, and I live at 626 East Lafayette Streeet, Ruleville, Mississippi, Sunflower County, the home of Senator James O. Eastland, and Senator [John] Stennis.

It was the 31st of August in 1962 that eighteen of us traveled twenty-six miles to the county courthouse in Indianola to try to register to try to become first-class citizens. We was met in Indianola by Mississippi men, highway patrolmens, and they only allowed two of us in to take the literacy test at the time. After we had taken this test and started back to Ruleville, we was held up by the City Police and the State Highway Patrolmen and carried back to Indianola, where the bus driver was charged that day with driving a bus the wrong color.

After we paid the fine among us, we continued on to Ruleville, and Reverend Jeff Sunny carried me four miles in the rural area where I had worked as a timekeeper and sharecropper for eighteen years. I was met there by my children, who told me the plantation owner was angry because I had gone down to try to register. After they told me, my husband came, and said the plantation owner was raising cain because I had tried to register, and before he quit talking the plantation owner came, and said, "Fannie Lou, do you know—did Pap tell you what I said?"

I said, "Yes, sir."

He said, "I mean that," he said. "If you don't go down and withdraw your registration, you will have to leave," said, "Then if you go down and withdraw," he said. "You will—you might have to go because we are not ready for that in Mississippi."

And I addressed him and told him and said, "I didn't try to register for you. I tried to register for myself." I had to leave that same night.

On the 10th of September 1962, sixteen bullets was fired into the home of Mr. and Mrs. Robert Tucker for me. That same night two girls were shot in Ruleville, Mississippi. Also Mr. Joe McDonald's house was shot in.

---

* "Testimony of Fannie Lou Hamer Before the Credentials Committee of the Democratic National Convention," 22 August 1964, Joseph Rauh Papers, Library of Congress.

And in June, the 9th, 1963, I had attended a voter registration workshop, was returning back to Mississippi. Ten of us was traveling by the Continental Trailway bus. When we got to Winona, Mississippi, which is Montgomery County, four of the people got off to use the washroom, and two of the people—to use the restaurant—two of the people wanted to use the washroom. The four people that had gone in to use the restaurant was ordered out. During this time I was on the bus. But when I looked through the window and saw they had rushed out, I got off the bus to see what had happened, and one of the ladies said, "It was a State Highway Patrolman and a chief of police ordered us out."

I got back on the bus and one of the persons had used the washroom got back on the bus, too. As soon as I was seated on the bus, I saw when they began to get the four people in a highway patrolman's car. I stepped off the bus to see what was happening and somebody screamed from the car that the four workers was in and said, "Get that one there," and when I went to get in the car, when the man told me I was under arrest, he kicked me.

I was carried to the county jail, and put in the booking room. They left some of the people in the booking room and began to place us in cells. I was placed in a cell with a young woman. . . . After I was placed in the cell I began to hear sounds of licks and screams. I could hear the sounds of licks and horrible screams, and I could hear somebody say, "Can you say, yes sir, nigger? Can you say yes, sir?"

And they would say other horrible names. She would say, "Yes, I can say yes, sir."

"So say it."

She says, "I don't know you well enough."

They beat her, I don't know how long, and after a while she began to pray, and asked God to have mercy on those people.

And it wasn't too long before three white men came to my cell. One of these men was a State Highway Patrolman and he asked me where I was from, and I told him Ruleville. He said, "We are going to check this." And they left my cell and it wasn't too long before they came back. He said, "You are from Ruleville all right," and he used a curse word, and he said, "We are going to make you wish you was dead."

I was carried out of that cell into another cell where they had two Negro prisoners. The State Highway Patrolman odered the first Negro to take the blackjack. The first Negro prisoner ordered me, by orders from the State Highway Patrolman for me, to lay down on a bunk bed on my face, and I laid on my face. The first Negro began to beat, and I was beat by the first Negro until he was exhausted, and I was holding my hands behind me at that time on my left side because I suffered from polio when I was six years old. After the first Negro had beat until he was exhausted, the State Highway Patrolman ordered the second Negro to take the blackjack.

The second Negro began to beat and I began to work my feet, and the State Highway Patrolman ordered the first Negro who had beat to set on my feet to keep me from working my feet. I began to scream and one white man got up and began to beat me in my head and tell me to hush. One white man—my dress had worked up high, he walked over and pulled my dress down—and he pulled my dress back, back up. . . .

All of this on account we want to register, to become first-class citizens, and if the Freedom Democratic Party is not seated now, I question America. Is this America, the land of the free and the home of the brave, where we have to sleep with our telephones off the hooks because our lives be threatened daily because we want to live as decent human beings, in America?

Alice Walker, Changed by the Movement

African Americans who participated in the Civil Rights Movement had their lives forever changed by the experience. Alice Walker (1944–), who worked in a voter registration project in Georgia, explains this metamorphosis in the following essay. Now a well-known novelist, her fiction often explores racial or feminist themes. Walker is best known for *The Color Purple*, which won the Pulitzer Prize in 1983, but other works, such as *Meridian* (1976), recreate movement days in the deep South.*

Someone said recently to an old black lady from Mississippi, whose legs had been badly mangled by local police who arrested her for "disturbing the peace," that the Civil Rights Movement was dead, and asked, since it was dead, what she thought about it. The old lady replied, hobbling out of his presence on her cane, that the Civil Rights Movement was like herself, "if it's dead, it shore ain't ready to lay down!" . . .

White liberals and deserting Civil Rights sponsors are quick to justify their disaffection from the Movement by claiming that it is over. "And since it is over," they will ask, "would someone kindly tell me what has been gained by it?" They then will list statistics supposedly showing how much more advanced segregation is now than ten years ago—in schools, housing, jobs. They point to a gain in conservative politicians during the last few years. They speak of ghetto riots and of the survey that shows that most policemen are admittedly too anti-Negro to do their jobs in ghetto areas fairly and effectively. They speak of every area that has been touched by the Civil Rights Movement as somehow or other going to pieces.

They rarely talk, however, about human attitudes among Negroes that have undergone terrific changes just during the past seven to ten years (not to mention all those years when there was a Movement and only the Negroes knew about it). They seldom speak of changes in personal lives because of the influence of people in the Movement. They see general failure and few, if any, individual gains. . . .

Six years ago, after half-heartedly watching my mother's soap operas and wondering whether there wasn't something more to be asked of life, the Civil Rights Movement came into my life. Like a good omen for the future, the face of Dr. Martin Luther King Jr. was the first black face I saw on our new television screen. And, as in a

* Alice Walker, "The Civil Rights Movement: What Good Was It?," *American Scholar* 36 (Autumn 1967).

fairy tale, my soul was stirred by the meaning for me of his mission—at the time he was being rather ignominiously dumped into a police van for having led a protest march in Alabama—and I fell in love with the sober and determined face of the Movement. The singing of "We Shall Overcome"—that song betrayed by nonbelievers in it—rang for the first time in my ears. . . . The life of Dr. King, seeming bigger and more miraculous than the man himself, because of all he had done and suffered, offered a pattern of strength and sincerity I felt I could trust. He had suffered much because of his simple belief in nonviolence, love and brotherhood. Perhaps the majority of men could not be reached through these beliefs, but because Dr. King kept trying to reach them in spite of danger to himself and his family, I saw in him the hero for whom I had waited so long.

What Dr. King promised was not a ranch-style house and an acre of manicured lawn for every black man, but jail and finally freedom. He did not promise two cars for every family, but the courage one day for all families everywhere to walk without shame and unafraid on their own feet. He did not say that one day it will be us chasing prospective buyers out of our prosperous well-kept neighborhoods, or in other ways exhibiting our snobbery and ignorance as all other ethnic groups before us have done; what he said was that we had a right to live anywhere in this country we chose, and a right to a meaningful well-paying job to provide us with the upkeep of our homes. He did not say we had to become carbon copies of the white American middle class; but he did say we had the right to become whatever we wanted to become. . . .

What good was the Civil Rights Movement? If it had just given this country Dr. King, a leader of conscience, for once in our lifetime, it would have been enough. If it had just taken black eyes off white television stories, it would have been enough. If it had fed one starving child, it would have been enough.

If the Civil Rights Movement is "dead," and if it gave us nothing else, it gave some of us bread, some of us shelter, some of us knowledge and pride, all of us comfort. It gave us our children, our husbands, our brothers, our fathers, as men reborn and with a purpose for living. It broke the pattern of black servitude in the country. It shattered the phony "promise" of white soap operas that sucked away so many pitiful lives. It gave us history and men far greater than Presidents. It gave us heroes, selfless men of courage and strength, for our little boys and girls to follow. It gave us hope for tomorrow. It called us to life.

Because we live, it can never die.

Asking Questions of the Documents

1. How did the Montgomery bus boycott differ from previous civil rights challenges, such as those sponsored by the NAACP?

2. What is nonviolent direct action? Explain the concept behind the strategy. What criticisms did white Alabama clergymen make of this strategy? How did Martin Luther King answer these charges? How successful was the strategy in ending Jim Crow in the South?

3. How did Mississippi whites use physical and economic intimidation to hamper the effectiveness of the voter registration campaign? What do you think prompted local blacks, such as Fannie Lou Hamer, to stand up to these threats? Why would the testimony of Hamer be particularly effective in bringing the problems of Mississippi blacks before a national audience?

4. How did the Civil Rights Movement change the lives of black participants? What do you think was the chief legacy of the Civil Rights Movement?

For Further Reading

Carson, Clayborne. *In Struggle: SNCC and the Black Awakening of the 1960s.* Cambridge, Mass.: Harvard University Press, 1981.

Crawford, Vicki L., Jacqueline A. Rouse, and Barbara Woods, eds. *Women in the Civil Rights Movement: Trailblazers and Torchbearers, 1941–1965.* New York: Carlson Publishing, 1990.

Garrow, David J. *Bearing the Cross: Martin Luther King, Jr., and the Southern Christian Leadership Conference.* New York: Random House, 1986.

Lawson, Steven F. *Black Ballots: Voting Rights in the South, 1944–1969.* New York: Columbia University Press, 1976.

McAdam, Doug. *Freedom Summer.* New York: Oxford University Press, 1988.

Morris, Aldon D. *The Origins of the Civil Rights Movement: Black Communities Organizing for Change.* New York: Free Press, 1984.

Weisbrot, Robert. *Freedom Bound: A History of America's Civil Rights Movement.* New York: W. W. Norton and Company, 1990.

16

Black Power, Black Nationalism

In the wake of its greatest legislative triumph, the Civil Rights Movement began to fragment. On 11 August 1965, less than a week after the passage of the Voting Rights Act, the black Los Angeles neighborhood of Watts exploded into a firestorm of looting and violence. When the riot ended, thirty-four people lay dead and property damage exceeded thirty-five million dollars. But Watts was only one incident in a half-decade of rage. From 1964 through 1968, the ghettoes of the North and West combusted in some three hundred riots involving at least a half million African Americans.

The riots illustrated the limits of the Civil Rights Movement. By the 1960s, a majority of African Americans lived in inner-city neighborhoods, most of them outside the South. They faced no Jim Crow laws or disfranchisement devices, only the economic ills and social alienation of places like Watts—widespread poverty, massive unemployment, welfare, inadequate housing and schools, and racist police. The boycotts, marches, sit-ins, and freedom rides had raised black awareness and expectations but could do little to ameliorate the conditions of ghetto life. Now many black activists, especially younger ones, searched for a different strategy.

"Black Power" became the new watchword. The term, coined by Stokely Carmichael in 1966, became a rallying cry for urban blacks increasingly alienated from the Civil Rights Movement. The idea derived from black nationalism—the belief that people of African descent share a common experience, culture, world view, and destiny. Most Black Power advocates were heavily influenced by Malcolm X, who urged African Americans to band together and take control of their communities "by any means necessary." Like Malcolm X, they generally eschewed the goal of integration and the strategy of nonviolence. But Black Power meant different things to different people. Most whites and some older blacks saw it as synonomous with violence. For younger black activists, it usually referred to self-reliance, race pride, and political and economic empowerment. The rising importance of Black Power became evident in 1966 when both SNCC and CORE embraced this more radical direction.

Black Power advocates shared a common goal—empowering black communities—but they differed on how that would best be achieved. Revolutionary nationalist groups, such as the Black Panther Party, called for armed struggle and espoused Marxist thought. Seeing racism as an inevitable product of capitalism, they welcomed alliances and coalitions with likeminded whites. Cultural nationalist groups, such as the Los Angeles-based US Organization, insisted that African Americans could liberate themselves from white domination only after they had adopted a cohesive culture, completely divorced from white ways. Its founder and leader, Maulana Ron Karenga, urged his fellow blacks to adopt African clothing and hairstyles, abandon their European surnames, learn Swahili, and celebrate distinctive holidays like Kwanzaa. He viewed Marxism as alien to the black struggle, rejected alliances and coalitions with whites, and maintained that armed struggle was impossible until blacks had rediscovered their cultural roots. By the time the Black Power Movement drifted into decline in the 1970s, both approaches had left their mark. Revolutionary nationalists had raised the political and economic consciousness of a generation of African Americans, while cultural nationalists had revolutionized their cultural values and practices. These changes were to be the chief legacies of Black Power.

Malcolm X, Black Nationalism and Black Revolution

Most Black Power advocates were inspired by the life and legacy of Malcolm X (1925–1965). Born Malcolm Little, he suffered through a troubled childhood, only to become a teenage hustler, pimp, and cocaine addict on the streets of Boston and Harlem. After a bungled burglary, he was sent to prison, where he read voluminously and converted to the separatist doctrines of Elijah Muhammad and the Nation of Islam. Released in 1952, he was appointed the minister of a Harlem mosque. Before long, his trenchant analysis of white racism, his confrontational language, and his charismatic style made him into the chief evangelist for the Black Muslims. But his growing popularity and independence brought estrangement from Muhammad and the Nation. After a 1964 pilgrimage to Mecca, Malcolm X became convinced of the possibilty of white redemption, rejected his unequivocal separatism, and considered politics as a possible vehicle for black empowerment. But to the end, he continued to preach the value of black nationalism and the likelihood of black revolution, as in the following 1964 speech. After his assassination one year later, *The Autobiography of Malcolm X* (1965) became a "nearly universal sacred text" for the Black Power Movement.[*]

Friends and enemies, tonight I hope that I can have a little fireside chat with as few sparks as possible being tossed around. Especially because of the very explosive condition that the world is in today. Sometimes, when a person's house is on fire and someone comes in yelling fire, instead of the person who is awakened by the yell being

---

[*] Malcolm X, "The Black Revolution," in *Two Speeches by Malcolm X* (New York: Merit Publishers, 1965).

thankful, he makes the mistake of charging the one who awakened him with having set the fire. I hope this little conversation tonight about the black revolution won't cause many of you to accuse us of igniting it when you find it at your doorstep. . . .

I'm still a Muslim but I'm also a nationalist, meaning that my political philosophy is black nationalism, my economic philosophy is black nationalism, my social philosophy is black nationalism. And when I say that this philosophy is black nationalism, to me this means that the political philosophy of black nationalism is that which is designed to encourage our people, the black people, to gain complete control over the politics and politicians of our own community.

Our economic philosophy is that we should gain economic control over the economy of our own community, the businesses and the other things which create employment so that we can provide jobs for our own people instead of having to picket and boycott and beg someone else for a job.

And, in short, our social philosophy means that we feel that it is time to get together among our own kind and eliminate the moral evils that are destroying the moral fiber of our society, like drug addiction, drunkeness, adultery that leads to an abundance of bastard children, welfare problems. We believe that we should lift the level or the standard of our own society to a higher level wherein we will be satisfied and then not inclined toward pushing ourselves into other societies where we are not wanted. . . .

By the hundreds of thousands today we find our own people have become impatient, turning away from your white nationalism, which you call democracy, toward the militant uncompromising policy of black nationalism. I point out right here that as soon as we announced we were going to start a black nationalist party in this country we received mail from coast to coast, especially from young people at the college level, the university level, who expressed complete sympathy and support and a desire to take part in any kind of political action based on black nationalism, designed to correct or eliminate immediately evils that our people have suffered here for 400 years.

The black nationalists to many of you may represent only a minority in the community. And therefore you might have a tendency to classify them as something insignificant. But just as the fuse is the smallest part or the smallest piece in the powder keg it is yet that little fuse that ignites the entire powder keg. The black nationalists to you may represent a small minority in the so-called Negro community. But they just happen to be composed of the type of ingredient necessary to fuse or ignite the entire black community. And this is one thing that whites—whether you call yourselves liberals or conservatives or racists or whatever else you might choose to be—one thing that you have to realize is, where the black community is concerned, although there the large majority you may come in contact with may impress you as being moderate and patient and loving and long-suffering and all that kind of stuff, the minority who you consider to be Muslims or nationalists happen to be made of the type of ingredient that can easily spark the black community. This should be understood. Because to me a powder keg is nothing without a fuse.

1964 will be America's hottest year; her hottest year yet; a year of much racial violence and much racial bloodshed. But it won't be blood that's going to flow only on one side. The new generation of black people that have grown up in this country during recent years are already forming the opinion, and it's a just opinion, that if there is to be bleeding, it should be reciprocal—bleeding on both sides. . . .

So today, when the black man starts reaching out for what America says are his rights, the black man feels that he is within his rights—when he becomes the victim of brutality by those who are depriving him of his rights—to do whatever is necessary to protect himself. An example of this was taking place last night at this same time in Cleveland, where the police were putting water hoses on our people there and also throwing tear gas at them and they met a hail of stone, a hail of rocks, a hail of bricks. [A] couple weeks ago in Jacksonville, Florida, a young teenage Negro was throwing Molotov cocktails.

Well, Negroes didn't do this ten years ago. But what you should learn from this is that they are waking up. It was stones yesterday, Molotov cocktails today; it will be hand grenades tomorrow and whatever else is available the next day. The seriousness of this situation must be faced up to. You should not feel that I am inciting someone to violence. I'm only warning of a powder-keg situation. You can take it or leave it. If you take the warning perhaps you can still save yourself. But if you ignore it or ridicule it, well, death is already at your doorstep. There are 22,000,000 African Americans who are ready to fight for independence right here. When I say fight for independence right here, I don't mean any non-violent fight, or turn-the-other-cheek fight. Those days are gone. Those days are over.

If George Washington didn't get independence for this country non-violently, and if Patrick Henry didn't come up with a non-violent statement, and you taught me to look upon them as patriots and heroes, then it's time for you to realize that I have studied your books well. . . .

This is a real revolution. . . . Revolution is never based on begging somebody for an integrated cup of coffee. Revolutions are never fought by turning the other cheek.

Revolutions are never based upon love your enemy, and pray for those who spitefully use you. And revolutions are never waged singing, "We Shall Overcome." Revolutions are based upon bloodshed. Revolutions are never compromising. Revolutions are never based upon negotiations. Revolutions are never based upon any kind of tokenism whatsoever. Revolutions are never even based upon that which is begging a corrupt society or a corrupt system to accept us into it. Revolutions overturn systems, and there is no system on this earth which has proven itself more corrupt, more criminal than this system, that in 1964 still colonizes 22,000,000 African Americans.

Julius Lester, The Attractions of Black Power

Malcolm X articulated the doubts stirring in the minds of many younger black activists about the Civil Rights Movement by the mid-1960s. One convert to Black Power, young Julius Lester (1939–), outlines the changing views of his peers in the following document. Lester left his white wife in 1966 to become an official with SNCC after the organization embraced black nationalism. He later authored *Look Out Whitey!: Black Power's Gon' Get Your Mama!* (1968), a popular movement tract. In recent years, he converted to Judaism and now teaches Judaic Studies at the University of Massachusetts.[*]

This is their message: The days of singing freedom songs and the days of combatting bullets and billy clubs with love are over. "We Shall Overcome" sounds old, out-dated. "Man the people are too busy getting ready to fight to bother with singing anymore!" The world of the black American is very different from that of the white American. This difference comes not only from the segregation imposed on the black, but it also comes from the way of life he has evolved for himself under these conditions. Yet, America has always been uneasy with this separate world in its midst. Feeling most comfortable when the black man emulates the ways and manners of white Americans, America has, at the same time, been stolidly unwilling to let the black man be assimilated into the mainstream.

With its goal of assimilation on the basis of equality, the Civil Rights Movement was once the great hope of black men and liberal whites. In 1960 and 1961 Negroes felt that if only Americans knew the wrongs and sufferings they had to endure, these wrongs would be righted and all would be well. If Americans saw well-dressed, well-mannered, clean Negroes on their television screen not retaliating to being beaten by white Southerners, they would not sit back and do nothing. . . . And the Reverend Dr. Martin Luther King Jr. was the knight going forth to prove to the father that he was worthy of becoming a member of the family. But there was something wrong with this attitude and young Negroes began to feel uneasy. Was this not another form of the bowing and scraping their grandparents had to do to get what they wanted? Were they not acting once again as the white man wanted and expected them to? And why should they have to be brutalized, physically and spiritually, for what every other American had at birth? .
. .

More than any other person Malcolm X was responsible for the new militancy that entered The Movement in 1965. Malcolm X said those things which Negroes had been saying among themselves. He even said those things Negroes had been afraid to say to each other. His clear, uncomplicated words cut through the chains of black minds like a giant blow-torch. His words were not spoken for the benefit of the press. He was not concerned with stirring the moral conscience of America, because he knew—America had no moral conscience. He spoke directly and eloquently to black men, analyzing their situation, their predicament, events as they happened, explaining what it meant for a black man in America.

America's reaction to what the Negro considered just demands was a disillusioning experience. Where whites could try to attain The Dream, Negroes always had to dream themselves attaining The Dream. But The Dream was beginning to look like a nightmare. They'd been living one a long time. They had hopes that America would

---

[*] Julius Lester, "The Angry Children of Malcolm X," *Sing Out* 17 (October-November 1966).

respond to their needs, and America had equivocated. Integration had once been the unquestioned goal that would be the proudest moment for Negro America. Now it was beginning to be questioned. . . .

When it became more and more apparent that integration was only designed to uplift Negroes and improve their lot, Negroes began wondering whose lot actually needed improving. Maybe the white folks weren't as well-educated and cultured as they thought they were. Thus, Negroes began cutting a path toward learning who they were. . . .

Now the Negro is beginning to study his past, to learn those things that have been lost, to recreate what the white man destroyed in him and to destroy that which the white man put instead. He has stopped being a Negro and has become a black man in recognition of his new identity, his real identity. "Negro" is an American invention which shut him off from those of the same color in Africa. He recognizes now that part of himself is in Africa. . . .

Many things that have happened in the past six years have had little or no meaning for most whites, but have had vital meaning for Negroes. Wasn't it only a month after the March on Washington that four children were killed in a church bombing in Birmingham? Whites could feel morally outraged, but they couldn't feel the futility, despair and anger that swept through The Nation within a nation—Black America. There were limits to how much one people could endure and Birmingham Sunday possibly marked that limit. . . .

What was needed that Sunday was ol' John Brown to come riding into Birmingham as he had ridden into Lawrence, Kansas, burning every building that stood and killing every man, woman and child that ran from his onslaught. Killing, killing, killing, turning men into fountains of blood, spouting until Heaven itself drew back before the frothing red ocean.

But the Liberal and his Negro sycophants would've cried, Vengeance accomplishes nothing. You are only acting like your oppressor and such an act makes you no better than him. John Brown, his hands and wrists slick with blood, would've said, oh so softly and quietly, Mere Vengeance is folly. Purgation is necessary.

Now it is over. America has had chance after chance to show that it really meant "that all men are endowed with certain inalienable rights." America has had precious chances in this decade to make it come true. Now it is over. The days of singing freedom songs and the days of combating bullets and billy clubs with Love. "We Shall Overcome" (and we have overcome our blindness) sounds old, out-dated . . . . As one SNCC veteran put it after the Mississippi March, "Man, the people are too busy getting ready to fight to bother with singing anymore." And as for Love? That's always been better done in bed than on the picket line and marches. Love is fragile and gentle and seeks a like response. They used to sing "I Love Everybody" as they ducked bricks and bottles. Now they sing:

> Too much love,
> Too much love,
> Nothing kills a nigger like
> Too much love.

Stokely Carmichael, Black Power Defined

In 1966 Stokely Carmichael (1942–), the new chairman of SNCC, gave the growing black nationalist sentiment among younger activists both a name and a slogan when he called for "Black Power." Born in the West Indies and raised in New York City, he became active in SNCC while a student at Howard University, then participated in Freedom Summer in Mississippi. In the following document, written in 1966, Carmichael defines and explains the need for Black Power. He later expanded this discussion in the volume, *Black Power: The Politics of Liberation in America* (1967), which he coauthored with a political scientist. Carmichael eventually adopted a Pan-African perspective, changed his name to Kwame Ture, and moved to the African nation of Guinea.[*]

We shall have to struggle for the right to create our own terms through which to define ourselves and our relationship to the society, and to have these terms recognized. This is the first necessity of a free people. . . .

Negroes are defined by two forces, their blackness and their powerlessness. There have been traditionally two communities in America. The White community, which controlled and defined the forms that all institutions within the society would take; and the Negro community which has been excluded from participation in the power decisions that shaped the society, and has traditionally been dependent upon, and subservient to, the White community.

This has not been accidental. The history of every institution of this society indicates that a major concern in the ordering and structuring of the society has been the maintaining of the Negro community in its condition of dependence and oppression. This has not been on the level of individual acts of discrimination between individual whites against individual Negroes, but as total acts by the White community against the Negro community. This fact cannot be too strongly emphasized—that racist assumptions of white superiority have been so deeply ingrained in the structure of the society that it infuses its entire functioning, and is so much a part of the national subconscious that it is taken for granted and is frequently not even recognized. . . . The ghetto itself is a product of a combination of forces and special interests in the white community, and the groups that have access to the resources and power to change that situation benefit, politically and economically, from the existence of that ghetto.

It is more than a figure of speech to say that the Negro community in America is a victim of white imperialism and colonial exploitation. This is in practical economic and political terms true. There are over twenty million black people comprising ten percent of this nation. They for the most part live in well-defined areas of the country—in the

---

[*] Stokely Carmichael, "Toward Black Liberation," *Massachusetts Review* 7 (Autumn 1966).

shanty-towns and rural black belt areas of the South, and increasingly in the slums of northern and western industrial cities. If one goes into any Negro community, whether it be Jackson, Miss., Cambridge, Md., or Harlem, N.Y., one will find the same combination of political, economic, and social forces are at work. The people in the Negro community do not control the resources of that community, its political decisions, its law enforcement, its housing standards; and even the physical ownership of the land, houses, and stores *lie outside that community.*

It is white power that makes the laws, and it is violent white power in the form of armed white cops that enforces those laws with guns and nightsticks. The vast majority of Negroes in this country live in these captive communities and must endure these conditions of oppression because, and only because, *they are black and powerless.* . . .

SNCC proposes that it is now time for the black freedom movement to stop pandering to the fears and anxieties of the white middle class in the attempt to earn its "good-will," and to return to the ghetto to organize these communities to control themselves. This organization must be attempted in northern and southern urban areas as well as in the rural black belt counties of the South. . . . We must organize black community power to end these abuses, and to give the Negro community a chance to have its needs expressed.

The Black Panther Party Platform

The leading black revolutionary nationalist group in the Black Power Movement was the Black Panther Party. Founded in Oakland in 1966 by Huey P. Newton and Bobby Seale, the organization blended black nationalism with Marxist thought. The Panthers quickly gained notoriety for their advocacy of violence. They openly displayed weapons, patrolled their neighborhoods to keep watch over the police, urged blacks to "off the pigs," stormed the California State Assembly to protest a pending gun control bill, and engaged in several widely publicized shootouts. Politicians and the media often overlooked their broader political agenda, much of which is expressed in the party's platform below. In Oakland, Chicago, and other cities where they set up chapters, they organized free breakfast and health care programs, taught courses in African-American history, and warned against the dangers of drug use. The Panthers became a main target of the FBI and other law enforcement organizations, prompting their rapid decline in the 1970s.[*]

---

[*] The Black Panther Party, "Platform and Program of the Black Panther Party" (October 1966).

The Platform

1. We want freedom. We want the power to determine the destiny of our Black Community. We believe that black people will not be free until we are able to determine our destiny.

2. We want full employment for our people. We believe that the federal government is responsible and obligated to give every man employment or a guaranteed income. We belive that if the white American businessman will not give full employment, then the means of production should should be taken from the businessmen and placed in the community so that the people of the community can organize and employ all of its people and give a high standard of living.

3. We want an end to the robbery by the white man of our Black Community.

We believe that this racist government has robbed us and now we are demanding the overdue debt of forty acres and two mules. Forty acres and two mules was promised 100 years ago as restitution for slave labor and mass murder of black people. We will accept the payment in currency which will be distributed to our many communities. The Germans are now aiding the Jews in Israel for the genocide of the Jewish people. The Germans murdered six million Jews. The American racist has taken part in the slaughter of over fifty million black people; therefore we feel that this is a modest demand that we make.

4. We want decent housing, fit for shelter of human beings. We believe that if the white landlords will not give decent housing to our black community, then the housing and the land should be made into cooperatives so that our community, with government aid, can build and make decent housing for its people.

5. We want education for our people that exposes the true nature of this decadent American society. We want education that teaches us our true history and our role in the present-day society.

We believe in an educational system that will give to our people a knowledge of self. If a man does not have knowledge of himself and his position in society and the world, then he has little chance to relate to anything else.

6. We want all black men to be exempt from military service.

We believe that black people should not be forced to fight in the military service to defend a racist government that does not protect us. We will not fight and kill other people of color in the world who, like black people, are being victimized by the white racist government of America. We will protect ourselves from the force and violence of the racist police and the racist military, by whatever means necessary.

7. We want an immediate end to POLICE BRUTALITY and MURDER of black people.

We believe we can end police brutality in our black community by organizing black self-defense groups that are dedicated to defending our black community from racist police oppression and brutality. The Second Amendment to the Constitution of the United States gives a right to bear arms. We therefore believe that all black people should arm themselves for self-defense.

8. We want freedom for all black men held in federal, state, county and city prisons and jails. We believe that black people should be released from the many jails and prisons because they have not received a fair and impartial trial.

9. We want all black people when brought to trial to be tried in court by a jury of their peer group or people from their black communities, as defined by the Constitution of the United States.

We believe that the courts should follow the United States Constitution so that black people will receive fair trials. The 14th Amendment of the U.S. Constitution gives a man a right to be tried by his peer group. A peer is a person from a similar economic, social, religious, geographical, environmental, historical and racial background. To do this the court will be forced to select a jury from the black community from which the black defendant came. We have been, and are being tried by all-white juries that have no understanding of the "average reasoning man" of the black community.

10. We want land, bread, housing, education, clothing, justice and peace. And as our major political objective, a United Nations-supervised plebiscite to be held throughout the black colony in which only black colonial subjects will be allowed to participate, for the purpose of determining the will of black people as to their national destiny. When in the course of human events, it becomes necessary for one people to dissolve the political bands which have connected them with another, and to assume, among the powers of the earth, the separate and equal station to which the laws of nature and nature's God entitle them, a decent respect to the opinions of mankind requires that they should declare the causes which impel them to the separation.

We hold these truths to be self-evident, that all men are created equal; that they are endowed by their Creator with certain unalienable rights; that among these are life, liberty, and the pursuit of happiness. That, to secure these rights, governments are instituted among men, deriving their just powers from the consent of the governed; that, whenever any form of government becomes destructive of these ends, it is the right of the people to alter or abolish it, and to institute a new government, laying its foundation on such principles, and organizing its powers in such form, as to them shall seem most likely to effect their safety and happiness. Prudence, indeed, will dictate that governments long established should not be changed for light and transient causes; and accordingly, all experience has shown, that mankind are more disposed to suffer, while evils are sufferable, that to right themselves by abolishing the forms to which they are accustomed. But, when a long train of abuses and usurpations, pursuing invariably the same object, evinces a design to reduce them under absolute despotism, it is their right, it is their duty, to throw off such government, and to provide new guards for their future security.

Amiri Baraka, The Role of the Black Artist

Black cultural nationalism took many forms within the Black Power Movement. One was a black arts movement in which black nationalist writers and artists coupled their art and their activism in an effort to raise the cultural and political consciousness of African Americans. Younger activists produced thousands of creative works in the late 1960s and early 1970s. The leader of this movement was Amiri Baraka (1934–), a prominent poet, essayist, and playwright. Attracted to black nationalism in 1965, he divorced his white wife, converted to Islam, abandoned his given name of LeRoi Jones, and moved to a black inner-city neighborhood in Newark. Baraka embraced a cultural nationalist perspective and advocated using drama, poetry, and fiction as tools to build the Black Power Movement. In the following essay, he explains the role that he believed black writers and artists should play in the movement. In 1974, as the movement was in decline, Baraka tempered his strident black nationalism and adopted a Marxist critique of western capitalism.*

The Black Artist's role in America is to aid in the destruction of America as he knows it. His role is to report and reflect so precisely the nature of the society, and of himself in that society, that other men will be moved by the exactness of his rendering and, if they are black men, grow strong through this moving, having seen their own strength, and weakness; and if they are white men, tremble, curse, and go mad, because they will be drenched with the filth of their evil.

The Black Artist must draw out of his soul the correct image of the world. He must use this image to band his brothers and sisters together in common understanding of the nature of the world (and the nature of America) and the nature of the human soul.

The Black Artist must demonstrate sweet life, how it differs from the deathly grip of the White Eyes. The Black Artist must teach the White Eyes their deaths, and teach the black man how to bring these deaths about.

---

* LeRoi Jones, "State/Meant," in *Home: Social Essays* (New York: William Morrow & Company, Inc., 1966).

Nikki Giovanni, Black Nationalist Poetry

Following the example of Baraka and others, Nikki Giovanni (1943–) emerged as one of the most effective black nationalist poets in the Black Power Movement. After drifting from SNCC to political conservatism in the early 1960s, she embraced black nationalism and used her poetry to raise the political and cultural consciousness of African Americans, performing on college campuses and in other centers of the Black Power Movement throughout the United States. The following poem demonstrates the method by which she blended her art with her political ideology. Giovanni remains a prominent literary observer of the African-American experience.*

Of Liberation

(Everyone is organized)
Black people these are facts
Where's your power

Honkies rule the world
Where's your power Black people
(There are those who say it's found in the root of all evil)
You are money
You are property
Own yourself
3/5 of a man
100% whore
Chattel property
All of us
The most vital commodity in america
Is Black people . . .

Honkies tell niggers don't burn
"violence begets you nothing my fellow americans"
But they insist on straightened hair
They insist on bleaching creams
It is only natural that we would escalate . . .

It has been pointed out:
"The last bastion of white supremacy is in the Black man's mind"

---

* Nikki Giovanni, "Of Liberation," in *Black Judgement* (Detroit: Broadside Press, 1968).

(Note—this is not a criticism of brothers)

Everything comes in steps
Negative step one: get the white out of your hair
Negative step two: get the white out of your mind
Negative step three: get the white out of your parties
Negative step four: get the white out of your meetings

BLACK STEP ONE: Get the feeling out (this may be painful—endure)
BLACK STEP TWO: Outline and implement the program
All honkies and some negroes will have to die

This is unfortunate but necessary

Black law must be implemented
The Black Liberation Front must take responsibility
For Black people
If the choice is between the able and the faithful
The faithful must be chosen
Blackness is its own qualifier
Blackness is its own standard
There are no able negroes
White degrees do not qualify negroes to run
The Black Revolution

The Black Liberation Front must set the standards
These are international rules

Acquaint yourself with the Chinese, The Viet Namese, The Cubans
And other Black Revolutions
We have tried far too long to ally with whites . . .

As all reports have indicated our young men are primary
On the job training is necessary
Support your local rebellion—send a young man into the streets . . .

Our choice a decade ago was war or dishonor
(another word for integration)
We chose dishonor
We got war

Mistakes are a fact of life
It is the response to error that counts
Erase our errors with the Black Flame
Purify our neighborhoods with the Black Flame

We are the artists of this decade
Draw a new picture with the Black Flame
Live a new life within the Black Flame

Our choice now is war or death
Our option is survival
Listen to your own Black hearts

      Nikki Giovanni

Asking Questions of the Documents

1. What is black nationalism? How did Malcolm X define black nationalism? Contrast his views (and those of other black nationalists) with those of Martin Luther King Jr. What tactics and goals did they advocate? What were Malcolm X's views on black revolution?

2. What impact did Malcolm X have on other African Americans in the 1960s? What impact does he appear to have today? What other influences prompted the rise of the Black Power Movement?

3. How did Stokely Carmichael define Black Power? How does this differ from Malcolm X's definition of black nationalism? What was the main goal of Black Power?

4. What was the agenda of the Black Panther Party? Which goals seem reasonable to you? Which seem unreasonable? Why? Why do you think the party appended the preamble to the Declaration of Independence to its platform?

5. What, according to Amiri Baraka (LeRoi Jones), should be the role of black artists in the Black Power Movement? How is that role illustrated in the poetry of Nikki Giovanni?

For Further Reading

Bracey, John H., Jr., August Meier, and Elliott Rudwick, eds. *Black Nationalism in America*. Indianapolis: Bobbs-Merrill, 1970.

Button, James W. *Black Violence: Political Impact of the 1960s Riots*. Princeton, N.J.: Princeton University Press, 1978.

Carson, Clayborne. *In Struggle: SNCC and the Black Awakening of the 1960s*. Cambridge, Mass.: Harvard University Press, 1981.

Haines, Herbert H. *Black Radicals and the Civil Rights Mainstream, 1954–1970.* Knoxville, Tenn.: University of Tennessee Press, 1988.

Perry, Bruce. *Malcolm: The Life of a Man Who Changed Black America.* Barrytown, N.Y.: Station Hill, 1991.

Pinckney, Alphonso. "Contemporary Black Nationalism." In *Black Life and Culture in the United States*, ed. Rhoda L. Goldstein, 243–262. New York: Thomas Y. Crowell, 1971.

Van Deburg, William L. *New Day in Babylon: The Black Power Movement and American Culture, 1965–1975.* Chicago: University of Chicago Press, 1992.

17

Half Empty, Half Full: African Americans Since 1968

The year 1968—which saw both the assassination of Martin Luther King and the passage of the last major piece of civil rights legislation by the U.S. Congress—is often viewed as the end of the era of the Civil Rights Movement. Since that time, African Americans have scored major gains, especially in the political realm. The Voting Rights Act of 1965 has brought dramatic increases in the size of the black electorate. African Americans have become an important voting bloc in most urban centers as well as in many areas of the rural South. The number of black elected officials has more than quadrupled. Black mayors govern many of our largest cities. Voters made Douglas Wilder the governor of Virginia and elected Carol Mosely Braun to the U.S. Senate from Illinois. And in 1984 and again in 1988, civil rights activist Jesse Jackson became a serious candidate for president.

Many blacks have also achieved significant economic and social gains. Due to affirmative action, laws prohibiting discrimination in employment, and greater access to higher education, a growing number of blacks have obtained professional and managerial jobs and entered the middle class. Likewise, the formal walls of segregation have fallen in employment, housing, education, and many other areas of American life.

But disparities persist between blacks and whites. One out of three African Americans still lives in poverty, many in inner-city communities plagued with inadequate schools, deteriorating housing, declining employment, dependence on welfare, high rates of drug use and violent crime, and a growing sense of hopelessness and despair. Their lives differ considerably from those of middle-class blacks.

The authors of *A Common Destiny* (1989), a recent analysis of the position of blacks in American society, observed:

> The status of black Americans today can be characterized as a glass that is half full—if measured by progress since 1939—or a glass that is half empty if measured by the persisting disparities between black and white Americans since the early 1970s. Any assessment of the quality of life for blacks is also complicated by the disparity between blacks who have achieved middle-class status and those who have not.

As African Americans look to the twenty-first century, they can point proudly to many recent gains but must recognize that their struggle for equality, empowerment, and racial justice continues.

Benjamin L. Hooks, Continuing the Struggle

Even with the impressive economic, social, and political gains which African Americans had achieved by the early 1970s, civil rights leaders continued to press for change. One of the most vocal was Benjamin L. Hooks (1925–), who followed Roy Wilkins as executive director of the NAACP from 1977 to 1993. During the 1980s, he was a major critic of the Reagan administration's avoidance of important racial questions and trimming of major social programs, including those designed to aid the poor. In the following remarks, which are excerpted from an address to the annual national gathering of the NAACP in New Orleans, Hooks offers a challenge to his fellow African Americans to continue the struggle for racial justice.*

I come humbled by the knowledge that as we assemble in this convention center, we stand on the shoulders of many giants who put their lives on the line in order that the racial progress we now enjoy could be made. We pay tribute to Medgar Evers who, 20 years ago on June 12, was cut down by an assassin's bullet. Medgar realized better than most that to stand up for justice in Mississippi was a dangerous and potentially fatal endeavor. Yet he stood boldly and tall, declaring to the world that it was better to die in dignity for a just cause than to live on one's knees as a supplicant. . . .

Today there are more elected black public officials in the State of Mississippi than in any state in the nation. Today, the face of race relations has been drastically altered by the surgical knife of self-denial and selfsacrifice by the thousands of men and women who met in churches off lonely roads [and] assembled around diningroom tables of shacks and shanties and who marched until [racist governors] gave way to elected officials who helped bring this state into the twentieth century. *Life is a struggle*. . . .

So it should come as no surprise that even though slavery has been officially over for more than 118 years, we still find ourselves struggling against slavery under new guises: racial discrimination in this country, apartheid and colonialism abroad. But as far back as we can read recorded history, life for every group has been a struggle. . . .

Here in America, from the *Mayflower* at Plymouth Rock to the men of war at Jamestown, life for the earliest settlers and their first slaves has been a struggle.

---

* Benjamin L. Hooks, "Struggle On!," *Crisis* 90 (August-September 1983).

Today, as our 74th Annual Convention assembles in this historic city, a city where blacks fought alongside Andrew Jackson . . . we find ourselves in a race in the struggle for survival.

One out of every three blacks in the country is officially listed below the poverty line.

One out of five black adults is unemployed. . . .

Black infant mortality is twice as high as that of whites. . . .

I cite these figures to highlight the fact that although we have made tremendous progress in the area of race relations, we still have a long way to go; and contrary to the glib assertions of the present Administration [of Ronald Reagan], much remains to be done if blacks are to share in the economic wealth and prosperity of this nation.

Yes, my friends, we are in the midst of a fierce struggle, one that becomes more difficult with the passing of each day. . . .

Anyone who has an appreciation for history should be cognizant of the fact that nations and great civilizations were not destroyed from without, but from within. When hopes are blasted, when expectations are doomed, when respect for government is shattered by the disparate treatment of groups of individuals; when people are left out— then a social order is doomed to destruction. Yes, social and economic destruction from within, not foreign aggressors, constitutes the greatest threat to our system of government. . . .

My brothers and sisters, as I close tonight, I want you to know that the struggle we will face through the remaining period of the '80s and on through the twenty-first century will not be an easy one. It is fraught with pitfalls and plagued with setbacks, but we as a people have developed a resiliency which has made it possible for us to survive slavery and various discrimination. We must never tire nor become frustrated. . . . We must transform stumbling blocks into stepping stones and march on with the determination that we will make America a better nation for all.

Michele Wallace, Becoming a Black Feminist

Some African-American women, like Sojourner Truth a century before, were increasingly aware by the 1970s that they faced not just racial injustice but the double bonds of racism and sexism. Several came to this realization as participants in the Civil Rights or Black Power Movements. A few became, and still remain, outspoken feminists (or "womanists" to use Alice Walker's term). In the following document, feminist scholar Michele Wallace (1952–) describes her development as a black feminist and her uneasy relationship with her white sisters in the women's movement.*

In 1968 when I was sixteen and the term Black consciousness was becoming popular, I started wearing my hair natural again. This time I ignored my "elders." I was too busy reshaping my life. Blackness, I reasoned, meant that I could finally be myself. Besides recognizing my history of slavery and my African roots, I began a general housecleaning. All my old values, gathered from "playing house" in nursery school to *Glamour* magazine beauty tips, were discarded. . . .

It took me three years to fully understand that Stokely [Carmichael] was serious when he'd said my position in the movement was "prone," three years to understand that the countless speeches that all began "the Black man . . ." did not include me. I learned. I mingled more and more with a black crowd, attended the conferences and rallies and parties and talked with some of the most loquacious of my brothers in Blackness, and as I pieced together the ideal that was being presented for me to emulate, I discovered my newfound freedoms being stripped from me, one after another. No I wasn't to wear makeup but yes I had to wear long skirts that I could barely walk in. No I wasn't to go to the beauty parlor but yes I was to spend hours cornrolling my hair. No I wasn't to flirt with or take shit off white men but yes I was to sleep with and take unending shit off Black men. No I wasn't to watch television or read *Vogue* or *Ladies' Home Journal* but yes I should keep my mouth shut. I would still have to iron, sew, cook, and have babies.

Only sixteen, I decided there were a lot of things I didn't know about Black male/female relationships. I made an attempt to fill myself in by reading—*Soul on Ice*, *Native Son*, *Black Rage*—and by joining the National Black Theatre. In the theatre's brand of a consciousness-raising session I was told of the awful ways in which Black women, me included, had tried to destroy the Black man's masculinity; how we had castrated him; worked when he didn't work; made money when he made no money; spent our nights and days in a church praying to a jive white boy named Jesus while he collapsed into alcoholism, drug addiction, and various forms of despair; how we'd always been too loud and domineering, too outspoken.

We had much to make up for by being gentle in the face of our own humiliation, by being soft-spoken (ideally to the point where our voices could not be heard at all), by being beautiful (whatever that was), by being submissive—how often that word was shoved at me in poems and in songs as something to strive for. . . .

The message of the Black movement was that I was being watched, on probation as a Black woman, that any signs of aggressiveness, intelligence, or independence would mean I'd be denied even the one role still left open to me as "my man's woman," keeper of house, children, and incense burners. . . .

In 1968 I had wanted to become an intelligent human being. I had wanted to be serious and scholarly for the first time in my life, to write and perhaps get the chance

---

*Michele Wallace, "A Black Feminist's Search for Sisterhood," in *All the Women are White, All the Blacks are Men, But Some of Us are Brave: Black Women's Studies*, ed. by Gloria T. Hull, Patricia Bell Scott, and Barbara Smith (Old Westbury, N.Y.: The Feminist Press, 1982). Copyright 1975 by The Village Voice, Inc.

Stokely and [James] Baldwin and Imamu [Amiri] Baraka (then LeRoi Jones) had gotten to change the world—that was how I defined not wanting to be white. . . .

I discovered my voice and when brothers talked to me, I talked back. This had its hazards. Almost got my eye blackened several times. My social life was like guerilla warfare. Here was the logic behind our grandmother's old saying, "A nigga man ain't shit." It was shorthand for "The Black man has learned to hate himself and to hate you even more. Be careful. He will hurt you." . . .

Whenever I raised the question of a Black woman's humanity in conversation with a Black man, I got a similar reaction. Black men, at least the ones I knew, seemed totally confounded when it came to treating Black women like people. Trying to be what we were told to be by the brothers of the "nation"—sweet and smiling— . . . young black female friends of mine were dropping out of school because their boyfriends had convinced them that it was "not correct" and "counterrevolutionary" to strive to do anything but have babies and clean house. "Help the brother get his thing together," they were told. . . .

When I first became a feminist, my Black friends used to cast pitying eyes upon me and say, "That's whitey's thing." I used to laugh it off, thinking, yes there are some slight problems, a few things white women don't completely understand, but we can work them out. In *Ebony*, *Jet*, and *Encore*, and even in *The New York Times*, various Black writers cautioned Black women to be wary of smiling white feminists. The women's movement enlists the support of Black women only to lend credibility to an essentially middle-class, irrelevant movement, they asserted. Time has shown that there was more truth to these claims than their shrillness indicated. Today when many white feminists think of Black women, they too often think of faceless masses of welfare mothers and rape victims to flesh out their statistical studies of woman's plight.

One unusually awkward moment for me as a Black feminist was when I found out that white feminists often don't view Black men as men but as fellow victims. I've got no pressing quarrel with the notion that white men have been the worst offenders but that isn't very helpful for a Black woman from day to day. White women don't check out a white man's bank account or stock-holdings before they accuse him of being sexist—they confront white men with and without jobs, with and without membership in a male consciousness-raising group. Yet when it comes to the Black man, it's hands off. . . .

Despite a sizable number of Black feminists who have contributed much to the leadership of the women's movement, there is still no Black women's movement, and it appears there won't be for some time to come. . . . For now, Black feminists, of necessity it seems, exist as individuals—some well known, like Eleanor Holmes Norton, Florynce Kennedy, Faith Ringgold, Shirley Chisholm, Alice Walker, and some unknown, like me. We exist as women who are Black who are feminists, each stranded for the moment, working independently because there is not yet an environment in this society remotely congenial to our struggle—because, being on the bottom, we would have to do what no one else has done: we would have to fight the world.

Molefi Kete Asante, Afrocentricity

The Black Power Movement of the 1960s continued to influence African-American culture in the decades that followed. One example is the body of Afrocentric scholarship that emerged in the interdisciplinary field of African-American Studies. Studying relevant topics from an Africa-centered perspective (known as Afrocentricity), it sought to avoid the racist biases inherent in Eurocentric scholarship on Africa and African Americans. It stressed the uniqueness and greatness of African cultures but generated controversy by attributing many of the achievements of the ancient Greeks to Egyptian origins. The leading advocate of Afrocentricity is Molefi Kete Asante (1942–), professor and chair of African-American Studies at Temple University, the only American college to offer a Ph.D. in the subject. He defines and defends Afrocentricity in the following essay.*

Afrocentricity is primarily an orientation to data. There are certainly data and facts which may be used by Afrocentrists in making analyses, but the principal component of the theoretical piece has to do with an orientation, a location, a position. Thus, I have explained in several books and articles that Afrocentricity is *a perspective which allows Africans to be subjects of historical experiences rather than objects* on the fringes of Europe. This means that the Afrocentrist is concerned with discovering in every case the centered place of the African. Of course, such a philosophical stance is not necessary for other disciplines; it is, however, the fundamental basis for African or African-American Studies. Otherwise, it seems to me that what is being done in African-American Studies at some institutions might successfully be challenged as duplicating in content, theory, and method the essentially Eurocentric enterprises that are undertaken in the traditional departments.

African-American Studies, however, is not simply the study and teaching about African people but *it is the Afrocentric study of African phenomena*; otherwise we would have had African-American Studies for a hundred years. But what existed before was not African-American Studies but rather Eurocentric study of Africans. Some of these studies led to important findings and have been useful. So the Afrocentrists do not claim that historians, sociologists, literary critics, philosophers, communicationists, and others do not make valuable contributions. Our claim is that by using a Eurocentric approach they often ignore an important interpretive key to the African experience in America and elsewhere. . . .

Like scholars in other disciplines, Afrocentrists . . . aim . . . to open fields of inquiry and to expand human dialogue around questions of social, economic, historical, and

---

*Molefi Kete Asante, "Afrocentric Systematics," in *Malcolm X as Cultural Hero and Other Afrocentric Essays* (Trenton, N.J.: Africa World Press, Inc., 1993).

cultural concern. Everything must be run through the sieve of doubt until one hits the bedrock of truth. Our methods, based on the idea of Afrocentricity, are meant to establish a clear pattern of discourse that may be followed by others. . . . Since the Afrocentric perspective is not a racial perspective but an orientation to data, anyone willing to submit to the rigid discipline of the field might become an Afrocentrist. . . . Afrocentric theories are not about cultural separatism or racial chauvinism. . . . Apart from the fact that one can be pro-African and not anti-white, the concept of Afrocentricity has little to do with pros and cons; it is preeminently about how you view phenomena. . . .

I believe that the white scholars who register a negative reaction to Afrocentricity do so out of a sense of fear. The fear is revealed on two levels. In the first place, Afrocentricity provides them with no grounds for authority unless they become students of Africans. This produces an existential fear: African scholars might have something to teach whites. The Afrocentric school of thought is the first contemporary intellectual movement initiated by African-American scholars that has currency on a broad scale for renewal and renaissance. It did not emerge inside the traditional white academic bastions. The second fear is not so much an existential one; it is rather a fear of the implications of the Afrocentric critique of Eurocentrism as an ethnocentric view posing as a universal view. Thus, we have opened the discussion of everything from race theory, ancient civilizations, African and European personalities, the impact of the glaciers on human behavior, and dislocation in the writing of African-American authors. We examine these topics with the eye of African people as subjects of historical experiences. This is not the only human view. If anything, Afrocentrists have always said that our perspective on data is only one among many and consequently the viewpoint, if you will, seeks no advantage, no self-aggrandizement, and no hegemony. The same cannot be said of Eurocentrism. . . .

The point is that Afrocentricity is nothing more than what is congruent to the interpretive life of the African person. Why should an African American see himself or herself through the perspective of a Chinese or white American? Neither the Chinese nor the white American views phenomena from the perspective of the African American . . . nor should they. Thus, to understand the African-American experience in dance, architecture, social work, art, science, psychology, or communication one has to avail one's self of the richly textured standing place of African Americans.

Rap Lyrics

While Afrocentric scholarship emerged in programs and departments of African-American Studies in American universities, another new black cultural form called rap developed on the streets of America's inner cities. Combining clever verbal wordplay with bold socio-political commentary, groups such as Grandmaster Flash and the Furious Five and Public Enemy conveyed the rage of black urban youth. The following rap lyrics are potent explorations of this rage. By the late 1980s, rap had become widely popular with youth across racial lines.[*]

The Message

It's like a jungle sometimes, it makes me wonder
How I keep from going under
It's like a jungle sometimes, it makes me wonder
How I keep from going under

Broken glass everywhere
People pissing on the stairs
You know they just don't care
I can't take the smell, can't take the noise
Got no money to move out, I guess I got no choice
Rats in the front room, roaches in the back
Junkies in the alley with a baseball bat
I tried to get away but I couldn't get far
'Cause the man with the tow truck repossessed my car
Don't push me 'cause I'm close to the edge
I'm trying not to lose my head
Ah huh huh huh huh
It's like a jungle sometimes, it makes me wonder
How I keep from going under . . .

You grow in the ghetto, living second rate
And your eyes will sing a song of deep hate
The place that you play and where you stay
Looks like one great big alleyway
You'll admire all the number book-takers
Thugs, pimps, and pushers and the big money makers
Driving big cars, spending twenties and tens
And you want to grow up to be just like them, huh
Smugglers, scramblers, burglars, gamblers
Pickpockets, peddlers, even panhandlers
You say, "I'm cool, huh, I'm no fool"
But then you wind up dropping out of high school
Now you're unemployed, all nonvoid
Walking 'round like you're Pretty Boy Floyd
Turned stick-up kid but look what you done did

[*] E. Fletcher, S. Robinson, C. Chase, and M. Glover, "The Message," copyright 1982 by Sugar Hill Music Publishers, Ltd.; Carlton Ridenhour, Keith Shocklee (James Henry Boxley), and Eric Sadler, "Fight the Power," copyright 1989 by Your Mothers Music/Def American Songs, Inc

Got sent up for a eight-year bid . . .

So don't push me 'cause I'm close to the edge
I'm trying not to lose my head
Ah huh huh huh huh
It's like a jungle sometimes, it makes me wonder
How I keep from going under . . .

(Dialogue)
What's that? A gang?
No!
Look, shut up! I don't want to hear your mouth
'Scuse me, Officer, Officer, what's the problem?
You the problem, you the problem
You ain't got to push me, man
Get in the car! Get in the car! Get in the godda—
Get in the car!

Grandmaster Flash and the Furious Five

Fight the Power

FIGHT THE POWER
We got to fight the powers that be

As the rhythm's designed to bounce
What counts is the rhyme
Designed to fill your mind
Now that you've realized the pride's arrived
We got to pump the stuff to make us tough
From the heart
It's a start, a work of art
To revolutionize, make change, nothin' strange
People, people, we are the same
No we're not the same
'Cause we don't know the game
What we need is awareness, we can't get careless
You say what is this?
My beloved, let's get down to business
Mental self-defensive fitness
(Yo) Bum rush the show
You gotta go for what you know
To make everybody see, in order to fight the powers that be
Lemme hear you say

FIGHT THE POWER
We've got to fight the powers that be

Public Enemy

Maxine Waters, Causes of the L.A. Riots

The rage of African Americans in the inner cities, so powerfully conveyed by the rappers, exploded into violence in South Central Los Angeles in April 1992. As in other inner cities, the growing inattention of the federal government, combined with an epidemic of crack cocaine, had hastened the deterioration and despair. Following the acquittal of four white police officers for allegedly beating Rodney King, a black man, protesters burned and looted sections of the city for four days. The riots resulted in 38 deaths, 3,700 burned-out buildings, and damages estimated at more than $500 million. In the following document, drawn from her testimony before the Senate Banking Committee, Congresswoman Maxine Waters (1938–), who represented South Central Los Angeles, explores the causes of the riots.*

The riots in Los Angeles and in other cities shocked the world. They shouldn't have. Many of us have watched our country—including our government—neglect the problems, indeed the people, of our inner-cities for years—even as matters reached a crisis stage.

The verdict in the Rodney King case did not cause what happened in Los Angeles. It was only the most recent injustice—piled upon many other injustices—suffered by the poor, minorities and the hopeless people living in this nation's cities. For years, they have been crying out for help. For years, their cries have not been heard.

I recently came across a statement made more than 25 years ago by Robert Kennedy, just two months before his violent death. He was talking about the violence that had erupted in cities across America. His words were wise and thoughtful:

> There is another kind of violence in America, slower but just as deadly, destructive as the shot or bomb in the night. . . . This is the violence of institutions; indifference and inaction and slow decay. This is the violence that afflicts the poor, that poisons relations between men and women because their skin is different colors. This is the slow destruction of a child by hunger, and schools without books and homes without heat in winter.

---

* Maxine Waters, "Testimony before the Senate Banking Committee," *Congressional Record* (1992).

What a tragedy it is that America has still, in 1992, not learned such an important lesson.

I have represented the people of South Central Los Angeles in the U.S. Congress and the California State Assembly for close to 20 years. I have seen our community continually and systematically ravaged by banks who would not lend to us, by governments which abandoned us or punished us for our poverty, and by big businesses who exported our jobs to Third-World countries for cheap labor.

In LA, between 40 and 50 percent of all African-American men are unemployed. The poverty rate is 32.9 percent. According to the most recent census, 40,000 teenagers—that is 20 percent of the city's 16 to 19 year olds—are both out of school and unemployed. . . .

We have created in many areas of this country a breeding ground for hopelessness, anger and despair. All the traditional mechanisms for empowerment, opportunity and self-improvement have been closed.

We are in the midst of a grand economic experiment that suggests if we "get the government off people's backs," and let the economy grow, everyone, including the poor, will somehow be better off. . . . The results of this experiment have been devastating. Today, more than 12 million children live in poverty, despite a decade of "economic growth," the precise mechanism we were told would reduce poverty. Today, one in five children in America lives in poverty. . . .

While the budget cuts of the eighties were literally forcing millions of Americans into poverty, there were other social and economic trends destroying inner-city communities at the same time.

I'm sure everyone in this room has read the results of the Federal Reserve Board's study on mortgage discrimination that demonstrates African Americans . . . are twice as likely as whites of the same income to be denied mortgages. . . .

In law enforcement, the problems are longstanding and well documented as well.

Is it any wonder our children have no hope? The systems are failing us. I could go on and on. . . . We simply cannot afford the continued terror and benign neglect that has characterized the federal government's response to the cities since the late 1970s.

Asking Questions of the Documents

1. Is Benjamin Hooks optimistic or pessimistic about the condition of African Americans in 1983? What kinds of racial injustices and inequalities remained to be addressed, prompting Hooks to challenge blacks to continue the struggle?

2. What prompted Michele Wallace to become a feminist? What problems did she encounter as a black feminist?

3. What is Afrocentricity? How does it differ in subject and approach from traditional western scholarship? Why does Asante believe many white scholars are critical of Afrocentricity?

4. What problems of inner cities are explored in the rap lyrics in this chapter? What did rappers such as Public Enemy urge blacks to do?

5. What caused the Los Angeles riots of 1992?

For Further Reading

Asante, Molefi K. *The Afrocentric Idea*. Philadelphia: Temple University Press, 1987.

Blauner, Bob. *Black Lives, White Lives: Three Decades of Race Relations in America*. Berkeley, Calif.: University of California Press, 1989.

Jaynes, Gerald D. and Robin M. Williams, Jr., *A Common Destiny: Blacks and American Society*. Washington, D.C.: National Academy Press, 1989.

Jones, Jacqueline. *Labor of Love, Labor of Sorrow: Black Women, Work, and the Family from Slavery to the Present*. New York: Free Press, 1985.

Lawson, Steven F. *Running for Freedom: Civil Rights and Black Politics in America Since 1941*. New York: McGraw Hill, 1991.

Morley, Jefferson. "Rap Music as American History." In *Rap: The Lyrics*, ed. by Lawrence A. Stanley, xv-xxxi. New York: Penguin Books, 1992.

Pinckney, Alphonso. *The Myth of Black Progress*. Cambridge: Cambridge University Press, 1984.

Credits

Grateful acknowledgment is made for permission to reprint:

CHAPTER 7

Page 81, Felix Haywood, The Death of Slavery: From B.A. Botkin, ed., *Lay My Burden Down: A Folk History of Slavery* (Chicago: University of Chicago Press, 1945). Reprinted with permission of the estate of B.A. Botkin.

CHAPTER 9

Page 96, Richard Wright, Living Jim Crow: "The Ethics of Living Jim Crow," from *Uncle Tom's Children* by Richard Wright . Copyright 1937 by Richard Wright. Copyright renewed 1965 by Ellen Wright. Reprinted with permission of HarperCollins Publishers, Inc.

CHAPTER 10

Page 120, John Hope, "Rise Brothers!": Reprinted with the permission of Simon & Schuster from *The Story of John Hope* by Ridgely Torrence. Copyright 1948 by Ridgely Torrence; Copyright renewed (c) 1975 by Ellen W. Dunbar.

CHAPTER 11

Page 126, Causes of the Migration: From Emmett J. Scott, "Letters of Negro Migrants of 1916-1918," *Journal of Negro History* 4 (July and November 1919). Reprinted with permission of the Association for the Study of Afro-American Life and History.

Page 129, Alain Locke, The New Negro: Reprinted with the permission of Simon & Schuster from *The New Negro: Voices of the Harlen Renaissance* edited by Alain Locke. Copyright 1925 by Alain Locke.

Page 132, Harlem Renaissance Poetry: From Claude McKay, "If We Must Die," in *Liberator* 2 (July 1919); Langston Hughes, "The Negro Speaks of Rivers," in *The Weary Blues* (New York: Alfred A. Knopf, Inc, 1926). From *Selected Poems* by Langston Hughes. Copyright 1926 by Alfred A. Knopf Inc. and renewed 1954 by Langston Hughes. Reprinted by permission of the publisher; Countee Cullen, "Yet Do I Marvel," in *Color* (New York: Harper and Brothers, Publishers, 1925). Copyright renewed 1952 by Ida Cullen. Copyrights held by the Amistad Research Center, Tulane University, New Orleans, Louisiana. Administered by Thompson and Thompson, New York, N.Y.

CHAPTER 12

Page 142, Mary McLeod Bethune, A Black Adviser to FDR: From Mary McLeod Bethune, "My Secret Talks with FDR," *Ebony* 4 (April 1949). Reprinted with permission of *Ebony* Magazine.

Pages 144, Roy Wilkins, A Black Assessment of the New Deal: From Roy Wilkins, "The Roosevelt Record," *Crisis* 47 (November 1940). Reprinted with permission of the NAACP.

CHAPTER 13

Page 153, Walter White, Race Relations in Wartime Detroit: From Walter White, "What Caused the Detroit Riots?." in *What Caused the Detroit Riots?* (New York: NAACP, 1943). Reprinted with permission of the Estate of Walter White.

CHAPTER 14

Page 161, Charles Hamilton Houston, Launching the Campaign: From Charles Houston, "Educational Inequalities Must Go!," *Crisis* 42 (October 1935). Reprinted with permission of the NAACP.

Page 163, Septima Clark, Black Schools in the Jim Crow South: From *Echo in My Soul* by Septima Clark with LeGette Blythe. Copyright (c) 1962 by Septima Poinsettia Clark. Used by permission of Dutton Signet, a division of Penguin Books USA Inc.

Page 167, Elizabeth Eckford, The First Day of School in Little Rock: From Elizabeth Eckford, "The First Day: Little Rock, 1957," in *Growing Up Southern: Southern Exposure Looks at Childhood, Then and Now*, ed. Chris Mayfield (New York: Random House, 1981). Reprinted with permission of Random House.

CHAPTER 15

Page 172, Rosa Parks, The Montgomery Bus Boycott: Reprinted by permission of The Putnam Publishing Group from Rosa L. Parks, "Recollections," in *My Soul is Rested: Movement Days in the Deep South Remembered*, by Howell Raines. Copyright (c) 1977 by Howell Raines.

Page 182, Alice Walker, Changed by the Movement: From Alice Walker, "The Civil Rights Movement: What Good Was It?," *American Scholar* 36 (Autumn 1967). Copyright 1967 by Alice Walker.

CHAPTER 16

Page 188, Julius Lester, The Attractions of Black Power: From Julius Lester, "The Angry Children of Malcolm X," *Sing Out* 17 (October-November 1966). Reprinted with permission of *Sing Out*.

Page 191, Stokely Carmichael, Black Power Defined: From Stokely Carmichael, "Toward Black Liberation," *Massachusetts Review* 7 (Autumn 1966). Reprinted with permission of *The Massachusetts Review*.

Page 195, Amiri Baraka, The Role of the Black Artist: From LeRoi Jones, "State/Meant," in *Home: Social Essays* (New York: William Morrow & Company, Inc., 1966). Reprinted with permission of William Morrow & Company, Inc.

Page 196, Nikki Giovanni, Black Nationalist Poetry: From Nikki Giovanni, "Of Liberation," in *Black Judgment* (Detroit: Broadside Press, 1968). Reprinted with permission of the Broadside Press.

CHAPTER 17

Page 202, Benjamin L. Hooks, Continuing the Struggle: From Benjamin L. Hooks, "Struggle On!," *Crisis* 90 (August-September 1983). Reprinted with permission of the NAACP.

Page 203, Michele Wallace, Becoming a Black Feminist: From Michele Wallace, "A Black Feminist's Search for Sisterhood," in *All the Women are White, All the Blacks are Men, But Some of Us are Brave: Black Women's Studies*, eds. Gloria T. Hull, Patricia Bell Scott, and Barbara Smith (Old Westbury, N.Y.: The Feminist Press, 1982). Copyright 1975 by the Village Voice, Inc. Reprinted with permission of Michele Wallace.

Page 206, Molefi Kete Asante, Afrocentricity: From Molefi Kete Asante, "Afrocentric Systematics," in *Malcolm X as Cultural Hero and Other Afrocentric Essays* (Trenton, N.J.: Africa World Press, Inc.. 1993). Reprinted with permission of Africa World Press.

Page 207, Rap Lyrics: From E. Fletcher, S. Robinson, C. Chase, and M. Glover, "The Message," copyright 1982 by Sugar Hill Music Publishers, Ltd. Reprinted with permission of Sugar Hill Music Publishers.; Carlton Ridenhour, Keith Shocklee (James Henry Boxley), and Eric Sadler, "Fight the Power," copyright 1989 by Your Mothers Music/Def American Songs, Inc. Reprinted with permission of Your Mothers Music/Def American Songs, Inc.